Y0-AFJ-653

# THE IMPACT OF INTERNET PORNOGRAPHY ON MARRIED WOMEN

# THE IMPACT OF INTERNET PORNOGRAPHY ON MARRIED WOMEN: A PSYCHODYNAMIC PERSPECTIVE

*Susan Cebulko*

## CAMBRIA PRESS

YOUNGSTOWN, NEW YORK

BRESCIA UNIVERSITY
COLLEGE LIBRARY

Copyright 2007 Susan Cebulko

All rights reserved
Printed in the United States of America

No part of this publication may be reproduced, stored in or introduced into a retrieval system, or transmitted, in any form, or by any means (electronic, mechanical, photocopying, recording, or otherwise), without the prior permission of the publisher. Requests for permission should be directed to permissions@cambriapress.com, or mailed to Permissions, Cambria Press, PO Box 350, Youngstown, New York 14174-0350.

Library of Congress Cataloging-in-Publication Data
Cebulko, Susan.
   The impact of Internet pornography on married women: a psychodynamic perspective / Susan Cebulko.
      p. cm.
   Includes bibliographical references and index.
   ISBN-13: 978-1-934043-17-2 (alk. paper)
   ISBN-10: 1-934043-17-6 (alk. paper)
   1. Married women—Psychology—Case studies. 2. Internet pornography—Psychological aspects—Case studies. I. Title.

   HQ759.C334 2007
   306.81—dc22

   2007005301

BRESCIA UNIVERSITY
COLLEGE LIBRARY

*To Tom, Kara, Nick, Kara, Natalie, and Brad*

# TABLE OF CONTENTS

# FOREWORD

In the Introductory Lectures (1915–1917), Freud introduced his theory of sexuality by describing it as an effort to extend our understanding of human sexuality beyond the realm of genital union. While Freud's theory of sexuality has been the target of a great deal of criticism, many of his ideas remain cogent: that sexuality has a lengthy developmental course, that we can observe differences in the ways men and women think about and express their sexuality, and that our entire history of relating to others becomes woven into our unique individual sexual expressions. Additional compelling ideas are that we have rich fantasy lives which inform our sexuality, that most people turn to sexual day dreams with great frequency and often our conscious fantasies seem to have little to do with actual "genital union."

The Standard Edition is full of examples of a wide variety of sexual expression and difficulties of sexuality between couples in Vienna at the turn of the century. Infidelity, fetishism, an inability to move into adult sexuality, incest, what we would now call child sexual abuse, are all detailed in Freud's works. Indeed there is good evidence that the idea of a Transference Cure came out of observations of temporarily restored mental health after a visit to a Spa—the treatment of choice for a wide variety of mental difficulties at that time. But careful listening to his patients led Freud to offer that the return to health had more to do with a sexual liaison while at the Spa rather than the many somatic treatments the facilities offered their patients. The "cure" was only temporary, as was the relationship and patients many times returned to their suffering. Something or someone sought after had been found, but the positive change in mental functioning did not last.

In this study, we see a realm of sexuality that Freud did not observe: sexuality on the Internet. We can observe over human history that sexuality regularly finds its way into evolving media—as is the case with the Internet. But we are also left to struggle with the fact that many people never turn to the Internet for sexual stimulations or intrigue. Weather sites, auction sites, sending out those annoying e-mail chain letters or pictures of children and grandchildren are but some of the possibilities that occupy the minds of Internet users.

Research can lead us to definitive answers and ideas for understanding and clinically approaching particular dimensions of the human experience. The research documented in this book offers to deepen and broaden our understanding of women who become embroiled in an ongoing, conflictual, disappointing but highly engaging battle with their husbands manifestly over their spouses' preoccupation with internet pornography, sexually charged "chat rooms" and other meeting sites.

Dr. Cebulko does not claim that she documents the experience of all women whose husbands use Internet pornography; rather it is a study of women who cannot say "No" and mean it when they discover their spouses using the Internet for sexual gratification and intrigue. Evidence suggests there are women who say no and mean no and that is it; and there are women who do not care. Each of these groups of women is interesting in its own right. For the women in this study, their husband's use of the Internet pulls them into something, and their accounts of their struggles pull us in as well. Dr. Cebulko has captured this pull, the ongoing struggle, the disappointment, the rage, the sadness, and despair. Most importantly, she details a cycle that keeps repeating; neither spouse knows how to end it, how to refocus their relationship on something more happy and productive.

This research is an important reminder that men who are drawn to the sexually charged regions of the Internet are not just single men. When men are married, their spouses are affected as well. Research that focuses solely on the user ignores the fact that people do not live in a vacuum. Except for people who are extremely emotionally isolated, we all live in a matrix of sustaining or potentially sustaining relationships. For a variety of reasons, men turn away from the possibilities of their marital relationships and turn to the sexual intrigue of the Internet. Something propels them into the realm of fantasy and sexual enactment. That *something* has been the topic of a great deal of analytic theorizing, novels and operas.

Dr. Cebulko's research is full of surprises: that the use of internet porn was but the tip of a much larger pattern of sexual enactment, and many times the least (for the lack of better word) "egregious," but became the focus of the martial conflict; that the women had a sense that something was wrong early on in the relationships but "chose" to overlook it; that the women become engaged in a cycle of disappointment with seemingly no way out; that they could not disengage. Clearly, the women in this study are participating in *something*, but what? Is the engagement solely around their husbands turning away from them, and engaging Internet porn?

And finally, we must wonder about the history of sexual abuse, rape and non-sexual chaotic childhood environments in the lives of these women. Many of the women in this study had experienced some sort of sexual boundary violation. None of them had treatment for their sexual trauma. Were the effects of their sexual trauma a factor in their inability to say "No" and mean it? Did it also play a role in their inability to take note of the warning signs they observed early on in their relationships? Does it play a role in their inability to disengage from the cycle?

The complexities of these findings are a powerful reminder to those who try and condense Internet porn into neat ideas such as addiction. Nothing in the realm of human experience is neat and tidy.

When the researcher and the clinician assume that the mind is an entity and the Internet is a separate entity then we can arrive at complex ideas to deal with complex situations. The mind has an unconscious; it has a self; it can be analyzed and motivations brought into the treatment setting. The Internet has no mind, hence no motivation. It is there in all its complexity, a library of immense proportion. We can pick and choose what we borrow, or what we purchase. Some people will go for purely intellectual stimulation or communication; others will be powerfully drawn to sexual stimulation and intrigue.

The reader will find many useful ideas to use when working with individuals or couples. This is not a "how to" or recipe book. It is for the clinician who uses research to inform the practice, and a powerful reminder that when part of a couple is involved in sexual intrigue, it effects their spouse and their spouse brings to the situation their own history, their own dynamics, their own disappointments, and their own hopes for something better.

Dr. R. Dennis Shelby
Research Director
The Institute for Clinical Social Work

# PREFACE

The tantalizing topic of Internet pornography generates a great deal of interest in academic spheres, the mainstream media, and on Capital Hill. A "Google" search produces not only links to heterosexual, homosexual, and child pornographic web pages, but links to screen tests to determine cybersex addiction, web pages offering assistance for cyberporn addicts, testimonies from individuals purporting to be recovered cyberporn addicts, multiple groups organized to curb the proliferation of the availability of Internet pornography, and various web pages devoted to a myriad of other aspects of Internet pornography. Daily perusal of newspapers, magazines, and television reveals an impressive amount of concentration on this particular topic. The majority of the focus is on the compulsive user and the negative effects on spouses and families.

My initial interest in the topic of Internet pornography was generated by my clinical work with a certain population of women who after months of psychotherapy, voiced distress about their husbands use of Internet pornography and their inability to convince their husbands to abandon the activities. At the same time, various members of the clergy expressed concern to me about this very problem in their congregations. At the time of the research, a survey of local colleagues revealed they were not encountering this issue in their practices, a fact I found to be curious. However, since the completion of the research in the spring of 2005, these same local colleagues have begun to notice that their clients are talking about Internet pornography as a major source of marital distress.

As I began my research on Internet pornography, I found that Internet pornography was examined from the perspectives of morality (Perkins, 1997), domination and oppression of women (Dines, Jensen, & Russo,1998), and violation of women's civil rights (Dworkin, 1989). However, the dominant model examined the issue from an addiction perspective (Carnes, Delmonico, Griffin, & Moriarity, 2001; Young, 2000; Schneider, 2000, 2001), which argues that individuals become addicted to the sexual stimulation of the Internet much as one becomes addicted to drugs or alcohol. In this model there is an addict and a co-addict. Treatment is prescribed for both addict and co-addict based on recovery from the addiction.

The addiction perspective increases our understanding of online behaviors and characteristics of the individual user from a particular vantage point. However, exclusive focus on Internet pornography use as an addiction has its limitations. The addiction model does not provide an in-depth understanding of individual human behavior and an exploration of unconscious motives. Nor does it always explain the role that compulsive use of Internet pornography may play in the complex marital relationship. Relying exclusively on an addiction model may obscure other important information such as the individual's underlying pathology, untreated trauma associated with sexual, emotional and physical abuse, developmental interferences, failures, and parental deficits. Individuals are complex, as are the relationships in which they are involved.

I deliberately chose to research the experiences of the wives of the user from a psychodynamic approach. A psychodynamic approach illuminates the experiences of women, not just as enablers, but also as active participants as a result of their own unconscious processes. Most research concentrates on the negative effects experienced by wives as a result of their husbands' preoccupation, but there is little concentration on women who bring their individual psychodynamics to a complex marital relationship. I conducted in-depth interviews with 16 women in an effort to comprehend how they understood and managed their husbands' Internet activities. I used grounded theory to analyze the women's experiences. The women in my study narrate a cycle of men's use of pornography and their own efforts to manage and cope with this knowledge. The wives find themselves locked in a cycle in their efforts to dissuade husbands from using the Internet. Repeated discoveries of Internet activity, confrontations with spouses, threats, promises and temporary behavioral changes on the part of husbands, and then more discoveries mark the cycle. It is a repetitive cycle, and for the most part, is an integral part of the marital relationship almost from its inception. Each person's individual psychodynamics contributes to and perpetuates this cycle. This highly charged cycle appears to be a permanent fixture in the relationship, and the women report an inability to break or affect permanent change. The presence of this cycle is an interesting aspect of the marital relationship and raises many questions about its unconscious function in the relationship.

Nine discrete yet related findings raise some interesting questions. These women report that accessing Internet pornography is a piece of a larger problem; viewing of online pornography is only the tip of the iceberg for many of the women. All the women in the study had prior untreated developmental deficits due to parental interferences, neglect, emotional and physical abuse, or sexual trauma. Deeper characterological issues contribute to participants' inability to say "No" (and mean it) or to disengage from the repetitive cycle. In addition, all the women describe problems that existed early in the relationship.

Since my study concluded in 2005, Internet pornography continues to generate academic, political, and popular interest. Much of the academic work remains focused on the user and on the addictive nature of Internet pornography, ignoring a psychoanalytic perspective. Philaretou, Mahfouz, and Allen (2005) examine Internet pornography and men's well being. Yoder, Virden, and Amin (2005) research

Internet pornography and user loneliness. Baird (2005) concentrates on clergy and cybersex (2005). Bird (2006) evaluates the role of marriage and family therapy in facilitating both individual and relationship healing, but only from an addiction perspective.

Additionally, there is a growing interest in child and adolescent exposure to pornographic material (Jochen & Valkenburg, 2006; Ybarra & Mitchell, 2005), which extends beyond academic circles and into the political sphere. In the past year, Congress has held hearings on the negative effects of Internet pornography, in which several experts have presented findings from their own research[1]. Senator Blanche Lincoln (D-AR) has sponsored a bill titled "Internet Safety and Child Protection Act of 2005" in an effort to provide protection for children[2].

Thus, while there has been some research on adolescents and pornography, the addiction perspective continues to be the most popular lens through which to view the problem of compulsive Internet pornography use. However, Wood (2006) proposes that a psychoanalytic perspective may offer a dimension to understanding the compulsive Internet user. She questions the unconscious meaning that pornography may hold for a specific individual and raises questions about the etiology and psychodynamics of the user. In my own work, I find that it is important to examine the phenomenon of Internet pornography beyond the addiction lens. Rather than being the causal source of distress in a marriage as the addiction model suggests, Internet pornography may serve an important function in the relational life of the couple as demonstrated by my findings.

Chapter One, the Introduction, outlines the purpose of the research. Chapter Two contains a review of the pertinent literature on the history of pornography, current research on pornography including Internet pornography, extramarital affairs, and various psychoanalytic

---

[1] See the Senate Judiciary's website for more information on the Hearings for Internet pornography, November 10, 2005. http://judiciary.senate.gov/hearing.cfm?id=1674
[2] See Sen. Lincoln (D–AR) website for more information. http://lincoln.senate.gov/press_show.cfm?id=241537

theoretical perspectives. In Chapter Three, I discuss participant recruitment, the qualitative and quantitative methodology, and limitations and generalizability. Chapter Four is an overview of the results of the research. The results are grouped into five major conceptual categories, which describe the repetitious cycle in which the women are embroiled. These five categories and their properties are discussed in Chapters Five, Six, Seven, and Eight. Two groups of women emerge from this study. There are women who discovered a support group, Co-addicts of Sex Addicts Anonymous and non-Co-addicts of Sex Addicts Anonymous women. Chapter Nine illuminates the differences between these two groups of women and Chapter Ten summarizes the results. Chapter Eleven discusses the findings and addresses the theoretical, clinical, and social implications of the research. Additionally, this chapter includes areas for future direction. More research needs to be conducted from a psychoanalytic perspective, deepening our understanding of the dynamics of the individual as well as the marital relationship. Ultimately, this theoretical perspective and analysis based upon it, can inform clinicians' treatment of clients for whom Internet pornography is voiced as a source of marital distress.

# ACKNOWLEDGMENTS

Many people were very helpful during the long process of interviewing, analyzing the data, and writing up the results of this study. First of all, I am deeply indebted to the women who dedicated their time and emotional energy to the interview process. These women were willing to candidly tell their stories in hopes that other women experiencing similar pain could find the assistance they needed. R. Dennis Shelby was a great mentor, providing not only encouragement but instilling confidence in me along the way. His quick mind was many times able to grasp what was difficult for me to see. He was constant in his attention, encouragement, and dedication to the process. When I was unable to maintain focus and excitement, I could count on Dennis to steer me in the appropriate direction. Barbara Berger and Marcia Adler were instrumental in assisting me in analyzing and interpreting the data. Both women offered considerable clinical expertise as well as theoretical knowledge. I want to extend a special thank you to these two women who were undergoing personal challenges and yet were able to maintain focus on my research.

I have been fortunate to have had access to excellent schools of higher learning. Each of these colleges and universities taught me critical thinking skills and prepared me for the challenge of research. Without the existence of the Institute for Clinical Social Work and the staff, faculty, and students, I could not have undertaken or completed this research.

My family was instrumental in the completion of this research. Tom, my husband spent many weekends and evenings as a single parent and household manager. He also kept me focused during this long process. Kara, Nick, and Brad provided entertainment, encouragement and much needed distractions. I hope I have inspired them and demonstrated that learning is a life long process. A special thank you to my mother for her gifts of curiosity, her love and excitement for learning, and her incredible stamina.

I also want to acknowledge those friends and colleagues who gave me valuable feedback and stimulation. Thank you to those of you who read my manuscripts and offered wisdom, interpretations, and knowledge.

# THE IMPACT OF INTERNET PORNOGRAPHY ON MARRIED WOMEN

# Chapter One

# Introduction

The original purpose of this study was to explore the experiences of Roman Catholic women whose husbands use Internet pornography. I surmised that there was a connection between the Catholic Church's education about matters of sex and sexuality and Catholic women's experiences of their husbands' use of pornography. However, after completing three one-hour in-depth interviews with five Catholic women, I found no religious derivatives in the raw data. In addition, the Roman Catholic women did not correlate Catholic teaching on morals and sexuality with their particular experiences of husbands' use of Internet pornography. The revised question became "What are the experiences of women whose husbands use Internet pornography?" During the same time period, I attended a Co-addicts of Sex Addicts Anonymous (COSA) meeting and several women volunteered for the research study. These women brought a different perspective. After consultation with the chair of the research, we decided that analyzing the variations in the COSA women would provide interest and be more cogent. Thus the Catholic Church approach was eliminated, and the study was expanded to include women who self-identified as co-addicts and attended COSA meetings. Questions from the General Social Survey measuring religious attitudes were no longer a factor and the responses were not incorporated into the findings. The research focused on the experiences of women whose husbands used Internet pornography and examined variations in women who attended COSA.

The proposal still contains the references and literature examining Catholic teachings on sex and sexuality as well as Catholic influence since this was an original part of the study and informed the early interviews.

I hypothesize that there is a relationship that exists among several factors, the psychosexual development of women, gender socialization, self-esteem, the particular dynamics of the marital relationship, and wives' unique responses to their husbands. The primary objective was to illuminate the experiences of women who suspect or know that their spouses use the Internet for pornographic purposes. The results of my research will aid social workers in therapeutic work with women who report that Internet pornography is causing marital distress and are in distress over this disruption in their lives.

Interest in the topic came from clinical experience with Roman Catholic women who had negative experiences with their husbands' use of Internet pornography. Approximately one-third of the women in my clinical caseload expressed concern about their husbands' use of Internet pornography. Priests from various parishes provided information on the growing problem in their congregations and pornography's affects on men and their families. A survey of local colleagues revealed that they were not hearing about this issue in treatment, which was also very curious. Meanwhile, Internet pornography was becoming a news item in the media.

Female clients repeated similar stories of their experiences with their husbands' use of the Internet for pornography. These narratives had many commonalities. All the women were impacted in negative ways by discoveries of their husbands' use of the Internet. All reported feeling betrayed, likening spouses' use of pornography to an affair.

Wives believed the pornography use negatively impacted the marital and sexual relationship. They were astonished at the availability of pornography, and the ease in which husbands (and often children) were able to access what they believed was objectionable material. Wives saw the Internet as the culprit and worried about husbands' sexual proclivities and moral decline as well as the effects on their children if they should discover pornographic Web sites. Many clients expressed unfamiliarity with computers and a lack of knowledge about the Internet. All were shocked at the accessible graphic material.

A reoccurring theme in therapy was the lack of success women had in convincing their husbands to relinquish Internet activity. They related the numerous, futile attempts and often explosive arguments that followed discoveries of husbands' Internet activity. Furthermore, many of them believed they were responsible for their spouses' pornographic use. They wondered if they had failed their husbands in the bedroom, if they were no longer "sexy" enough, or if something was wrong with them because the husbands were "looking" elsewhere.

Prior to the availability of the Internet, men had to sneak off to an "adult" bookstore, peep show, or certain movie theaters usually located in seedier parts of the city. Pornography was available only underground, not in the "respectable" areas. Men brought home magazines, *Playboy*, being the most popular and more socially acceptable. However, with the ascent of the Internet, men had access to a less-visible, readily available media source in the relative privacy of the home. They could easily access pornography with a click of the mouse.

Discourse in the public domain on the subject of pornography focuses on issues of morality, domination and oppression of women, and violation of women's civil rights. Religious leaders, moral educators, and social feminists dominate the discussion. However, the issues of pornography are far more complex and cannot be understood through a limited lens.

Earlier forms of obtainable heterosexual pornography concentrated on the nude female form. The Internet opened up areas of pornographic viewing not previously or easily accessible. Available pornographic visuals now include heterosexual, homosexual, child, sadomasochistic, and bestiality. The literature review examines all the forms of sexual activity offered via the Internet.

Internet pornography was an unknown phenomenon 20 years ago. Since the mid-1980s, its growth has been exponential. Most middle to upper middle class families have personal computers and Internet service available in the home. This is especially true for the population that I treat. Computer technology continues to grow and change almost on a daily basis. The easy access to pornography and other sexually related activities on the Internet has spawned new areas of inquiry into what some therapists are terming "Internet addiction."

This research will concentrate on formulating a psychodynamic understanding of women's experiences with husbands who use Internet pornography. Thus, the inquiry will examine the relationship between wives' issues of self-esteem and their lack of efficacy. The exploration of female psychosexual development and its impact on wives' experiences with their husbands will contribute additional knowledge.

I initially chose Roman Catholic women because that is the population I serve. Additionally, I have been raised in the Roman Catholic Church and share a common background with these women. However, with the lack of religious derivatives in the material, the study eliminated the Roman Catholic angle and concentrated on the comparisons and differences between two groups of women, non-COSA and COSA women. While an interesting subject, it is beyond the scope of this research to formulate a psychodynamic understanding of the husbands' preoccupation with pornography. I am solely interested in how wives understand and manage their husbands' Internet activities.

# CHAPTER TWO

# BACKGROUND

The broad nature of this question requires some background study on existing forms of pornography and theoretical contributions to psychosexual development. The examination of the pornography literature explores various media, Internet sexual content and activities, pornography's effects on spouses and families, and social feminist critique of pornography. Works from diverse theorists will encompass reviews of an analytic feminist understanding of the psychology of women, object relations theory, issues of intimacy, and forgiveness and hope. The original research was to focus on Catholic women; the review will therefore include the Catholic Church's teachings on sex and sexuality. This background study will help determine which psychodynamic understanding best illuminates the experiences of women in the research study.

It is not the intent of this research to examine compulsions of husbands and their normative or pathological development. Nor is the intent to understand the intricacies of the marital relationship beyond how women understand the impact of pornography use on the marriage. These concepts will be considered on a limited basis as they relate to the experiences of women.

## HISTORY OF THE LITERATURE ON PORNOGRAPHY

The issues surrounding pornography have traditionally been framed in terms of sexual morality issues (Perkins, 1997), First Amendment rights (Dworkin, 1989), or issues of offensiveness or obscenity (Dines et al., 1998). In 1988, Andrea Dworkin and Catharine McKinnon, radical feminists, attempted to obtain an anti-pornography ordinance in Minneapolis. They centered the pornography debate on the civil rights of women (Dworkin, 1989) and sought ordinances prohibiting pornographic material. However, the federal courts rejected the ordinance on First Amendment grounds. In support of her civil rights debate, Dworkin (1989) examines the meaning of pornography and the system of power in which pornography exists. Dines et al. (1988) address the production and consumption of pornography in a social, political, and economic context.

Pornography has existed in Western Civilization since Greek and Roman periods. Early pornography consisted of physical artifacts such as frescoes depicting sexual acts including a satyr having sex with a goat, giant erect phalluses, and etchings of nude bodies in the act of sex (Kendrick, 1996). These depictions were not widely disseminated, available only to a select group of individuals. The invention of the printing press expanded the media of pornography from the visual to include the written word and provided opportunities for a larger population. As subsequent new technologies emerged, resourceful entrepreneurs discovered unique ways to manufacture pornography, either in the written word or in audio-visual format. In fact, pornographers have always been the first to exploit the new technology (Griffiths, 2000). Pornography is now available in books, magazines, photographs, film, and videos.

Dines et al. (1998) trace the growth and development of the modern heterosexual pornography industry with the appearance of the first issue of *Playboy* in 1953. This magazine played a major part in transforming the industry from a sleazy under the counter business to a multibillion-dollar industry. The invention of the camera and moving pictures offered yet other ways of producing and disseminating pornography. The advent of the Internet, originally created for military and perpetuated for academic communication (Young, 2000), has emerged as the technology of the 2000s for creating and distributing pornography.

Internet pornography was an unknown phenomenon just 20 years ago. However, since the mid-1980s, the growth of the Internet has been exponential. The price of personal computers has dropped and Internet browser software has become readily available (McKenna & Bargh, 2000). For enterprising individuals this proved to be an inexpensive and effective media to market pornography. Suddenly pornography was available with a click of the mouse and enjoyed almost immediate success. In fact, the pornography Internet sites were the first sites to generate an income (Rossetti, 2002). Internet pornography generated $1 billion in revenues in 1988 alone. According to Probe Ministries Website (www.leaderu.com), it is now an $8 billion a year business. A 1995 popular news magazine article on cyberporn estimated that 83.5% of all photos on the Internet were pornographic, although this story relied on data that was of questionable validity (Rossney, 1995). Nevertheless, the article generated public interest on the subject of Internet pornography. The rapid expansion of Internet availability has tremendously altered previous definitions, meanings, and understandings of heterosexual pornography. What was once available to a select few is now available to virtually any child or adult, male or female, who has access to a computer and the Internet; and many individuals are obtaining it. Schneider (2000), citing an Oct. 23, 2000 edition of the New York Times states "in 2000, one of four regular Internet users, or 21 million Americans, visited one of the more than 60,000 sex sites on the Web at least once a month" (p. 250). The number of users has grown since 2000. Cybersex activity is quite seductive due to its anonymity, affordability, and accessibility or what Schneider refers to as "the triple A engine" (2000, p. 250).

The relatively uncensored nature of the Internet provides a range of options that make it the ideal medium for transmitting sexual material.

Not only can the large entertainment industry take advantage of the Internet, but also any individual who desires to build amateur Web sites can avail himself of this avenue. The word "sex" is the number one searched keyword on Web browsers (Young, 2000). The availability of pornography and the number of users obtaining it has led to new types of problems for individuals in society. According to Schneider (2000), "with the rapidly enlarging role of computers in homes and offices, psychotherapists and addiction counselors are increasingly seeing clients with a new problem: cybersex addiction" (p. 250). Schneider recruited 45 men and 10 women who self-identified as cybersex participants to complete a brief online survey. All participants had experienced adverse consequences from their online sexual activities. Some respondents in Schneider's study described a swift progression of a previously existing compulsive sexual behavior problem. Others who had no history of sexual addiction found themselves rapidly involved in an escalating pattern of cybersex. The "triple A engine" and risk-free chance of contracting a sexually transmitted disease make the Internet an ideal medium for sexual involvement. These characteristics also make the Internet well suited for hiding one's activities from the spouse because it leaves little evidence of sexual encounters (Schneider, 2000).

Unlike Schneider's study, this study will concentrate on wives whose significant others are preoccupied with pornography rather than on the pornography users themselves. In order to understand the experience of wives, it is important to understand the dominant frame in which Internet pornography use is discussed among psychologists and researchers. Most experts in the field (Carnes et al., 2001; Young, 2000; Schneider, 2000, 2001) refer to cybersex as an addiction. The general population is familiar with this characterization of cybersex, as it has been presented in the mainstream media. Therefore, an understanding of the subject from the point of view of an addiction model is important for understanding the impact of men's perceived addictions on the wives.

Various researchers characterize compulsive use of the Internet as an addiction (Carnes et al. 2001; Schneider & Weiss, 2001; Young, 1998, 2000). These authors claim that the Internet has a strong appeal that can become as habit-forming as substances. Thus, they recommend interventions similar to those used to treat chemical substance abuse. According to the addiction model, a combination of neurochemical and behavioral bases explain addictive behavior. The addictive substance increases the dopamine levels in the brain, which leads to a craving for the substance in order to make one feel good and / or to prevent the self from feeling discomfort.

In an addicted family, there is always the addict and an enabler. Therefore, if the cybersex addict is married, the spouse is named as the enabler. In keeping with the addictions model, Carnes et al. (2001) have devised a "Cybersex Codependency Inventory." The inventory helps an individual determine if she or he has become part of the partner's compulsive or addictive behaviors. Answering 18 or more of the 35 questions determines one's codependency behaviors.

The characteristics of addictions include increased tolerance, withdrawal symptoms, time spent in activities necessary for pursuit of the substance, loss of control or compulsivity, continuation despite adverse consequences, and preoccupation (Schneider & Weiss, 2001). Other compulsive disorders have been categorized as "addictions," including gambling, overeating, shopping, and high-risk sexual behaviors. Online users can become addicted to the Internet much as one could become addicted to drugs or alcohol (Young, 2000). Whether it is an addiction or a compulsion, compulsive use of the Internet for pornography is not under the control of the conscious ego.

Griffiths (2000) describes a type of addiction called technological addiction. These are "operationally defined as non-chemical (behavioral) addictions that involve human-machine interaction" (p. 538). These addictions can be either passive or active, and usually contain "inducing and reinforcing features that may contribute to the promotion of addictive tendencies" (p. 538).

Schneider (2000) defines three distinct levels of cybersex users:

> Level 1: Recreational users.
> Level 2: At-risk users or those individuals who have some predisposition for dealing with emotional issues through sexual means.

> Level 3: Compulsive or addicted users or those individuals who have a history of intimacy and relationship concerns and a previously established pattern of sexual acting out.

Various researchers (Schneider, 2000; Cooper, 2002; Young, 2000) have documented the effects of cybersex on the compulsive user. These effects include: risk of job loss, guilt and shame, loss of interest in sex with the spouse, increased preoccupation with sex, increased objectification of people, lost sense of self, increased interest in deviant sex, and risk of arrest.

Cybersex behaviors include viewing and downloading of pornographic material, viewing and downloading illegal or deviant sexual images, visiting sexually oriented chat rooms, viewing, downloading, and / or chatting while engaging in masturbation, reading and writing sexually explicit letters and stories, exchanging sexually explicit e-mails with others, exchanging visual images via digital cameras, placing ads to meet sexual partners, and engaging in interactive online affairs. The cybersex consumer may engage in these activities with opposite sex individuals or with same sex individuals. While many of these activities are free, users often have to pay for access or use of these sites. Often, those engaging in cybersex pursue activities offline with individuals they have met while online, including phone sex and skin-to-skin sex. Some cybersex users participate in illegal or paraphilic online activities such as sadomasochism and domination / bondage, bestiality, viewing child pornography, and having sex with underage persons or those who claim to be underage.

Numerous studies have concentrated on non-Internet pornography and its effects on participants (Dines et al., 1998; Perkins, 1997; Dworkin, 1989; Schneider, 2000). Some have focused on the possible effect of heterosexual pornography on aggressive behavior and on the families of consumers of pornography (Zillmann & Bryant, 1988). Other studies have explored Internet relationships (Carnes et al., 2001; Civin, 2000; McKenna & Bargh, 2000; Schnarch, 1997; Young, 1998; Weber-Young, 2001). However, research into the participant's preoccupation with cybersex and how this affects spouses and partners is in the early stages. Schneider's 2000 study focuses on the adverse consequences for spouses that result from use of the Internet for some sort of sexual activity. Matheu and Sobotnik (2001) briefly address the impact on the spouse and family.

Zillman and Bryant's (1988) findings demonstrated that subjects reported less satisfaction with their intimate partners after viewing heterosexual pornography. The dissatisfaction extended to their partners' affection, physical appearance, sexual curiosity, and sexual performance. In addition, the participants assigned increased importance to sex without emotional involvement. The researchers quantitatively measured the dissatisfaction using the Indiana Happiness Inventory and Marital Satisfaction Inventory (Zillman & Bryant, 1988).

According to research conducted by Blair (1998), Kibby and Costello (2001), not all cybernet sex had negative consequences. Blair examined the phenomenon of Internet sex and the implications it has for female power roles. Kibby and Costello studied interactive sex entertainment sites using CU-SeeMe video-conferencing software. CU-SeeMe was developed by Cornell University for educational purposes and distributed as freeware. Like all new communication technologies, those seeking erotica rapidly colonized CU-SeeMe. Kibby and Costello (2001) propose that interactive CU-SeeMe sex entertainment blurs the boundaries between image and act and this suggests that online interactive sex entertainment allows for the possibility of rewriting codes of sexuality. This study provides useful information on the experiences of the participants, but gives no insight into the consequences for participants and their partners.

Schneider (2000) performed a qualitative study of cybersex participants and looked at the implications for therapists. Approaching cybersex participation from an addiction model, Schneider explored gender differences, recovery issues and meanings for therapists. She discovered that many therapists were uninformed about the nature and extent of sexual activities available online and,

> (1) minimized the significance of cybersex behavior
> and did not accept it for the powerful addiction it

was, (2) failed to make it a priority to stop illegal or
self-destructive behaviors, and (3) did not consider
the effect of the cybersex involvement on the spouse
or partner (p. 250).

While effects of Internet pornography have not been sufficiently
studied, Zillman and Bryant's (1988) findings suggest that compulsive
use of Internet pornography may negatively impact sexual satisfaction
for the user. Furthermore, Schneider (2000, 2001) demonstrated that
there are negative consequences for the spouse and families of those
men who participate in cybersex. Excessive use of the Internet for sexual activity can result in adverse consequences for the individual as well
as his family (Schneider, 2000, p. 256). These consequences include
depression and other emotional problems, social isolation, career loss
or decreased job performance, and other financial difficulties. There also
may be a "worsening of their sexual relationship with spouse or partner,
harm done to their marriage or primary relationship" (p. 250). These
consequences affect not only the individual, but also his family.

The subject of Internet sex, cybersex, and Internet pornography
needs to be further studied. As the Internet continues to grow at an
exponential rate, so will the number of cybersex participants. Marketers
of pornography will continue to develop innovative and creative
means to attract consumers to the specific Web sites and chat rooms.
As several studies have indicated, there are consequences for the
participants and families of those who excessively use the computer
for sexual activities. Thus, it is essential that therapists develop an
understanding of the Internet and sexual activity on the Net. It is also
important for therapists to understand the experiences and effects that
this activity has on the families of those participants.

Observations from clinical practice indicate that many women are
aware on some level of their husbands' preoccupation with Internet
pornography. They struggle with ways to manage their relationships
with their husbands and the preoccupation with the Internet. Women
employ various psychological defenses and respond with a myriad of
behaviors in their efforts to cope with their spouses' chosen pastime.

Often women defend against any knowledge of their husband's behaviors by using the defense of denial. Others disavow their husband's Internet behaviors, which allow them to tolerate their husband's activity and manage the marital relationship. Other responses to husbands include ignoring the behavior, detective work to uncover the use, arguments about the material, bargaining with their husbands, using detective software to reveal cybersex activities, deleting Web sites, controlling computer access, increasing sexual activity and repertory of sexual activities, retaliating by spending money or engaging in extramarital affairs, and withdrawing from the relationship. Some women generate conflict about issues seemingly unrelated to their husbands' Internet activity. Many women confront their husbands directly only after the children are exposed to the material. Rarely do women confide in others due to intense shame about their spouse's use of pornography. Women's awareness level is not reflective in their coping strategies.

The relationships women have with their husbands are complex and complicated. Although they claim to find the Internet behavior reprehensible, some women rationalize an inability to make spouses relinquish this activity. All wives struggle internally and externally with this issue. It impacts their spiritual, emotional, sexual, intellectual, and relational lives. There are underlying psychological reasons that explain the difficulty of establishing firm, clear boundaries. How do women manage in the relationship? How are some women able to establish and maintain boundaries while other women feel powerless? Why is it that some women participate in the activity and other women withdraw? How do the psychosexual development, socio-educational background, and religious beliefs affect women in how they manage?

To understand this phenomenon, this study will examine various analytic theoretical perspectives, commencing with current day theorists and ending with Freud. The literature review will begin with the social feminists and their contribution to the understanding of pornography. While this is a limited view, it provides context and social history. Once the social environment for the use of pornography is established, the literature will move into the psychoanalytic realm and explore multiple theories. The theories will include analytic feminist, relationalist, object relations, Freudian, and literature on affairs. This literature review will offer some possible explanations as to how wives manage their lives.

## CURRENT RESEARCH ON PORNOGRAPHY

### Social Feminist Theory

Prior to the 1980s, discourse in the public domain focused on issues of morality in relation to pornography. The radical feminists removed the discussion from moral grounds and placed it in the context of abuse and oppression of women. This view was a reaction to the proliferation and availability of the pornographic material. Although the Social Feminist view is a limited lens through which to examine this phenomenon, it is important in terms of its historical significance and expansion of the discussion beyond morality.

Social feminists (Dines et al., 1998; Lederer, 1980) are not the only feminists to examine the meaning of heterosexual pornography from the context of the system of power, some radical feminists (Dworkin, 1989; MacKinnon, 1987) also do. The radical feminists argue that sexuality is not innate, but a social construct (Dworkin, 1989; MacKinnon, 1987). Gender is a hierarchy based on power in which men dominate and women submit. Pornography is a "core constitutive practice of gender inequality" (MacKinnon, 1987, p. 149). Steinman argues that pornography is "about power and sex-as-weapon" (Stoller, 1991, p. 1088). According to MacKinnon's theory, the contents of pornography "speak to the male compulsion to dominate and destroy that is the source of sexual pleasure for men" (1987, p. 149). Many of these radical feminists believe that men are sexual predators by nature, desiring their sexual lives to be like the fantasy lives depicted in pornography.

MacKinnon (1987) proposes that pornography has a large role in a system that subordinates and oppresses women. According to MacKinnon, pornography objectifies all women, making them into "cunts" (p. 223). Men treat women as pornography depicts women to be. These feminists maintain that women do not participate in this objectification, but are coerced.

Dines et al. (1998) also see issues of pornography embedded in a larger system and discuss the consumption and production of pornography from a social, political, and economic context. From their perspective, women are objects in pornographic representations. The authors view pornography as part of an oppressive, patriarchal sexual system that perpetuates injustice. Like MacKinnon (1987) and Dworkin (1989), Dines et al. (1998) believe that this pattern of "dominance and submission ... ... has been incarnated as sexuality in each of us" (p. 6).

According to Laura Lederer (1980), only two sides of the pornography issue had been presented as of 1980. She proposed that the conservative approach, which declares pornography to be immoral, and the liberal approach, which presents pornography as an aspect of our expanding human sexuality, have not addressed the culture's debasement of women in pornographic images and films. Like other social feminists (Dines et al., 1998; MacKinnon, 1987; Dworkin, 1989), Lederer (1980) views women as victims in the pornography debate. Lorde (1980) expands the discourse by examining the role of desire and eroticism in pornography. She believes women have learned to suppress eroticism as a result of being immersed in a patriarchal culture.

In his contribution to the discourse on pornography, Khan (1979) evaluates pornography from an aesthetic and psychological perspective rather than focusing on the judicial and ethical. He criticizes the "ecriture" of pornography for its repetition, and lack of literary style imagination, and monotony. It is not that it is immoral but that it is "pathetically bad literature" (Khan, 1979, p. 221), which alienates an individual from himself and from the other. Pornography is not about intimacy. It appears to be about sensuality and orgiastic pleasure, but is really about a physical manipulation of one's own body and the other's bodily organ. He agrees with radical feminists in equating pornography with rage, humiliation, and submission. "The true achievement of pornography is that it transmutes rage into erotic somatic events" (p. 222). Rather than stimulating desire, it paradoxically is about a lack of desire. Compulsive use of pornography inhibits the inner capacity for growth.

*Analytic Feminist Theory*

Analytic feminists (Benjamin, 1986, 1988, 1995; Chasseguet-Smirgel, 1988) approach the problem of pornography from an alternative perspective than the position articulated by the social feminists. These theorists are keenly interested in feminine developmental issues, object relationships, and the role of pornography. Many of these theorists believe the development of women's sexuality and the specific problems that women experience in relationships are neither entirely biologically nor socially determined. Their arguments put forward the idea that sexual development is highly complex and cannot be reduced to either biology or culture.

Benjamin (1986, 1995) takes exception to Dworkin's (1989) discussion on the subject of pornography because if Dworkin believes that all men derive sexual pleasure from dominating and destroying, then men are by nature the dominators. Thus, women's participation in this sexual domination means that women's nature is as pornography depicts it, submissive. Benjamin concludes, "If men inevitably are what they are, then how can women not be what they are?" (1995, p. 177). She wonders if the social feminists really want to see women as inherently victims.

According to Benjamin (1995), pornography is not simply a social, political construct that perpetuates the oppression of women. Nor are pornographic representations expressions of concrete contents of desire; instead, they express a relation between sexual excitement and the realm of fantasy. Pornography can be felt as a confrontation with some dangerous and exciting otherness. This fantasy or reality has the power to create internal excitement, which can be either repulsive or pleasurable to women.

Benjamin's difficulty with MacKinnon (1987) is that her discussion of the gender domination is too simplistic. MacKinnon "flattens the most difficult problem into the proposition that 'violence is sex'" (Benjamin, 1995, p. 177). Although MacKinnon acknowledges that women experience sexual pleasure in the context of abuse, she does not attempt to understand what makes powerlessness exciting. The social and radical feminists associate women with submissiveness. However this leads to the question, if women are victims how will they be able to challenge the status quo of the patriarchal power? Benjamin believes that MacKinnon relies on social definitions of men and women and fails to understand the psychological intricacies of the sexual relations between men and women.

Benjamin (1988, 1995) seeks alternative explanations to the understanding of gender domination / submission. She begins by questioning why these particular concepts shape the relationship between sexes and argues that the problem of domination / submission appears to be anchored so deep in the psyche that it seems to be inevitable that men will dominate and women will be submissive. Benjamin wonders about the origins of the particular problem and begins with an observation of Freud. Freud accepted this pattern as normative. He saw the interplay between domination and submission in terms of the Oedipal struggle between father and son. Mature feminine development meant that women would embrace submission, while men would be dominant.

Benjamin (1988, 1995) begins with the assumption that the problem of domination / submission is a dualism that permeates Western culture and continues to shape the relationship between men and women despite society's formal commitment to equality. In western culture, it is usually the female who provides primary care to children of both sexes. Thus, both the little girl and boy find their first object in the mother. Benjamin (1988, 1995) theorizes that as the first object, the mother influences patterns of identifications and object relations that create gender identity. The little girl's identification with the mother may compromise her struggle for independence while the boy's may compromise his dependency needs. According to Benjamin (J. Benjamin, personal communication, August 8, 2003), this theory of human development is generalizable to many women and men. Although she has been criticized for this generalization, it is beyond the scope of this research to critique this theory.

Submission to an idealized other is a key component of masochism. According to Benjamin (1995), Freud's explanation of female sub-mission and male dominance as biologically determined is too one-dimensional. She is also critical of the tendency in feminism to view the woman as victimized by male aggression. Women actually derive something from the interplay of domination / submission. Love and domination are complementary, involving the participation of both the one who has power and the one who is willing to submit to power. Benjamin (1995) believes that submission is the "desire of the domi-nated as well as their helpless fate" (p. 52). She takes the position that women have an internal propensity toward masochism while men have one toward sadism. "I suggest that the patterns of gender identifications and separation-individuation that arise from female parenting creates a feminine proclivity to masochism" (Benjamin, 1995, p. 461).

The domination / submission dilemma lies in the fact that women are alienated from their own sexual desire. Power for the woman does not reside in her own desire for another, but in her desirability. This desirability is based on how the culture defines what is desirable. Since the woman cannot claim her own desire, she must seek it in another. The woman searches for a powerful, idealized lover in whom she can vicariously experience desire. Benjamin's discussion of the prob-lem of domination and submission is pertinent to researching the experiences of women whose husbands are preoccupied with Internet pornography.

The early mother / infant relationship is the foundation for domi-nation / submission pattern observed in men and women in western culture. Domination and submission are the result of the infant's inability to tolerate the necessary tension between dependence and independence. In developmental progression, infants must build up a gradual and imperfect capacity for mutual recognition of the parents. This ability to recognize the other is crucial to normative development. By recognition, Benjamin (1995) means the capacity to see the other as a subject. Recognition begins with the other's confirming response. This response informs infants that meaning has been created. As development proceeds, there is a tension that must be maintained between asserting one's own reality and denying the reality of the other. In progressing toward this dialectic, infants must give up the fantasy of omnipotence in exchange for acknowledging the reality of the other. If a maturing individual fails to navigate this developmental step, she will be unable to engage in mutual recognition of the other and the development of a healthy self will be compromised.

According to Benjamin (1995), there is a subject-object complementarity present in the early infant / mother relationship that must eventually give way to a relationship of mutuality. The infant has to relinquish the fantasy of the mother as the all-powerful object and begin to recognize her as a person in her own right. If the mother / infant dyad is unable to manage this tension, the complementary structure continues and becomes a template for future interactions between the self and the other. However, as long as mother remains the omnipotent object, the infant is engaged in a power struggle. This omnipotent mother becomes the basis for the "dread and retaliation that inform men's exercise of power over women" (Benjamin, 1995, p. 195). The adult relation between men and women becomes the locus of the great reversal, turning the tables on the omnipotent mother of infancy. Man becomes the dominator, while woman is in the complementary position of submission.

The relationship between self and other includes a tension between sameness and difference. No one can be truly independent of another, but individuals also need to be recognized. By recognition, Benjamin (1995) means, "the other is mentally placed in the position of a different, outside entity but shares a similar feeling or state of mind" (p.184). The infant must maintain this tension of dependence and independence. However, this can feel threatening to the developing infant as recognition, the ability to truly see the other, threatens the existence of the self. In response, the self may move toward the polarity of independence, denying one's dependency needs, and toward domination. Splitting occurs when dependence is devalued and independence is idealized.

According to Benjamin (1988), one sees the "pure culture" (p. 52) of domination and submission in sadomasochistic fantasies and relationships. The "fantasy of erotic domination includes both the desire of independence and the desire for recognition" (Benjamin, 1988, p. 52). If the infant is unable to surrender the fantasy that he is omnipotent and can magically control the object, the infant may believe that he can become independent without recognizing the other. Benjamin stresses that in order to achieve independence; there must be mutual recognition, a sharing of like feelings and intentions. Without this mutual recognition, the child continues to believe that he can control the other who is not a separate individual. The developing individual fails to recognize his dependency.

The masochist fears independence as independence means abandonment and separation. Her sense of self is shaped by her identification with the self-sacrificing mother. If the woman acknowledges that she is different from her mother, the woman risks destroying the beloved other. She can protect the "all-good, all-powerful maternal object" (Benjamin, 1988, p. 79) by retreating into compliance and submission. The fear of separation and difference is transformed into submission. By submitting to the sadist, by taking on the fault, the masochist protects the other from hurt and pain and reenacts the early relationship with the mother.

"Controlled practice of sadomasochism portrays a classic drama of destruction and survival" (Benjamin, 1988, p. 68). The excitement for the sadist lies in the survival of the masochist. If the masochist can survive the attack, the sadist can then experience love and experience freedom. As the sadist experiences this as love, so does the masochist. The woman shares the deep psychic pain; "the opportunity to give over pain in the presence of a trusted other who comprehends the suffering he inflicts" (Benjamin, 1988, p. 68). Both masochist and sadist derive something out of the arrangement.

Benjamin (1995) examines the differences in gender development to understand the phenomenon that associates femininity with masochism and masculinity with sadism. For both sexes, the woman is the primary caretaker and the first object. Differentiation in relation to the primary object poses a special difficulty for the male child. He must define himself as a different gender in order to differentiate from his primary love object. The male child cannot grow up to become his mother; he can only have her as his mother. To achieve masculinity, boys deny their original identification with the mother. This process of disidentification often prevents the young male child from recognizing his mother as a separate person. In confirming himself as a separate individual, the boy may see mother as the other, an object rather than a subject. The little boy's male identity emphasizes separation, difference, and independence. In achieving this masculine identification, he denies his dependence on the mother and may lose his capacity for mutual recognition. As Benjamin (1988) argues, when one denies the recognition of the other as an individual, one persists in seeing the other as object "to be done to and violated, to be separated from, to have power over, to denigrate" (p. 77).

Both the young female and young male desire to escape the threat of mother engulfment. In western culture, mother is a desexualized figure whose only power resides in servility to others. She has power over the child, but not power over her own destiny. The phallus, in the form of father, represents desire, liberation, and freedom from dependency. For Benjamin (1988), the phallus is symbolic and not actual. It is important because of what it represents to children of both sexes, power.

It is in the phallus that individuals find the excitement. Since women have suppressed their own sexual desire, they often seek it in another. Finding a powerful lover and choosing subordination are expressions of a woman's desire. Desire is also expressed through submission and envy, products of idealization. If the female can identify with an ideal other, she can experience being desired (Benjamin, 1988).

Chasseguet-Smirgel (1988) also addresses the question of a woman's desire and the difficulty she has in achieving sexual satisfaction. She posits that the root of the problem with female desire can be traced to a particular developmental phase of object change in the Oedipal phase. This change of objects is important in psychosexual development. The pitfalls present in this object change may induce in an adult female guilt over anality. When Chasseguet-Smirgel (1988) refers to anality, she is referring to women's inability to achieve satisfaction in her own personal, professional, and social successes. Anality is power and due to the guilt about that power, women sublimate their anality. A woman who is capable of claiming her own agency is able to relate to a man who is able to respect and take her contributions seriously. Claiming self-agency empowers the woman to confront the man without fearing that her aggression will annihilate him. Chasseguet-Smirgel (1988) differs from Benjamin (1988) in that Benjamin understands idealization of the other who has the power to be a specific component of alienation of women's desire.

Chasseguet-Smirgel (1988) locates the problem in the developing mother-daughter relationship and a need for idealization of the paternal penis as part of feminine development. The growth of idealization is an initial step in the change of objects from mother to father. The young woman's aggressive instincts toward her father and the penis are in direct conflict with her need to idealize. She cannot both experience idealization and aggression simultaneously. Thus, she experiences guilt that makes psychosexual development problematic.

For change of object to occur, a new good object capable of alleviating the shortcomings of the first object must exist (Chasseguet-Smirgel, 1988). The little girl needs to project good aspects of the primary object onto a secondary object while simultaneously projecting bad aspects onto the original primary object. Thus for Chasseguet-Smirgel, splitting is an important component in this process. The mother's task is to provide optimal frustration and the father's is to provide a solid personality. If these two conditions are met, then the woman will not experience guilt over her own or sense of power. However, if these two conditions are not met, the little girl will be unable to establish a non-conflictual identification with her mother, resulting in an over-idealization of the father. This idealization process profoundly impacts the little girl's future psychosexual development. In order to safeguard idealization of father, the little girl represses aggression toward her father (and toward the penis) and maintains identification with bad aspects of the first object.

The guilt the developing girl feels toward her father vis-à-vis aggression affects both her sexual development and her development

in areas that assume an unconscious phallic significance. The little girl
will retain a primitive over-idealization of the penis and a devaluation
of herself. This over-idealization is problematic in adulthood as the
young woman experiences difficulty in intellectual, professional, and
creative arenas. For example, intellectual, professional, and creative
achievements could mean the adult woman has not only surpassed
her own mother by appropriating her father's penis, but she may also
have "castrated the father" (Chasseguet-Smirgel, 1988, p. 101). Thus,
a woman may experiences enormous guilt about her own agency, and
this guilt could manifest itself in various somatic symptoms.

If the little girl's mother is too omnipotent and / or too domineering,
the young girl may feel helpless and envious. Although the woman
may retain unconscious images of the phallic mother, the daughter
realizes it is the father who possesses the actual penis. She turns
from mother toward father in an effort to liberate herself from the phallic
mother who in her omnipotence has narcissistically injured the little
girl. Chasseguet-Smirgel (1988) claims the little girl realizes that the
possibility of healing the narcissistic wound resides in possessing the penis.
In this context the penis serves both as an organ and as a phallus that
symbolizes "treasure of strength, integrity, magic power, or autonomy"
(Chasseguet-Smirgel, 1988, p. 111). Penis envy is not about envy of
the penis for its own sake, but for the attributes it appears to offer
and has its origins in mother conflict. Since the little girl lacks this
power, she envies the one who possesses the penis. The girl seeks
satisfaction by turning her aggression toward the new love object;
father. "Any achievement which provides her with narcissistic pleasure
will be felt as an encroachment on the father's power, thereby leading
to many inhibitions" (Chasseguet-Smirgel, 1988, 111). These inhibitions
manifest themselves later in the realm of sexuality where the woman
may be unable to fully take pleasure in sexual experience.

Other analytic feminist theorists are critical of developmental
theories that assume mature development means the infant moves
from total dependence on mother to separation, individuation, autonomy, and self-reliance. These theorists postulate that development of
a self takes place within the context of a relationship (Miller, 1984;

Chodorow, 1978, 1980; Gilligan, 1982, 1986; Surrey, 1991). Maintenance of this relationship with another is primary for women. According to Miller (1984), gender differences are predominantly a societal construct. The young child learns that her own sense of agency comes not in doing for the self, but in doing for another. An adult female derives a sense of self-esteem from being part of a relationship and tending to that relationship. Indeed, the woman is likely to believe that "all activity should lead to an increased emotional connection with others" (Miller, 1984, p. 39).

In contradiction to Benjamin's (1988) assertion that society is committed to equality, Miller (1984) believes that western culture remains sexually bifurcated with definite understood roles for men and women. A young woman receives a strong message from culture that if she develops a sense of agency, her chances for a satisfying emotional experience will be jeopardized. The sense of self becomes organized around establishing and maintaining relationships. Surrey (1991) refers to development of self in the female as organized around "self-in-relation." Early in life, the little girl is encouraged to develop abilities to "feel as the other feels" and to learn about other individuals. Even the threat of disruption of a relationship can be perceived as more than a loss of a relationship; it can be perceived as a total loss of self (Miller, 1984).

Like Benjamin (1988), Miller (1984) notes that a woman learns her own sexual sensations and desires do not emanate from inside the self, but are brought forth by and for the male. A woman is unable to claim her own sexual desire, and instead, experiences sexual stirrings as wrong, bad, or shameful. However, a man is encouraged and permitted to be sexual, to desire and to act upon their desires, while this same activity for a woman is discouraged.

Chodorow (1978, 1980) disagrees with 19th and 20th century feminists who argue that if one could degender society, male dominance would be eliminated. One side of this argument maintains that gender differences are acquired, while an alternate view claims that differences are innate. Gender differences are both socially and psychologically created according to Chodorow (1978, 1980). Therefore, the issue of domination / submission is both psychologically and socially created. Differences, especially gender differences are created within the context of relationship. The infant experiences herself as both cognitively and libidinally merged and continuous with the primary caretaker. An essential early task in her psychosexual development is the establishment of a separate sense of physical and psychological self. Like Benjamin (1995), Chodorow (1978, 1980) believes separation-individuation takes place within a relationship with the primary other. Adequate separation means the infant must perceive a subjective sense of other, to experience mother as "not me." This other has needs, feelings, and desires that are separate from those of the developing infant. If the infant does not learn to perceive the subjectivity of her mother, then the mother will continue to be perceived as an object.

The central core of self is "internally, a relational ego, a sense of self-in-good relationship" (Chodorow, 1980, p. 427). This "true self" or "central self" emerges through the experience of continuity that the mother provides. Once this continuity is experienced, the child can develop a sense of self-agency. The more secure the individual, the less need to define oneself as separate from others. "Differentiation is not distinctness and separateness, but a particular way of being connected to others" (Chodorow, 1980, p. 428).

Mothers are often experienced in ambivalent ways by both infants and adults. Attitudes toward mothers and expectations of what it means to be a mother have their origins in the early differentiation process. Differentiation and separation are inherently problematic for both genders as the mother is viewed as other, or an object. This view of the mother as object has the potential to remain into adulthood due to early internalized object images and feelings about self in relation to mother. The difficulty for women in establishing a sense of an independent self is not due to development of core gender identity, but is a product of both a society that devalues the specific gender and an ambivalently experienced mother.

Chodorow (1980) cites the Oedipal conflict along with broader object-relational and ego processes as informative in defining gender-related issues. She views this period as important in "constituting different forms of relational potential" (Chodorow, 1978, p. 167) in the different genders. Based on retention of preoedipal attachment to her mother, a girl comes to define and experience herself as continuous with others. She also emerges from this period with a greater degree of empathy than her male counterpart and more preoccupation both with her external world and her internalized object-relationships. "The basic feminine sense of self is connected to the world, the basic masculine sense of self is separate" (Chodorow, 1980, p. 169).

While feminine identity is formed based on attachment to the mother, masculine identity formation is based on a denial of attachment to the mother and focus on separation. This denial of attachment results in repudiation and devaluation of all that is feminine. Masculine personality comes to be founded "more on the repression of affect and the denial of relational needs and a sense of connection than feminine personality" (Chodorow, 1989, p. 73).

Chodorow's (1980) discussions of the father / daughter dyad and the role of idealization correspond to that of Benjamin's (1995), but Chodorow offers added clarity. The young girl's relation to her father is important during her early development. The original mother relation is seductive as it offers possibility of blissful unity. However, this blissful unity is also frightening because of the fear of complete dependence and the potential for loss of self. In contrast to her mother, the father has always been known as a separate person with separate interests. The infant has not had to rely completely upon this other. The father's presence is important as he affirms development of feminine self.

Chodorow (1989) notes that Chasseguet-Smirgel (1988) speaks to the "peculiar duality of men's secondary yet at the same time primary importance to women" (Chodorow, 1989, p. 71). The fathers, and men in general, are emotionally secondary and not exclusively loved, but they are idealized. The father represents escape both physically and intrapsychically from maternal omnipotence. However, in western culture, a father is often distant and in an ideological position of authority in the family. Mother usually contributes to her husband's position of authority. The young girl may not really come to know her father with his real strengths and weaknesses. She is unable to see his limitations, yet must count on a feeling of being loved. Her attachment to him is based to a large extent on fantasy and idealization. This idealization of the father leaves her with a distorted image of him and affects future relationships with men.

*Object Relations Theory*

The theory of object relations offers another perspective for examining the experiences of women who are married to men who use Internet pornography. According to this perspective, the early infant mother relationship becomes the template for later adult relationships. A discussion of object relations' theory will contribute to the discourse as to how adult relationships become problematic for particular women.

Children develop an interpersonal world by forming object attachments with significant others. These early relationships form the basis of self-structure and are affected by limitations of that relationship. The templates that are laid in infancy influence later choices of objects. These later attachments are formed to minimize anxiety and pain. Any attachment, no matter how painful, is preferable to loss of contact (Fairbairn, 1943; Summers, 1994). A child will choose painful attachments in order to avoid isolation and anxiety of annihilation (Kernberg, 1975; Fairbairn, 1943; Klein, 1937). In her adult relationships, she may establish a pattern of choosing object relations that appear to be pathological. This pattern is driven by an infantile need to look for the object who will help regain "the lost unity of the self" (Armstrong-Perlman, 1994).

Fairbairn's (1943) conception of the internalization of a bad object is useful for understanding dynamics of individuals who find themselves in relationships that do not adequately meet their needs or are frustrating those needs. It may also explain how wives cope with husbands' cybersex use. Fairbairn theorizes that ego is present from birth and libido is a function of ego. It [libido] is of "secondary importance in comparison with object-relationships" (Fairbairn, 1943, p. 60). The ego and libido are fundamentally object seeking. "A relationship with the object ... is the ultimate aim of libidinal striving"

(Fairbairn, 1943, p. 60). A whole ego is present at birth, and this "pristine" ego serves the function of searching for a gratifying object. From birth, the infant is oriented toward relationships with others. If these external others are unable to provide a satisfying relational experience, the infant will need to internalize the "subjectively experienced aspects of the real external parents" (Fairbairn, 1943, p. 69). In order to maintain a much needed connection to the other. These internalized aspects are experienced as bad or depriving.

For Fairbairn (1943, 1949), aggression is not primary; it is a reaction to frustration or deprivation. If the infant experiences the primary caretaker as a frustrating object, it becomes too painful to long for or depend upon the physically or emotionally absent object. In order to cope with disappointment and maintain a connection to the object, the infant unconsciously splits and internalizes aspects of the real external parents. Once this object is internalized, the exciting and frustrating aspects are split off from the "main core of the object and repressed by the ego" (Grotstein, 1994, p. 51). The libidinal ego becomes attached to the "needed-exciting" internal object and the antilibidinal ego becomes attached to the frustrating object. This internalization of a bad object is the infant's attempt at regaining control over the deprivation of the environment. These internalized objects are substitutes for unsatisfying relationships with real external mothers. Furthermore, the infant becomes the bad one, while the real external objects remain good. Fairbairn (1943) stressed that this defense mechanism, the "moral defense against bad objects" (p. 65), is an adaptive response to disappointment in the environment.

According to Fairbairn (1943), once these objects are internalized, they provide a template for future relational engagements, including choice of one's spouse. These endopsychic structures are so powerful that they shape all future external relationships. In addition, the ego identifies to varying degrees with these "bad" internalized objects. The experiences of the internal object relations and the projection of them onto an external other produce pathological suffering (Greenberg & Mitchell, 1983, p. 173). The frustrating or exciting internal objects are projected onto the other in an effort to regain control. This cathexis of ego to object makes it exceedingly difficult for an individual to separate from the depriving, disappointing or exciting other. The tantalizing and frustrating object has a particular hold on the individual, as the individual tenaciously holds on to hope that the bad object will offer something good.

Guilt is also employed as a defense against release of bad objects. The deepest source of resistance is "fear of the release of bad objects from the unconscious" (Fairbairn, 1943, p. 69). If an individual were to release bad objects, the world would become too terrifying because bad objects would be external and no longer within the control of the individual. An individual is better able to retain internal bad objects than to live with terror of what is not in one's control.

Klein (1937) is also interested in internalization of objects and the pathology that develops as a result of a fixation at a particular developmental phase. According to Klein, the love / hate conflict that appears in early infancy is active all through one's life. A constant tension exists between hate and love. The little girl may unconsciously seek in her spouse or her lover attributes of her early relationship with her mother. The father also plays an important part in the little girl's early life and her relationship to him may influence her later love relations. For Klein, the most important development in human relations is the "capacity for identification with another person ... ... and is also a condition for real and strong feelings of love" (Klein, 1937, p. 311). In making sacrifices for another whom one loves, one has the ability to be both a good parent and a good child to the parent. The complexity of the relationships an individual experienced with her parents is reenacted in adult love relationship.

Klein (1937, 1946, 1975) emphasizes the importance of object relationships in development and psychopathology. Unlike Fairbairn (1943) who stresses the real external bad objects, Klein (1975) views the origins of bad objects as a product of the phantasies of the infant and places more emphasis on the internal world of the infant. The unconscious phantasies overcome reality considerations of real people. In the paranoid position, the developing infant is threatened by her own sadistic phantasies involving the fears that she will destroy the object and relationship to the object. Splitting results from efforts to manage hatred and aggression. To protect the good object, the infant splits the object into a good and a bad object and simultaneously projects destructive impulses outward onto the object. The bad object is then experienced as persecutory and evil. However, as Grotstein (1994) argues, the badness perceived in an object is a "by-product of the infant's own greed, envy, and / or destructive hate upon them" (p. 135). By perceiving the object as bad, the infant is then safe from her own destructiveness; the baby will not destroy the mother, the mother will destroy the infant. In order to manage the accompanying fear of this bad mother, the infant idealizes the persecutory object.

Now that the threat comes from outside the infant, she is able to introject the bad object in an effort to control danger and reduce anxiety. This cycle of projection-introjection allows the infant to manage aggression and reduce the anxiety. This projection-introjection cycle builds up the internal world of the infant and enables her to control the constant frustration and gratification she experiences with the object.

If the infant's maternal environment offers enough of a positive experience, the infant will be able to internalize a solid good object. The paranoid position gives way to the next phase of development, the depressive position, as the infant gradually begins to recognize that good and bad objects are the same. Splitting is no longer relied on as a major defense once the objects are integrated. The infant becomes aware of her own capacity to inflict harm on the object she loves and on whom she depends for gratification. The desires, wishes, and phantasies that the infant previously projected onto the object are now owned as originating in the infant. Guilt over this desire to harm the object accompanies anxiety. If this guilt is unresolved during this phase it can lead to difficulties in later adult life. Depressed adults may find it exceedingly difficult to separate from their object whether they are good objects or bad objects (Summers, 1994).

*Self-Psychology*

The phenomena of the vertical split may contribute another perspective on the complex relationship of cybersex user and spouse.

Goldberg (1999) explains the phenomenon of the vertical split, describing it as "being of two minds" or the practice of disowning parts of the self that one finds distasteful (Goldberg, 1999). This is the phenomenon in which the individual intensely claims to dislike particular behavior and beliefs, yet tolerates or even participates in these same behaviors and actions. Disavowal is the defense that maintains the structure of the vertical split.

The vertical split consists of an experience, in which there are coexisting feelings that lead to different and opposite results. During the course of development, an individual must learn to reconcile the contradictions that are present in life. One early defense mechanism is that of splitting. This defense allows the individual to preserve the relationship with the caretakers and reconcile the contradictions. The aim of disavowal is to maintain self-cohesion.

There are two forms of splitting that Goldberg (1999) observed in his patients. The first form is that which is seen in the borderline disorders where there has never been a sense of unification. The second form of splitting occurs in individuals where unification of the self has been achieved.

Vertical splits are not necessarily problematic, but can become pathological when fantasy life becomes so divided from reality that it takes on a life of its own. The fantasy life becomes reality and the individual begins acting out of this reality. As a result, the split in self becomes even more accentuated and feelings associated with fantasy become split from reality. This phenomenon is not simply a form of denial or suppression; disparate parts of the personality actually exist side by side. These separate personality attitudes may have "different goal structures, different pleasure aims, different moral and aesthetic values" (1999, p. 67).

The vertical split may be a defense used by women whose husbands' play out their sexual fantasies in the world of cybersex. Wives often lack efficacy; they are unable to convincingly order husbands to stop activities they find objectionable. Thus, it is possible that women are both simultaneously stimulated and repelled by cybersex. Women probably had some awareness of husbands' use of pornography prior to marriage, yet they pursued marriage. By using the defense of disavowal, wives are able to manage relationships. Husbands' may also use the defense of the vertical split that leads them to engage in excessive Internet use in relative privacy. Due to their abilities to disavow feelings and behaviors, husbands and wives together participate in the vertical split.

*Feminine Masochism*

The topic of feminine masochism is an idea that was introduced by Freud (1905) and elaborated by numerous other theorists (Menaker, 1953; Reik, 1941; Benjamin, 1986). Masochism can be expressed either in the form of a sexual perversion or as a life attitude. An earlier discussion of Benjamin's (1988) overview of sadism and masochism or domination / submission has already provided some insight into this concept, but additional literature will further illuminate the problem of masochism. Since it is possible that wives whose husbands are preoccupied with Internet pornography tolerate this behavior due to their masochistic natures, it is necessary to explore a discussion of masochism and its complement, sadism.

Sadism is the "most common and the most significant of all the perversions" (Freud, 1905, p. 157). Freud defines sadism as the "desire to inflict pain upon the sexual object," (p. 157) and masochism as its reverse. Sadism is not only characterized by physical violence toward the sexual object, it also includes pleasure in humiliating or subjugating the other. Freud considers sadism to be the active form, while masochism was the passive form.

For Freud (1905), masochism is the expression of the death instinct. Its aim is the gratification of the unconscious need for self-punishment stemming from guilt over forbidden sexual impulses. He views masochism as a passive component to sexuality. Masochism is sadism turned inward. Freud (1905) observes that most males have a desire to "subjugate" by means other than traditional "wooing" of the opposite sex. He claims that sadism is an active component of sexuality. The most remarkable feature of sadism / masochism is that it seems to occur together in the same individual. "A person who feels pleasure in producing pain in someone else in a sexual relationship is also capable of enjoying as pleasure any pain which he may himself derive from sexual relations" (Freud, 1905, p. 159).

Freud (1905) believes that sexuality of most males contains the need to aggressively overcome resistance. Thus, sadism corresponds to this aggressive component that has become exaggerated. Freud (1933) links sadism with masculinity and masochism with femininity. Normative development for the little girl means that she must abandon a certain amount of activity for passivity. If she fails to accept that her clitoris is inferior and exaggerates her "previous masculinity, clings to her clitoridal activity" (1933, p. 130), she emerges with a great amount of activity that is characteristic of a male and this may influence her choice of object. This clinging to "activity" is problematic for the female in the development of her femininity. Although Freud (1933) acknowledges that women display "great activity in various directions" (p. 115) he believes that they give preference to passive aims. Women are both constitutionally as well as socially inclined toward masochistic impulses.

Since Freud (1933), many theorists have perpetuated the notion of feminine masochism. Benjamin (1986) cites the works of Deutsch and Bonaparte as furthering the idea that masochism, narcissism, and passivity are "decisive tendencies in women's sexual and psychic life" (Benjamin, 1986, p. 457). Deutsch relies on Freud's theories of feminine development. Freud (1933) believes that women are born into this world already castrated. In order to move into mature femininity, the female must give up her "active-aggressive stand" that focused on the clitoris. This aggression must go somewhere and the Oedipal female, turns the aggression inward. This inward aggression takes the form of a wish to be castrated by the father and to be penetrated by him. Women's acceptance of pain and humiliation are crucial to a sexual relationship with men.

Kernberg (1975) views sadomasochism as an important element in erotic desire. While masochism can be viewed as a healthy capacity for self-sacrifice, it also can become a perversion when played out in the sexual realm. For Kernberg (1975), masochistic psychopathology centers on unconscious conflicts concerning sexuality and the superego and masochism as sexual perversion involves experiences of pain, submission, and humiliation to obtain sexual gratification. Punishment is the consequence of unconscious forbidden Oedipal activity that is a part of genital sexuality.

### Effects on Wives of the Husband's Preoccupation with Pornography

This section will explore the literature on effects of Internet pornography on wives of cybersex consumers. Although pornography has been in existence for hundreds of years, research addressing Internet pornography is in beginning stages. Schneider (2000, 2002), Carnes et al. (2001), and Young (2000) are leaders in this new field. This study will be using this literature to understand the impact on wives and their particular developmental histories.

Schneider (2000, 2002) explores the effects of cybersex on spouses and families of the user. Initially, women may attempt to ignore or explain away peculiar behaviors and obsession with the Internet they observe in their spouses. However, at some point wives discover their husbands' preoccupation, either accidentally or after a deliberate investigation. This discovery results in shock, betrayal, anger, and pain. Hopelessness, confusion, and shame accompany the cycle of confrontation and broken promises (Schneider, 2002).

Women often find it difficult to deal with their partners' Internet compulsions. Shame, self-blame, and embarrassment are features women often share. Many wives attempt to cover up the problem or take actions that Schneider terms "codependent." They use various mechanisms to cope with husbands' Internet preoccupations. These include attempts to control access to the computer, ultimatums, and the increase of frequency and repertory of sexual activities. The husbands' engagement in cybersex affects marital relationships as the wives report feeling lonely, ignored, unimportant, neglected, and angry. The women's self-esteem also may be affected. Fear, mistrust, suspicion, decreased level of intimacy occurs, and physical abuse may become a problem. Several wives have even engaged in their own extramarital affairs in order to seek revenge or shore up self-esteem.

Some women compare the devastating emotional impact of cybersex to the emotional impact of an affair. The same feelings of "hurt, betrayal, abandonment, devastation, loneliness, shame, isolation, humiliation, and jealousy are evoked" (www.jenniferschneider.com). For most women, lying is a major cause of distress. The women compare themselves unfavorably with online images and felt an inability to compete with the images.

The sexual relationships of couples are also affected. Two-thirds of Schneider's respondents describe sexual problems that coincide with the apparent beginning of cybersex activities. These wives report that the cybersex users avoid intimate sexual activity, blame women for sexual problems, urge women to participate in objectionable sexual activities, and are emotionally detached during sex, interested only in their own pleasure. Often both partners lose interest in sex. Furthermore, Schneider (2000, 2001) finds that cybersex is a major contributing factor to separation and divorce.

While these studies provide insight into the consequences of cybersex on the marital relationship, the particular dynamics of the relationship have not been explored in depth. Many questions remain unexplored. "When does this begin? What is happening in the relationship at the time of the increase in Internet activity? What is the nature of the couple relationship? Are there any precipitators, either in the marriage or outside of the marriage?" These are areas that must be researched.

## Relevant Literature on Affairs

Often, women compare husbands' preoccupation with pornography to extramarital relationships. They experience some of the same feelings of hurt, jealousy, loneliness, and confusion as if husbands were having physical affairs. Based on these women's reports, the literature examining affairs will further increase the understanding of this subject. It is beyond the scope of this research to reach a psychodynamic understanding of motives of husbands who engage in cybersex.

Research by Schneider (2000, 2001) indicates that partners of those who engage in cybersex often experience the activity as an affair.

There are vast amounts of self-help literature addressing issues of affairs. A search of Barnes and Noble's Web site reveals 74 books covering such topics as managing affairs and avoiding discovery, recovery from an affair, and discovering an affair. Most of the literature is aimed at women, examining and offering advise on how to handle the "perils and pitfalls" for them in relationships with men who are unfaithful. Smalley (1996), a Christian author, encourages women to win back their husbands by honoring their spouse, increasing communication, and managing boundaries with husbands.

There is a dearth of psychoanalytic literature that examines aspects of affairs. Some of the literature, which does address affairs, does so from the perspective of the unfaithful partner. However, there is a lack of literature that examines infidelity from the perspective of the one who is betrayed. Kernberg (1995), Kramer (1996), and Frank (1996) examine infidelity and connect it with concerns of intimacy. Their assumption is that intimacy issues impact fidelity issues. The desire for intimacy is inborn (Alperin, 2000). Citing research by Prager, Alperin (2000) lists advantages to those individuals who develop intimate relationships. They are "less likely to develop psychological symptoms, have a lower mortality rate, have fewer accidents, and are at lower risk of developing illnesses than those who lack intimate relationships" (Alperin, 2000, p. 138). Mitchell (2003) is interested in the role that romance plays in relationships.

Kramer (1996) connects infidelity with developmental difficulties of impaired capacity for intimacy and eventual fidelity. These theorists connect intimacy with fidelity, but it should be noted that intimacy is a psychological term, while fidelity is a social value or ideal. Citing Eisenstein, Kramer (1996) states, "emotionally immature people are incapable of experiencing satisfactory interpersonal intimacy, including heterosexual activity" (p. 16). Meyers (1996) believes that intimacy is not a psychoanalytic concept but an "observable interaction between two people" (p. 94). Meyers (1996) and Kramer (1996) view unfaithful individuals as having an inability to be fully intimate. Others cite the ability to enter into affairs as proof of intimacy.

Although Kernberg (1995) does not use the term "intimacy," he discusses deep and lasting relations between two people. The deep and lasting relations require that both people have the capacity for empathy and understanding for one's self and for the other. Intimacy is a component in mature sexual love where one can experience and maintain an exclusive love relation with another. The integration of tenderness and eroticism is crucial to this maintenance.

Kernberg (1995) notes differences between men and women in their ability to tolerate discontinuities in love and sex. Men appear to be capable of maintaining a sexual relationship with a woman even if they no longer love that woman. Women, on the other hand, seem to need an emotional connection in order to engage in sexual relations. Men find it easier to function sexually without love or affection toward the particular woman, while women need to care for the man. Women will often cease sexual relations if they no longer have strong feelings for their partner. Kernberg's (1995) observations of differences between men and women can provide insight into dynamics of women in the study.

Intimacy is an intersubjective experience that involves two or more people. As such, each individual's psychic structure is important in the experience (Frank, 1996). Difficulties that arise during separation-individuation can disrupt intimacy. An individual should emerge from this separation-individuation phase with both a sense of clear boundaries between self and object and a sense of self and identity. This successful individuation is a prerequisite for object relatedness, closeness, and intimacy. The essence of intimacy is a physical and psychical merger between two individuals. Involvement in intimacy is the simultaneous experience of being both separate and merged.

Alperin (2000), citing Hatfield, defines intimacy as a "process by which a dyad—in the expression of thought, affect and behavior—attempts to move toward complete communication on all levels" (p. 138). Western emphasis on individualism and self-sufficiency inhibits development of strong attachments, as do intrapsychic factors in experiencing intimacy. Hence, not all individuals are capable of this type of intimacy experience.

Capacity for intimacy develops in infancy as a result of the mother-infant relationship. Individuation-separation issues are important in understanding the experience of intimacy (Alperin, 2000; Akhtar & Kramer, 1996). Successful separation-individuation process and the establishment of secure boundaries between the self and other and formation of separate self and identity are prerequisites for the capacity for intimacy.

Strean (1976) examines extramarital affairs from the point of view of the one engaging in the affair. Given the fact that society encourages individuals to enjoy new "id pleasures," he does not find it unusual that individuals indulge their "narcissism, grandiosity, and omnipotent fantasies" (Strean, 1976, p. 102). Strean links fidelity with mature ego functions and infidelity with impulsive gratification of libidinal pleasure.

Mitchell (2003) contributes to the literature on affairs by introducing a new concept. He believes that romance is an integral part of relationships. He defines romance as "a mode of relating to another person, which generates emotions, stimulates imaginative play, and nurtures devotion to ideals" (p. 27). Romance is the erotic component of a love relationship. Falling in love is closer to romance than actually being in love. However, there is an inherent stability in romance; it fades over time as it relies on novelty, mystery, and danger.

According to Mitchell (2003), affairs may be the result of difficulty in managing long-term relationships and continuing to experience and sustaining romance. Romance gives meaning to lives and thus, individuals continually seek romance. The sustaining of romance is difficult and rather than diminishing over time, it actually becomes more dangerous. Intense desire is involved in romance and this desire generates a sense of deprivation. Romance involves fantasy as well as reality, sameness and otherness, and love and hate.

There is a dialectical relationship between attachment and danger, and individuals have a need for both (Mitchell, 2003). Danger provides an element of excitement, while attachment provides much needed security. The task for adults is to maintain tensions between the two. Humans seek out stability, continuity, and the familiar since these are qualities that provide security and allow for deep and secure attachment. Individuals demand that objects of attachment remain unchanged and stable. However, this stability is contrary to danger, as a stable, secure, grounded object does not evoke an element of danger. The element of danger is excitement in ordinary living.

The relationship between attachment and danger has its origins in the infant / mother dyad. The developmental task of the child is to be able to assert her independence while remaining dependent on mother. There is danger and excitement involved in maintaining tensions between independence and dependence. If the child is too dependent on mother, she risks loss of self in a merging. If she attempts to become too independent, she risks loss of the object.

According to Mitchell (2003), love involves elements of idealization, aggression, guilt, self-pity, and commitment all of which have roots in early infant experiences of envy and greed. He claims that idealization of the other does not dissipate over time, but as the individual becomes better acquainted with various aspects of his spouse, he may become more disappointed. In addition, society places a great deal of pressure on marriage to provide couples with enjoyable and frequent sex. Expectations for sexual gratification are high and it is very difficult for marriages to fulfill these expectations. As marital relationships develop, couples find themselves disappointed. Adults also discover how much they depend on the other to meet various security needs. The deepening of dependency needs makes idealization of the other a dangerous prospect. It is safer to fantasize about what one does not have than to fantasize about what is real. If an individual desires his partner sexually, he is in the position of needing the partner. This need can feel quite dangerous. Indeed, this longing for the other can evoke a sense of humiliation.

Aggression is an important component of desire (Mitchell, 2003). In order to fully feel one's own desire, one must feel aggression. Inhibition of aggression also inhibits desire. An individual can regulate his aggression through "segregation and reversals." The man can claim that he is really quite independent and that it is the wife who is dependent and needy. He stays with her because she needs him. There is an intricate two-step that takes place in maintaining this dynamic. The wife must play the part of the dependent, passive person while the husband plays the active, independent individual. Cultural tradition provides bifurcation along gender lines that make this role-playing easier for both parties.

This theory contributes to the body of information regarding the complexity of the subject of cybersex. According to Mitchell (2003), pornography offers stimulation and desire that is risk free. Desire connected to pornography cannot feel out of control. Viewing pornography protects the viewer from his own vulnerability, romantic longings, and dependency needs. Pornography functions to both gratify sexual desire and to generate arousal. It is not just a measure or consequence of naturally occurring sexual desire, it is a medium through which individuals can control their desire through "contrivance." This contrived way of stimulation means that one is never "surprised" by spontaneous desire.

*Roman Catholic Teachings on Sex and Sexuality*

This section explores some of the Roman Catholic Church's teachings on sex and sexuality. Roman Catholic women have been educated by the Church and have particular understandings of how sex and sexuality operates in their lives. Their approach to sexual issues will be flavored by the Church's teachings. Although some of the Church documents were published in the 1990s, the teachings remain constant since the early days of the Church. The recent documents have been updated to account for developing technologies and societal changes.

The mission of the Church is to guard the "deposit of faith ... which the Lord entrusted to His Church, and which she fulfills in every age" (*Catechism of the Catholic Church*, 1994, p. 1). According to Catholic teaching,

> A catechism should faithfully and systematically present the teaching of Sacred Scripture, the living Tradition in the Church and the authentic Magisterium, as well as the spiritual heritage of the Fathers, Doctors, and saints of the

Church, to allow for a better knowledge of the Christian
mystery and for enlivening the faith of the People of God
(Catechism of the Catholic Church, 1994, p. 4).

The Church has always believed that catechesis is the Church's
"sacred duty and inalienable right" (John Paul II, 1979, para. 14).
The name "catechesis" is given to any and all efforts on the part of the
Church to make disciples and to educate and instruct those Disciples
of Christ. According to Pope John Paul II (1979), the primary objective of catechesis is to,

Lead the person to study this mystery (mystery of
Christ) in all its dimension: to make all men see what
is the plan of the mystery ... comprehend with all
the saints what is the breadth and length and height
and depth–know the love of Christ which surpasses
knowledge (para. 5).

The aim of catechesis is to put the individual in communion with
Jesus Christ. With this as her directive, the Church has outlined in
various documents the particulars related to catechesis. There are
texts devoted to catechesis with children, adolescents, youth, young
people, handicapped, adults, and young people without religious support, quasi-catechumens (unbaptized individuals inquiring about
baptism), and the elderly. The documents specify how the church
should go about imparting the truth of the faith to the various groups.
The documents specify the sources, the language one uses, who can
transmit the catechism, and how to train an individual to be a catechist.

The concept of sin is an integral part of the Church's teachings.
The Church defines sin as "an offense against reason, truth, and right
conscience, it is failure in genuine love for God and neighbor"
(*Catechism*, 1994, p. 505). Sin can be divided into two categories,
venial and mortal. Venial sins are lesser sins. Mortal sins are grave
violations of God's law. It is a turning away from God, saying "no"
to God. Venial sin offends and wounds, but is not a grave violation
and does not destroy charity in the hearts of individuals. Venial sin

does not break the covenant with God. However, deliberate and unrepented venial sin can lead little by little to mortal sin. Violation of the Church's teachings means that one has sinned. Sins pertaining to every aspect of sexuality may be categorized as venial or mortal.

A large part of catechesis is devoted to sexuality. The Church has produced 55 documents addressing issues of sexuality. The church acknowledges the human person is profoundly affected by sexuality. Sex is necessary for procreation and to transmit those characteristics, which make an individual a man or woman. Sexual matters are frequently discussed in all forms of social communication.

According to *Persona Humana* (1975), the "corruption of morals has increased" (para. 1) and one indication of this is the "unbridled exaltation of sex" (para. 1). The Church acknowledges that some educators have been able to pass on appropriate values. However, there are others who have "put forward concepts and modes of behavior which are contrary to the true moral exigencies of the human person" (para. 1). The Church is greatly concerned that teachings, moral criteria, and modes of living be preserved.

In *Truth and Meaning of Human Sexuality* (1995), the Pontifical Council for the Family produced an Ecclesial document focused on sexuality. Although many families of the past did not provide specific sexual education, the general culture was permeated by respect for fundamental values. The culture preserved and protected these values. With the decline of traditional models, children were left without consistent and positive guidance and parents were unprepared with answers. The present culture has commercialized sex and the mass media has provided depersonalized and recreational information. This information does not factor in the different stages of information and development of children. It is also influenced by an individualist concept of freedom and lacks the basic values of "life, human love, and the family" (para. 3).

Often, the public school system has endeavored to provide sex education programs. The Church states that this imparting of information takes the place of the role of the family. Sometimes "this really leads to the deformation of consciences" (Pontifical Council for the Family, 1995, para. 1).

The Church offers pastoral guidelines to help parents with the teaching of sexuality. Indeed, the Church believes that it is the sacred duty and right of parents to be the principal educators of their children. In forming her view of sexuality, the Church draws on Christ's admonition concerning the sixth commandment (Exodus 20:14; Deuteronomy 5:18).

> You have heard that it was said, "You shall not commit adultery." But I say to you that every one who looks at a woman lustfully has already committed adultery with her in his heart (Matthew 5:27–28). (Pope Pius XI, 1930, para. 21).

The Church takes seriously that God created man and woman in God's own image. According to Genesis 1:27, "He blessed them and said, 'Be fruitful and multiply.'" Sexuality affects all aspects of the individual. Sexuality affects the capacity to love, the ability to procreate, and the ability to form bonds with others. Each individual must acknowledge and accept his or her sexual identity. The Church views sexuality as a gift and that gift must be used with discretion and regard for one another.

The preceding biblical passage is the foundation for the Church's view of sexuality. Because each of the two sexes is an image and likeness of God, the "union of man and woman in marriage is a way of imitating in the flesh the Creator's generosity and fecundity" (*Catechism*, 1994, p. 620). The Church catechism addresses the vocation to chastity, the virtue of chastity, and offenses against chastity. Chastity is defined as "the successful integration of sexuality within the person and thus the inner unity of man in his bodily and spiritual being" (p. 620).

The focus of *Persona Humana* (1975) is to repeat the church's doctrine on certain points in view of "the urgent need to oppose serious errors and widespread aberrant modes of behavior" (para. 7). The doctrine makes clear that every genital act must be within the framework of marriage. The church does not allow premarital sex even if one is intending to celebrate marriage or if circumstances prohibit marriage. Sexual intercourse must be safeguarded in the stability of marriage. Sexual union is legitimate if a definitive community of life has been established between a man and a woman.

Homosexual relations are a focus of the Catholic Church's teachings on morality and sexuality. She cautions that the homosexual person must be treated "with understanding and sustained in the hope of overcoming their personal difficulties and their inability to fit into society" (*Catechism*, 1994, p. 625).

Traditional Catholic doctrine defines masturbation as the "deliberate stimulation of the genital organs in order to derive sexual pleasure" (*Catechism*, 1994, p. 623). It constitutes a "grave moral disorder." The Church acknowledges that psychology and sociology believe that it is a normal phenomenon of sexual development. However, the Church still believes that masturbation is wrong in that "the deliberate use of the sexual faculty outside of marriage is contrary to its purpose" (*Catechism*, 1994, p. 624). Masturbation occurs outside the context of mutual self-giving and human procreation. The Church instructs that "the affective immaturity, force of acquired habit, conditions of anxiety, or other psychological or social factors" (*Catechism*, 1994 p. 624) must be taken into consideration when judging the culpability of the sin.

The Catechism of the Catholic Church condemns lust or "the disordered desire for inordinate enjoyment of sexual pleasure" (1994, p. 623). Sexual pleasure should not be sought for itself "isolated from its procreative and unitive purposes" (p. 623). The Church considers marriage to be a sacrament. The physical intimacy shared by the spouses is a sign and a "pledge of spiritual communion" (p. 626). Physical intimacy is an integral part of love and these marital acts are considered to be noble and honorable and bring the couple not only joy and pleasure, but foster self-giving.

These lengthy documents explore various aspects of sexuality, how one teaches sexuality, what is it, who is it reserved for, etc. Typically, sex education is taught to sixth graders during their religious formation. Every Catholic child learns that sexual intercourse is only for married couples, masturbation falls short of God's design for sexuality, and looking lustfully at another constitutes sin.

Roman Catholic teaching addresses the production and consumption of pornography and its effects on humanity in *Pornography and Violence in the Communication Media* (The Pontifical Council for Social Communications, 1989). She assigns some of the responsibility for the violation of human dignity and rights to the media. While the media is capable of producing much that is positive, it is also capable of depicting a life that is deformed. The Church is aware of the "widespread increase of pornography and wanton violence in the media" (para. 5) and this increase reflects the darker side of human nature. While pornography and violence have always been elements of the human condition, the growth of these commodities in the last 25 years has made it more easily accessible to a wide array of the population including young children.

Pornography is a violation of the right to privacy of the individual human body, and it reduces the human body to an anonymous object for the purpose of gratifying one's lust. Pornography affects individuals in that it has the capacity to cause injury and to corrupt those under its influence.

> Pornography and sadistic violence debase sexuality, corrode human relationships, exploit individuals—especially women and young people—undermine marriage and family life, foster antisocial behavior and weaken the moral fiber of society (Pontifical Council for Social Communications, 1989, para. 10).

Individuals who indulge in the use of pornographic material may become preoccupied with fantasy and acting out behavior resulting from the fantasy. Pornography interferes with "personal moral growth" (para. 15) and the development and nurturing of appropriate healthy relationships. It impacts the trust and openness in marriage and family life.

Those who engage in the use of pornography or contribute to its production and dissemination indulge in a "serious moral evil" (para. 11) and are considered to be sinning. Exposure to pornography can have a desensitizing effect on individuals as it renders the individual insensitive to the rights and dignity of others. The Church uses an addictions model to understand the habit-forming effect of pornography and individual's propensity to seek out harder core and more perverse material.

The Church assigns reasonability for the spread of pornography in the media to capitalism, "bad libertarian arguments" (para. 20) that promote free speech at the cost of protection of the innocent and the right for each individual to be treated with dignity, the legal system, and confusion and apathy on the part of many.

*Definitions of Pornography*

The etymology of the word "pornography" stems from the Greek words, "porno," meaning prostitutes, and "graphos," meaning writing (http://www.m-w.com/dictionary/pornography). Kendrick (1996) claims that pornography of the Western civilization is a little over two centuries old and traces its origins to Pompeii. The Roman emperor Tiberius compiled a personal library containing pornography, but because sex was a taboo subject under Judeo-Christian tradition, there were limited depictions of pornography until the 20th century (Microsoft).

Dines et al. (1998) recognize that the term "pornography" cannot be defined with precision. What is pornographic to some may not be pornographic to others. However, they purport that there is a widely understood definition of pornography in the culture. "Pornography is the material sold in pornography shops for the purpose of producing sexual arousal for mostly male consumers" (p. 3). Dworkin (1989) relies on an old definition of pornography as "the graphic depiction of whores" (p. xii). Stoller (1991) provides another definition: "pornography is material produced with the intent to excite erotically" (p. 1984). He includes romance novels in this definition since women use these books to excite themselves. In its definition, *Microsoft Encarta Encyclopedia* includes any "written, graphic, or oral depictions of erotic subjects intended to arouse sexual excitement in the audience" (Microsoft, 1997). The *Canadian Dictionary of the English Language* defines it as "sexually explicit material (that) sometimes equates sex with power and violence" (Hoggs, 1990). Mitchell (2003) claims that pornography functions both to gratify sexual desire and to generate arousal.

The previous definitions denote pornography as material that is used for sexual voyeuristic purposes. However, since the arrival of the Internet, pornography has undergone a transformation. The Internet provides individuals with opportunities for shared interaction that traditional media pornography does not. The term for this sexual participation is "cybersex." Schneider describes cybersex as,

> The use of digitized sexual content (visual, auditory, or written), obtained either over the Internet or as data retrieved by a computer, for the purpose of sexual arousal and stimulation. (p. 250)

A Carnegie Mellon study (1995) adopts the definition of pornography that computer pornographers use in everyday practice. Pornography is defined as: "depiction of actual sexual contact (hard-core) and depiction of mere nudity or lascivious exhibition (soft-core)." (http://business.enotes.com/business-finance-encyclopedia/ethics-information-processing).

*Statement of Assumptions*

The following assumptions will guide and organize the study.

1. For clinical theoretical purposes, the human mind is comprised of internal object relationships. Human beings are intrinsically relationship seeking. Individuals depend on these complicated relationships for emotional and physical satisfaction and support. Elements of these can be sexualized.
2. The Internet is a complex medium for exchanging information, some of which is pornographic. Individual's use of the Internet is a reflection of internal psychodynamics.

3. Depictions of pornography date back more than two centuries. Various mediums have been employed through which to portray this pornography. The 1980s saw the rise of the Internet, which has become the new medium of the 2000s for the distribution of pornography. Certain husbands have become preoccupied with sexual activity involving the Internet and are bringing the pornography into the home. This phenomenon is different from the former pornographic material, which included peep shows, magazines, and videotapes in several ways. Many of the former forms could be hidden from view in the trunk of a car or locked in a file cabinet. In addition, zoning laws prevented certain types of pornography from appearing in middle and upper class neighborhoods. The Internet, however, easily crosses boundaries that people have erected.

4. Many women have various levels of awareness of their husbands' Internet preoccupations. They may be consciously aware, in denial, or disavow the reality. These sexually related activities may be disruptive to the spousal relationship and to the family.

5. Often, there is a time lag between the wives awareness of the activity and confrontation of their husbands. If and when they confront, these women often have an inability to make their husbands stop the activity.

6. The Roman Catholic Church and their teachings on sex and sexuality may have some impact on the experiences of the women. These women have been influenced by the Church's teachings on morality, marriage, and sexuality. The teachings impact how the women understand their spouse's use of the Internet.

7. These women have a unique, recognizable, and describable experience that they will be able to convey. The methodology used in the study assists in capturing, identifying, organizing, and describing these experiences.

8. Since I am a clinician trained in systems theory and object relations psychodynamic theory, this orientation will influence how I organize, analyze, and interpret the data. My personal

value system will influence this study. I have a bias against pornography as I view it to be an objectification of women.

9. I assume that my participants will be able to convey the complexity of their experiences and that my methodology will assist me in analyzing, describing, and conveying the complexity of the experiences.

CHAPTER THREE

# METHODOLOGY

## INTRODUCTION

This study used a mixed methodology consisting of quantitative and qualitative analysis. Strauss and Corbin (1998) advise the use of qualitative methods when "the research is attempting to understand the meaning or nature of experiences of persons with problems such as chronic illness, addiction, divorce, and the act of coming out" (p. 11). According to Strauss and Corbin, qualitative research lends itself to the researcher getting out in the field and discovering what people are doing and thinking. Initially, the research question to be explored was: "What Are The Experiences of Roman Catholic Women Whose Husbands Use Internet Pornography?" However, when no derivatives of religious experiences materialized, the questions became "What Are The Experiences of Women Whose Husbands Use Internet Pornography?" The study was interested in the experiences of women with husbands' pornography use, the impact on the self, the various coping methods used, and emotions that were activated. The goal was to find results that explained the experiences and to develop a theory that would be relevant for clinical social work.

The qualitative method employed grounded theory procedures, whereby the theory is derived from the data. I did not undertake this research with a preconceived theory in mind, but allowed the theory to emerge through the systematic gathering and analysis of data. Grounded theory techniques provided opportunity for a deep, rich, and thick description of the phenomenon. Grounded theory employs creative thinking, a chance for the researcher to work closely with the data with possibilities for both creativity and science.

The quantitative methodology relied on a simple demographic questionnaire and a lengthier attitudes questionnaire. The demographic questionnaire was used to gather information on the socioeconomic status of participants. The second survey consisted of specific questions gleaned from the General Social Survey and Indiana Happiness Inventory and Marital Satisfaction Inventory (Zillman & Bryant, 1988). The questions were designed to examine attitudes toward religious beliefs, happiness, marriage, and pornography.

## PARTICIPANT RECRUITMENT

Letters were sent to area therapists and Catholic parishes requesting that the enclosed flyers (Appendix A) be placed in an area where women would notice them. Initially, recruitment flyers advertised for Catholic women whose husbands used the Internet for sexual purposes. Most therapists and priests were co-operative although there were priests and therapists who were reluctant to have the flyers in common areas. I also contacted and personally spoke to selected therapists who specialized in addictions. The local Catholic newspaper featured an article discussing my intended research. Letters and flyers were mailed to the contact couple for Retrovaille, a weekend retreat devoted to marriage building.

Approximately half the participants read the article in the Catholic newspaper and contacted me. Local therapists referred several more women. The remaining women were recruited from a local

Co-addicts of Sex Addicts Anonymous (COSA). Some of the women volunteered after hearing about the research from other participants.

## DESCRIPTION OF PARTICIPANTS

Sixteen women volunteered for the study and were interviewed in three one-hour segments. Each woman signed an informed consent statement before beginning the interview process (Appendix B). Fifteen women completed either fully or partially both the qualitative and quantitative parts of the research. The sixteenth woman excused herself after the first interview due to an emotional "upset." She was in treatment and pre- ferred to return to her psychotherapist for debriefing. All women were married during the interview process although one was in process of obtaining a divorce. No others were considering a divorce. One hundred percent of participants were still living with their spouses.

Participants ranged in age from 26 to 80 years in age, with 58% between ages 33 and 50. All but one had children, averaging two to six children. Seventeen percent of women were retired, 29% self-identified as homemakers for their primary occupation, while the remaining 52% were employed outside the home. Occupations reported included teachers, managers, pharmacists, and nurses, 76% had some college education or had completed college, with the remainder high school graduates and one with vocational training. All women were white with an average income of $104, 286, with their incomes ranging from $40,000 to $175,000. All the women reported some type of religious affiliation with 58% claiming Roman Catholicism and the remaining were Protestant and Jewish. Participants were offered up to three debriefing sessions. One woman returned for all three sessions and eventually found a therapist.

Of the 16 women, seven attended COSA meetings and ten did not. Of the ten non-COSA women, only one was familiar with the 12-Step group. Ten of the women had been in some form of therapy or were presently in therapy. The women who participated in therapy were not the same subset of women who attended COSA.

## DATA COLLECTION

The data was gathered using a semi-structured, face-to-face interview and questionnaires. This interview process consisted of three one-hour interviews concerning participant's subjective experiences of their husbands' use of the Internet for sexually related activities. The number of women was determined by theoretical saturation, when stories became redundant. Each interview began with the question as to why, the women, they agreed to participate. This question was followed by an invitation for them to relate their experiences with husbands. Of particular interest was the wives' current experience with their spouses, their understanding of what it means to be a woman in western culture, their understanding of husbands' use of pornography, and the impact on the relationship. The respondents' replies to initial questions guided subsequent questions. Tentative analysis and conclusions of prior interviews generated additional questions. Each interview was audio taped using digital technology and transcribed verbatim. Detailed notes were taken that not only captured the content of the interviews, but recorded impressions, observations, thoughts, interpretations, and questions for future interviews.

The quantitative instruments consisted of a simple demographic survey (Appendix C) and a questionnaire (Appendix D) containing specific categories selected from the General Social Survey (Queens College, 1972) and the Inventory of Personal Happiness (Zillmann & Bryant, 1988). The General Social Survey is a personal interview survey containing over 3260 different questions covering a wide range of variables. The questionnaire for this study included variables addressing personal happiness, value of marriage, and religious and pornographic attitudes. This questionnaire is part of the public domain and can be accessed via the Internet (www.soc.qc.edu). The Indiana Inventory of Personal Happiness is designed to measure perceptions and evaluations of sexuality and is also part of the public domain.

Upon completion of the face-to-face, each participant was given the questionnaires and offered the option of completing and returning it anonymously via an addressed, stamped envelope provided by me.

Fifteen of 16 respondents completed the questionnaires and mailed them to me. Several women left some questions unanswered in the survey with no explanation provided. The sixteenth woman left the study and declined to complete the surveys.

## DATA ANALYSIS

*Qualitative*

The data in this study consisted of words phrases, sentences contained in the interviews as well as journal notes and memos made by me. The demographic and attitudes questionnaires were used to augment and further understand the collected data. Grounded theory was used in data analysis (Strauss & Corbin, 1998) as it allowed for dynamic and fluid process. Analysis of the data at each stage influenced the line of questioning, allowed for tentative theory building, increased my understanding of the complexities of participants' experiences, and opportunities to test the theory. Initially, the research focused only on the experiences of Catholic women. Only after analyzing the first several interviews with the Catholic women, did I understand that either Catholic women saw no connection between Catholic upbringing and experiences or it was not relevant to their experiences. Thus, limiting findings to just Catholic women became unnecessary and the study needed to expand to include other women. Grounded theory techniques permitted me to expand understanding and seek out additional participants with other experiences. This led to inclusion of women who attended COSA meetings and an opportunity to compare and contrast experiences of COSA and non-COSA women.

As data was analyzed and preliminary conclusions were reached, I followed up with respondents to test out these theories. Data retrieved from subsequent interviews was brought back to the original data for clarification, conceptualization, and comparison. Specific phenomena, or central ideas were generated from the analyzation of the data. These central ideas were organized into categories, "concepts that stand for phenomena" (Strauss & Corbin, 1998, p. 101). This ensured that the emerging categories accurately reflected women's experiences. Initially, there were numerous categories. Gradually, as more data was analyzed, the categories were condensed and refined. Some categories became properties while other categories were confined to produce.

Atlas-ti is a software program designed to manage large bodies of audio, graphical, and textual data. It uses a variety of tools to assist in uncovering the complex phenomena embedded in the data. The program provides a section for memoing, formulating categories and properties of those categories. It has the capacity to organize data with more sophisticated tools than this researcher deemed necessary. However, it was invaluable for organizing quotes into specific categories and importing those quotes into the word document.

The three major analytic tools are open, axial, and selective coding. The first several interviews were analyzed using open coding, which is defined as "the analytic process through which concepts are identified and their properties and dimensions are discovered in data" (Strauss & Corbin, 1998, p. 101). In fragmenting the data, I examined each word, phrase, and line through a microscopic lens. Open coding broke the data down into manageable subsets making it easier to establish initial categories and their properties and dimensions. In open coding, I compared discrete parts to each other looking for differences and similarities. Fragmenting data by open coding guarded against pushing through the data so quickly as to overlook valuable information. At this juncture, all categories were tentative; nothing was permanent. Initially, the categories were descriptive; they were used to organize data. The software program was eminently helpful in open coding as it organized and contained all interviews in easily accessible files.

Once the data had been fragmented, the process of axial coding began. Axial coding is "the process of relating categories to their subcategories" (Strauss & Corbin, 1998, p. 123). This process involved coding around the axis of previously defined categories, linking those categories at the level of properties. It is at this point the fractured data was reassembled and coded in order to understand the phenomena. Categories and properties were named, often with words provided by participants. Categories were related to subcategories. How did these conditions influence or mitigate the phenomena? Axial coding allowed for examination of relationships between various properties. The properties were then linked to categories in an effort to determine additional relationships. Several properties ran through more than one category. These properties were analyzed to determine how they varied throughout categories. In this step of analysis, I was building a provisional theory. This emerging theory was compared to the original data searching for confirmation or negation. Memoing continued as relationships, ideas, considerations, and thoughts occurred. In order to account for my bias, consultations continued with my professional colleagues.

Selective coding, "the process of integrating and refining the theory" (Strauss & Corbin, 1998, p. 143) marked level three. Categories and their properties were generated in open coding and systematically developed and linked with subcategories in axial coding. At this point theory began to materialize. Category development reached theoretical saturation, no new properties, dimensions, or relationships emerged. In selective coding, a central category was selected that represented the main theme of the research. All other categories (and their variations) organized around the central category. Once the central category was identified, reviewing for internal consistency and holes refined the theory. Poorly developed categories were expanded. Other categories were discarded and properties combined. Previous memoing proved invaluable in the integration process.

An important step in this level was the validation of the theoretical scheme. This was accomplished by having selected participants comment on the emerging story. Theory was constantly compared to original data searching for flaws, inconsistencies, and variations in order to further its validation. At this point, the material was organized into a written document that had been consistently compared to the raw data and grounded in that data.

The final step in analyzing the data was to choose several participants to review the material for quote and context accuracy (Lincoln & Guba, 1985). I chose several women to read the document and make comments. This process enriched and validated the text, and added to the integration of the theory.

*Quantitative*

General Survey Questionnaire

The quantitative portion of the data included a short demographic survey as well as questions extracted from the General Survey Questionnaire and the Indiana Happiness Inventory and Marital Satisfaction Inventory (Zillman & Bryant, 1988). The questionnaire contained attitude scales that examined perceptions, and attitudes toward pornography, the role of religion, and marriage. The survey questionnaires contributed to an expanded portrait of the women. The results were not used to test or to score. The results were tabulated and provided a system for comparing the questionnaires and the interviews. Descriptive statistics were used to analyze results of the questionnaire and demographic survey.

The results of the questionnaires were compared to the qualitative section searching for consistency in the data. Any discrepancies that appeared were accounted for in the discussion of results. Often there appeared to be a conflict between what participants related in interviews and how they answered the survey questions. The comparisons provided a portrait of the women's beliefs, attitudes, and values in regard to personal happiness, religion, pornography, and marriage. I used clinical judgment to assess subjective discrepancies. The information from this survey was used to develop a theory as to how the participants negotiate and manage with their husbands' sexually related Internet activity.

The religious attitudes portion of the General Social Survey proved to be irrelevant in light of the expansion of the study to include COSA women. At this point, religious affiliation and attitudes were extraneous to understanding the similarities and differences between COSA and non-COSA women. The entire questionnaire is included in Appendix D.

## LIMITATIONS AND GENERALIZABILITY

There are several possible limitations to this study. Initially, I intended to use a specific sample of women, women who are Roman Catholic and are impacted by pornography. If I discovered that the teachings of the Church influenced the ways in which these women cope, then the findings would not be generalizable beyond Roman Catholic women. However, early in the study after coding many interviews, it became apparent that the participants did not connect Roman Catholic teachings on sexuality with their current dilemma. I also encountered a group of women who attended COSA meetings. This group of women provided additional interest and the study expanded to include a comparison of the two groups.

The participants were Caucasian, middle to upper middle class women, and most had some college education. All women could afford personal home computers and Internet capability. The study is not generalizable beyond married women; it does not address women in committed relationships either heterosexual or homosexual.

The major limitation of this study is the size and homogeneity of the population. The sample study was small, 16 women began the study and only 15 completed. Larger samples may provide different results.

I anticipated that my initial bias and value system would impact this study. I am opposed to pornography on the basis that it objectifies women. I intended to manage these biases and any other emergent ones through continuous discussions with the chair of the research study. However, as the research unfolded and findings became clearer, I realized that pornography was incidental in comparison to other sexually related activities. While the women believed that viewing pornography leads to more egregious activities, I do not. Viewing pornography is quite separate from other sexually related activities.

## PROTECTION OF PARTICIPANTS

The research conformed to the standards, policies, and procedures of the Institute for Clinical Social Work, including those of the Ethical Standards for Human Research. Participants were fully informed, signed and were given a copy of the "Individual Consent for Participation in Research" (Appendix C). Participants were offered the opportunity to terminate involvement at any point. One woman declined further participant after the first interview. She was in psychotherapy and referred back to the therapist. She declined a debriefing session.

The anticipated risks involved were possibilities of negative emotional responses arising from examination of this issue. Three debriefing sessions were offered. One participant took this opportunity. After the three debriefing sessions she was referred to a therapist.

An unanticipated side effect was the negative emotional response experienced by two transcribers. During the process of transcribing, each discovered their significant other accessing Internet pornography. I debriefed each woman and referred her to a psychotherapist. One transcriber elected to discontinue the work, while the second chose to continue. The latter transcriber noticed she was behaving like the participants in the study in relation to her significant other. She found a therapist and also began therapy. She insisted on psychodynamically informed therapy.

Confidentiality for participants (and transcribers) was guaranteed and maintained. Each participant was identified by a code. Transcribers were not given actual names, only codes and were committed to confidentially. While direct quotes were used in the written document, all efforts were made to conceal any identifying characteristics. Names of participants were not used in the word document and references to places, people, and events were also disguised. The original digital recordings as well as the transcriptions are in my possession and will remain in a secure location for three years.

# CHAPTER FOUR

# INTRODUCTION TO THE RESULTS

> "I was living it. I was living a cycle of that. And it was just oh, gosh, destructive, destructive."

The study results are grouped into five major conceptual categories. These categories describe experiences of women whose husbands use the Internet for sexually related activities. In efforts to manage and deal with their husbands' use of Internet pornography and other related sexual activities, women continually looped through a cycle that Just Keeps Happening. Women reported an inability to disrupt this circle.

> Like I said, it's just a cycle. I would find out this stuff; we'd have this big argument. He'll sleep on the couch for a while. And I told him it's just like we cycle. He sleeps on the couch for a while, and it's just, he wants it to go away. Like nothing ever happened. Then the cycle just keeps happening.

Internet pornography is not an isolated event in the life of marriage; it had its origins in the beginning of the relationship and continued for months and years. The category, *In the Beginning*, illustrates the origins of pornography and other sexually related activities that were present early in the relationship. The following three categories form the repetitious cycle

- *Temporary Peace*
- *Something is Definitely Up*
- *The Big Discovery*

These categories are not necessarily sequential and can occur in any order in the life of the cycle. In the final category, two groups of women emerge: COSA women and non-COSA women. Each category contains several properties that elaborate the particular phenomena. Some properties are unique to the category while other properties appear in each category.

Many women articulated and described the chain of events and its variations. Participants reported lacking efficacy in their abilities to achieve substantive changes in men's behaviors. Periodically, husbands would make minor changes and the cycle would deviate, but there was no permanent disruption or transformation. "That's what I'm saying, it just keeps cycling and cycling. It never gets dealt with. He just puts it on a shelf for awhile and it comes back and something worse happens."

Not only did the circle keep recurring with no positive changes, but participants also experienced the situation as deteriorating and their husbands' sexually related activities as increasing.

> It goes in cycles, so as far as his use of pornography. And he'll get caught. You know, I'll find stuff, and then he'll swear he's going to stop, and then it will stop for a while, and then he'll start up again. Then he'll get caught and it just cycles like that. And every time it's gotten worse as far as what he's getting into, so.

The cycle continued for months and years. Women did not know how to interrupt and reported a feeling of being "stuck." They coped and managed with this problem in their lives. Their methods of coping did not bring about a positive change in the marital relationship. "I [am] just kind of in a rut. I don't go forward and I don't go backward. Maybe a little more backward than forward I would say."

About half the women began their narratives by relating how the husbands' use of pornography and the Internet began. The other half of women began with *The Big Discovery*. All participants reported they were aware of their husbands' use of pornography *In the Beginning* of their marriage, if not in early in the relationship. This category comprises ten categories: Family of Origin, Experience of Pornography, Separate Lives, Collecting Evidence, Small Confrontations, Excuses, "It's My Fault," "Alluring Power," Dealing With It, and Forgiveness and Hope. The first property considers participants' family of origin histories. All wives came from disorganized homes and experienced sexual, emotional, and physical boundary violations. They brought previous experiences of exposure to some form of pornography into the relationship. Separate Lives explores the independent lives the couples had been living for some time. Husbands who exhibited questionable behavior prompted wives to clandestinely search for evidence and tentatively confront their spouses. In this category the husbands gave excuses and wives seemed to accept evasive answers and justifications. The property of "It's My Fault" looks at women's beliefs that they were to blame for their husbands' activities. Wives reported feeling that they had lost both their "alluring power" and their struggles to cope. Forgiveness and Hope addresses wives' attempts to forgive and the ongoing hope for change.

A *Temporary Peace* follows the category of *In the Beginning* when a relative calm ensued. The properties in this category are: Collecting Evidence, Covering for Him, Keep Talking, Tolerance, Vigilance, and Forgiveness and Hope. Although it appeared that domestic life was peaceful, women continued to collect evidence. As they collected proof of the sexually related activities, women covered for their husbands with family, friends, and even with themselves. In this category they did not directly confront their husbands. Instead, they kept the dialogue going with their husbands because of their desire to keep talking. Over a period of time, wives were able to tolerate more awareness of their husbands' behaviors. The temporary peace in the house did not prevent women from remaining vigilant. Forgiveness was easier to grant due to the relative calm, and hope was increased.

In the third category, women realized that *Something Is Definitely Up*. As they discovered increasing amounts of evidence, they could not continue to ignore this evidence. The properties in this category are: the Big Confrontation, Idle Threats, Desperate Solutions, Consequences, Seeking Help, and Forgiveness and Hope.

Wives could not explain why one specific piece of evidence prompted them to confront their husbands. They issued threats or ultimatums during the big confrontation, but were unable to follow through. Husbands' appeased their wives with small changes, and the women eventually relented on their idle threats. Wives became their husbands' babysitters, hoping to prevent reoccurrences of sexually related activities. Women resorted to desperate solutions in efforts to cope with their feelings.

Both wives and husbands experienced consequences after the big confrontation. The consequences had marital, family, and social implications. At this juncture, women sought outside assistance. Seeking outside help provided women with increased hope, which enabled them to forgive their husbands.

Again, a *Temporary Peace* was established that could not be maintained. It was eventually broken by *The Big Discovery*. This discovery was so traumatic women reported internal and external chaos. The properties in this category are: Major Betrayal, Raw Emotions, "I Don't Know Him: He Doesn't Know Me," Confrontation, Cyber Detective, Consequences, "I Know: I Don't Know," Dealing With It, and Forgiveness and Hope.

All women experienced *The Big Discovery* as a major betrayal. Raw emotions of anger, confusion, doubt, fear, sadness, helplessness, isolation, despair, shame, insecurity, and betrayal emerged. The nature of the major betrayal prompted many women to wonder if they really knew their husbands and if their husbands knew them. With the discovery and the surfacing of intense emotions, wives realized they must finally deal with this issue, and the issue was much larger than they previously believed. This category included a big confrontation. At this point, women became cyber detectives, even those women who were previously computer illiterate. There were consequences associated with the big discovery that went beyond the disrupted marital relationship.

Women realized they could no longer ignore the sexually related activities, and they admitted to both knowing and not knowing simultaneously. The property of dealing with it took on new significance as women struggled to find additional coping methods. Those who had not previously sought outside help now pursued assistance. The women divided into two groups as one group sought assistance in a 12-Step program called COSA. Forgiveness and Hope were present in *The Big Discovery*, but the ability to forgive was greatly diminished. However, women experienced an increase in hope after pursuing outside assistance.

The final category in the cycle, COSA Women addresses a variation in the population of women. In *The Big Discovery*, several women were directed to COSA meetings. The properties in this category are: A New Language, COSA as Ritual, Work Your Own Program, "I'm No Longer Isolated," Abundance of Information, Marriage Enhancement, and Forgiveness and Hope. Often, spouses of the COSA women joined the addicts group, Sex Addicts Anonymous (SAA). COSA women adopted a new language that helped them understand and articulate what was occurring in their marital relationships. Just as non-COSA women who were religious turned to religious rituals, the 12-Step groups provided COSA women with necessary rituals. The property of Work Your Own Program assisted COSA women in focusing on their own behaviors and emotions rather than on that of their husbands. A major difference for COSA women was the discovery of support, which ameliorated the sense of isolation. COSA women demonstrated more knowledge of their husbands' activities than their non-COSA counterparts. Most women in this group expressed the importance of enhancing the relationship. The property of Forgiveness and Hope was intricately connected to attendance for both husbands and wives at their respective self-help groups. However, in spite of differences between the two groups of women, the cycle that Just Keeps Happening remained virtually unchanged.

The cycle that Just Keeps Happening is repetitive. There were numerous discoveries, confrontations, excuses, and instances of relative peace. The properties of hope and forgiveness as well as raw emotions were consistent in each category and changed somewhat from category to category. Although this cycle manifested itself for each of the participants, there were variations to the theme. The women were individuals, and as unique people, they managed and coped with the disruption in their intrapsychic and interpersonal lives.

# CHAPTER FIVE

# IN THE BEGINNING

## INTRODUCTION

"Okay, I'll start from the beginning."

The category, *In the Beginning*, describes wives' experiences of pornography that dated from early in the relationship. All women acknowledged that husbands had used pornography early in the relationship. According to most women in the study, magazines were the most available and most commonly used form of pornography. *Playboy* was the most popular of the magazines, as all women mentioned it as a source of interest to husbands. However, over time, husbands engaged in a variety of behaviors that went well beyond the use of pornographic magazines. Many men perused pornographic Web sites featuring women, gay males, children, sadomasochism, and bestiality. Some men established online relationships with both women and men, entered chat rooms, participated in Internet sexual encounters, and for more than a few, engaged in physical encounters with other women and men.

Wives had a variety of experiences and reactions to their husbands' use of pornography. What some women reacted to as offensive was not considered offensive for others. "It was in the beginning; we hadn't been married very long" was a common thread through the stories. For all women, the Internet was another form of pornography use and a common denominator that brought this issue to the forefront. "It was years [of] accumulating things that have taken place throughout the years that, that, have been red flags to me." "I suspected something."

*In the Beginning* tells the story of women's experiences with husbands' use of pornography. The properties in this category are: Family of Origin, Experience of Pornography, Separate Lives, Collecting Evidence, Small Confrontations, Excuses, "It's My Fault," "Alluring Power," Dealing With It, and Forgiveness and Hope.

Women reported childhood developments that were greatly affected by disorganized home lives. This disorganization included boundary violations, alcohol and drug abuse, infidelity, combative parents, and divorce. The family of origin property explores those particular issues that affected women's lives. The second property, experience of pornography, explores familiarity women had with pornography prior to the marriage as well as in the marriage. Most women tolerated the presence of pornographic magazines in the marital household. The third property, separate lives, addresses the couple's ability to exist in the same household and engage in different tasks apparently unaware of the life of the other. Behavior that appeared suspicious to wives provided impetus for them to begin searching and collecting evidence. Armed with evidence, wives tentatively approached and confronted their husbands. Inevitably, husbands offered excuses which wives appeared to accept. Not knowing what to do with the information, women were left with a sense of "this is my fault." Women confessed to fearing a loss of their "alluring power;" that ability to attract husbands and maintain their interest. Women reported they used various methods to deal with these phenomena. The final property in this category is the short cycle of forgiveness and hope.

## FAMILY OF ORIGIN

"I grew up in a dysfunctional home."

Most women in this sample study reported childhoods and early adult years that were disorganized and traumatic. Psychosexual development was compromised by numerous parental failures. As children, a majority of women experienced boundary violations that were sexual, emotional, and physical in nature. Problems in the home were not limited to boundary violations, but included alcohol and drug abuse, neglect, extramarital affairs, early death of a parent, mental illness, and combative parents. Several women were consciously aware of their disruptive family backgrounds. "The majority of wives have come from either strict family backgrounds, very religious backgrounds, or families that had substance abuse, and parents that were alcoholics."

Participants described mothers as physically or emotionally absent. Other times, mothers were too present, "smothering" and rescuing daughters. They shared inappropriate information, especially information pertaining to marital discord. "I was probably 17 when we began talking in depth [about my father's extramarital affairs]." Some mothers were unable to demonstrate affection or love. "Being raised a Catholic all of my life, my family was not open. They were very cold." Some mothers were physically and / or emotionally abusive. "My mom yelled at us to keep from hitting us ... she didn't want to hit us like she was hit. So, she yelled at us, she might as well as hit me because the fear is the same." Participants observed mothers focusing more attention on husbands than on their children. They saw their mothers tolerating husbands' disrespectful behaviors and simultaneously trying to please husbands.

> My mom took care of my dad. He had an affair when I was 18 months old. After that, she said she didn't know if he was staying or going for a year. She became anorexic and would do anything she could to make my dad happy so that he wouldn't leave. And she continued that until I was 12 or 13.

When mothers were absorbed with fathers and domestic turmoil, daughters were ignored. Some mothers grew tired of domestic disputes and left husbands. "But my mother had had enough … enough of the politicking. She fell in love with someone else." Premature death claimed other mothers, causing emotional distress for developing girls. "My mom died when I was 16, she had cancer and I think I spent the next 7 years rebelling."

More participants focused on major disappointments with their fathers than with mothers. A consistent theme was the absence of fathers. This absence was due to a variety of factors such as career choices, alcoholism, extramarital affairs, illness, or even death. Many women had fathers who worked long hours or traveled for business purposes. "I don't know, we were brought up so close, because my father was in the army so, it was just the three of us." "He was gone all the time. He worked all of the time." If careers did not pull fathers from home; the local bar or other women captured attention. "He was powerful and such a handsome man. I think my dad was a womanizer." Some fathers were simply emotionally absent. "My dad who never before wanted to be in our lives before, because he was a real workaholic."

Alcohol abuse was another contributing factor in father absence. "He would come home and just be blasted." Whether fathers frequented bars or drank at home, they were still unavailable to developing girls. "I just know that he [my father] didn't come home from work, so we assumed he was out drinking and when he would come in he would go to bed."

Even while admitting paternal failings, many women idealized fathers. "So when he was home, it was like, 'oh daddy's home.' Like, 'daddy was so special.' They [fathers] were very big. They were very big and to be held in awe I guess." Daughters often observed that fathers were admired not only by family members, but also by the community. "He was hugely liked and popular. He was good at what he did, really good."

Women told of fathers who mistreated mothers and were disrespectful. "At one point, my father was physically abusive to my mother and caused a lot of pain. There was a lot of hate and fear between my mother [and father]." Some fathers repeatedly lied to mothers and had extramarital affairs. Many households were contentious with mothers and fathers constantly arguing. "My parents had a very rocky relationship and my mother suspected my father many times of being with somebody else."

Frequently, women admitted to feelings of loneliness that accompanied them from early childhood. They were unable to attribute these feelings to any one factor. Some claimed loneliness was a result of the family dynamics. "My parents, they were always arguing, fighting." Others were reluctant to locate this loneliness in the family and preferred to think it was more of a social problem. "I always felt left out, not part of the big club."

A large percentage of women in the study were molested by family members or raped in early adulthood. Several parents failed to protect daughters from sexual violations by family members. "I had been sexually molested by my grandfather when I was three or four." Continued sexual violations by family members increased the traumas. "I was molested by a brother-in-law when I was 12 or 14. My brother raped me when I was 16." Others fathers sexualized the father / daughter relationship. "He's always told us inappropriate things. He has said that he and my mom … didn't have sex with him for the last 6 years before they divorced."

Women reported generational histories of physical, sexual, or emotional abuse. "My mother was an adult child of alcoholics. She was molested and beaten by my grandfather." "My dad was brought up by his aunt and uncle because his mother died when he was three months old. His father was an alcoholic and was in and out of prison for that."

In addition to sexual violations by family members, some women experienced further trauma later in adolescence or young adulthood. "When I was 16, I was orally raped by a guy down at college. It was pretty awful. I never thought it was sexual assault. I figured it happened to a lot of people." The women did not report these rapes to parents or authorities.

Several women in the study were teenage mothers. "I was married right out of high school." "I was married, and I was a teenage pregnancy. Had to get married because that was the Catholic thing to do. I thought about giving up the baby." Teenage mothers producing daughters who became teenage mothers was a reoccurring theme. "She was pregnant with me when she was 16 years old."

Women witnessed violence at home. "And they would break things, and throw things." Divorce was experienced as traumatic. "My parents divorced when I was 5 or 6." "My parents were divorced when I was about 16." In these families young daughters had to figure out how to cope and became the peacemakers or fixers. "I am a peacemaker." "I guess I'm a fixer like my mother."

Childhood trauma was not confined to neglect or abuse. Often, perceived abandonment was cited as traumatic. "My whole issue comes from having a medical trauma at 18 months old. I had a cleft pallet and was left at the hospital in Saint Louis for 2 weeks without my parents." Critically ill parents adversely affected some women. "My mother had breast cancer and she lost her breast." A mentally ill parent also posed difficulties for developing women. "My two sisters both have pretty significant mental disorders that they inherited from my dad."

Neglect, abuse, and abandonment were not the only interferences in psychosexual development. Over involved parents were seen by some women as contributing to poor decision-making processes in adult years. "They're more enablers because they don't let you figure out things on your own. They're there to help. And really, their helping is really hurting you."

Husbands were not immune to traumatic childhoods. Most women knew information concerning their husbands' background prior to marriage. Husbands' family issues were strikingly similar to those of wives. Alcohol, violence, divorces, extramarital affairs, combative parents, and absent fathers were the common themes in the husbands' stories. Again, these patterns were repeated generation to generation.

Fathers-in-law exposed young sons to sexual material, which wives believed to be inappropriate. "His dad had taken him to strip places a couple of times. His dad had porn magazines." Fathers-in-law were often sexually aggressive toward participants. "You know, because he's several times tried to touch me and different things." Wives believed husbands' fathers had sex addictions based on behaviors they observed. "And, his father was a sex addict." Many fathers-in-law had extramarital affairs. "I don't know how his father was. I do know his parents divorced. His father had a girlfriend. God knows, and so it's kind of like that whole cycle."

Alcohol abuse and other addictive behaviors permeated husbands' families of origin. "Because of the addictive behavior that seems to be a pattern throughout my husband's family with his dad—probably an alcoholic, his grandpa an alcoholic."

With their understanding of husbands' family backgrounds, many women found explanations for husbands' aberrant behaviors. "His father left when he was four. I knew that he was abusive and now I've come to learn the rest of the story."

Some women made the correlation between their own disorganized families of origin and their husbands' families of origin. "His parents divorced. His father had a girlfriend and my parents had a very rocky relationship. My mother suspected my father many times of being with somebody else, and so it's kind of like that whole cycle."

Many women exhibited a history of involvement with men who displayed behaviors that were questionable. "I dated him from the age of 15 until I was 21. We quit dating because he was cheating on me." Yet, they married men they knew had questionable histories. "He asked me to marry him within 2 weeks. He was divorced. He had two children. And, he was very broken at that time. He was very, you know, humbled by his divorce." Women frequently entered into relationships with men who were controlling, abusive, and had a history of addictions. "He's a recovering addict. But looking back, I should have said, oh he hasn't been sober long enough. I thought he was charming, I mean, saying all the right things. And he made me feel good." Several women admitted marrying men out of desperation.

"Also, my own fault is that I'd been divorced before. I come from this Catholic family. A two-time loser with an infant. I mean, how in the hell did [I] get [myself] into that situation?"

Women disclosed that they divorced first husbands because of turbulent, objectionable behavior. "But I was afraid of him. And he was a weirdo, and we had a restraining order on him." Yet, they conceded they had married men of a similar caliber. Many women were forthcoming with their own history of addictions. "I told you I'm a recovering alcoholic." "We both used to drink and smoke together."

Alcohol and drug abuse, boundary violations, combative parents, divorce, death, and mental illness were pervasive difficulties in childhood development both for study participants and husbands.

## EXPERIENCE OF PORNOGRAPHY

> "It was in the beginning ... we hadn't been married very long."

According to wives, men gradually introduced more and varied forms of media, expanding beyond magazines. As they narrated their stories, women often admitted to knowledge of husbands' pornography use prior to marriage while other times, they insisted it appeared only after the marriage. A majority of woman knew their husbands came into marriage with previous experience of pornography. For most women, the Internet had not yet been expanded to its present point of development in the early years of marriage. Thus, magazines and videos were common sources of pornography, with *Playboy* being the most popular. According to women's accounts, they tolerated the magazines believing that viewing them was normal behavior. Some had grown up in homes where their fathers had subscriptions. "But my dad had *Playboy*, so I just thought that, well, it's just kind of normal to have *Playboys* around the house." Although their parents had often hid magazines from public view, many women had been aware of their existence. However, other women denied knowledge of their fathers' use of pornography.

> "When we met 11 years ago, he [her husband] was
> getting his *Playboy* delivered to his parents' house."
> Many husbands brought their magazine collection into
> the marital home. These men claimed they had a sub-
> scription to *Playboy* because they "liked the articles."
> Some women not only accepted *Playboy*, but also
> even admitted that they too enjoyed the articles. "And
> I thought they were, you know, some of them were
> very interesting."

Most women did not require that their husbands totally dispose
of the pornography collection. Several allowed husbands to retain
possession of a partial stock, but demanded they discard all others.
However, this demand was generally ignored. "But I always told him
it wasn't coming to our new home when we got married and it wasn't
invited into our relationship. It had to go."

According to wives, husbands graduated from magazines containing pictures and stories. Men rented X-rated movies (upon invention
of the home video player / recorder) watched risqué cable shows,
visited "titty" bars, and in some cases, met with prostitutes. All men
left small clues indicating activities. Women discovered hotel and
video receipts in jacket pockets, cartoon videotapes that also contained the Playboy Channel, and sometimes, rented pornography
videos in the VCR. With the rise of the Internet in the 1990s, husbands gradually began using the readily available Internet to pursue
their activities. Women were aware it "would open up a whole new
world for him."

In the beginning, women attempted to rationalize. They appeared
to have awareness that husbands were accessing material of which
they disapproved and chose to ignore this information. Wives hoped
it would not develop into a larger problem, and that eventually, their
husbands would give up pornography viewing.

> So, the first 6 years, when these things would come
> up, um, I never contemplated—is this going to take
> you somewhere else, are you going to, you know? Is
> this beginning of problems, you know?

## SEPARATE LIVES

"There was a distance."

A common theme throughout the stories was the retrospective observation that wives and husbands had been living separate lives for
a period of time. The separation period varied from months to years.
The first several years seemed to be good for most couples. However,
some women noticed a distance early in marriage. As children came
along and lives got busy, women reported feeling that the couple
appeared to be moving in opposite directions. Couples were caught in
their own worlds, living separately under one roof, each unaware of
what was going on in the partner. As time passed, women were spending more time taking care of children, pursuing careers, attending to
household activities, and volunteering in various community efforts.
Husbands were also busy establishing careers, and time together
in the evenings was decreasing. Due to active lives, women found
themselves exhausted at the end of each day and frequently retreated
to other rooms in the house. They watched television in one room
while husbands spent time perusing the Web. Wives also engaged in
domestic chores independent of husbands' assistance. Husbands and
wives were gravitating toward separate spheres in the house. For the
most part, social life outside the home remained active, but time in
the home was spent independent of one another.

Retrospectively, women realized there was not enough in depth
communication. Discussions centered on everyday activities, logis-
tics of running a household, and raising children. There was a reduc-
tion in sexual activity that accompanied separate lives. "We have sex
less often. Sometimes it's because I'm tired, sometimes it's because
I don't want to."

In some cases life situations forced the couple into separate lives.
Chosen careers dictated that husband or wife travel. "Two years ago, he
got a job out of state and lived with a friend of ours and his girlfriend."
In other cases a problematic pregnancy necessitated bed rest. "I was
pregnant again, and I was on bed rest. And I was on bed rest for three

months. It was a very stressful time in our marriage." Other stress issues for couples included infertility, unemployment, or ill health. "We have been married for 15 years and for ten years we were unable to conceive."

Conflict between couples also caused distance for several women. Many women noticed their husbands appeared to be initiating arguments with them as the use of pornography was increasing. Time and time again, women reported they were confused by skirmishes, but nonetheless were drawn into conflict. "He would blame it on all sorts of things. And then the fights started." Husbands blamed their use of pornography on infrequency of sex and lack of innovation in sexual relationships.

Other women noticed subtle changes in their husbands. "He just started changing. He seemed preoccupied." Some husbands lost weight, appeared depressed, became more irritable, and retreated from family life and social activities. "Then he started losing weight. He lost 15 or 20 lbs."

A preoccupation with computers was a common occurrence. All women noticed spouses were spending increasingly large amounts of time on the computer. "In my mind, I wondered what was going on. For years, he has been preoccupied, being back there on the computer." Initially, women assumed it was work related, "He was always pulling things out of interest, or research, etc."

As previously mentioned, some women identified difficulties in the marriage from the beginning. "He was at the gym for 3 hours [obsessing over] body building [drinking] protein powder." For these women, pornography was an extension of other issues in the marriage. These problems centered on over indulgence of alcohol, controlling behavior, abuse of illegal drugs, mismanagement of finances, gambling problems, social difficulties, and preoccupations with religion, work, or other activities. Due to their activities, some men could not maintain employment. "He's never done drugs, never been into alcohol. But his spending has been a problem." Although women cited pornography as the central problem in the marriage, there were numerous indications there were other serious issues.

## COLLECTING EVIDENCE

> "[I'd be] coming back down to see when he was
> coming to bed [and] I would catch him now and then
> looking at pornography on the Internet."

Many women had a vague sense something was "a bit off" in their husbands' behavior. Prior to the availability of the Internet, wives discovered magazines hidden away, children's cartoon tapes containing Playboy Channels, or husbands changing television stations when wives entered the room. Once the Internet was available in the home, wives often walked downstairs in the evening and noticed husbands rapidly changing computer screens. They also observed their husbands blocking computers so that a casual passerby could not easily see the screen. Many women reported that husbands spent hours on the computer and took inordinate amounts of time to shut it down. As time passed, women observed their husbands remaining awake long after wives had retired to bed.

Collecting evidence was not confined to just pornographic viewing material. Other wives noticed credit card charges that were dubious, bank passwords that had been changed, hotel receipts, and video receipts in pants pockets. "I came across chatting, notes. I came across secret accounts. I came across hotel receipts." Other women found pornographic material in unlikely places, including a child's book bag. A common piece of evidence was discovery of 1–900 numbers on the phone bill indicating that men had been calling for phone sex.

Women reported occurrences of pop up messages on computer screens. "Hi, I'm Lisa, do you remember me?" These pop up messages were messages from other women and / or men or advertisements for additional pornography Web pages. Windows would open featuring advertisements for pornography *"Bare Naked Teen Sluts, Horny Housewives*, etc." Women also accessed previous Web sites frequented by husbands while surfing the Net. Many wives spoke of stumbling on objectionable material while checking their own e-mail or searching history to recapture visited sites. "So I turned on the computer and wanted to check my e-mail. Well, when I opened that arrow that shows that's what happened, the recently opened addresses, I could just see that there were different kind[s] of addresses."

Some women tentatively questioned husbands while others just ignored the behaviors. However, many women developed suspicions concerning unexplained behaviors on the part of husbands. Although they could not identify the problem through their collections of evidence, women would relate, "I just felt that something was wrong." They spoke of, "something inside of me." Gradually, these doubts and vague feelings gave way to more concrete suspicions. "I became more and more suspicious." As uncertainties continued to rise, women became more intentional in their task of collecting evidence. Based on their knowledge that something was not quite right in the marriage, many women began watching for signs of aberrant behavior. "I got to the point where I wanted to know. So, I became snoopy in my own right by seeking out ways to figure out exactly what he was up to."

According to the narratives, women were not always aware they were intently observing their husbands. In describing their focus on husbands' behaviors, women consistently expressed their search for proof in passive voices rather than active voices: "It eventually happened," "It was somehow I found," "I was able to come across." These passive voice constructions made it appear as though wives were not intent on actively searching for evidence. "I was able to come across in a pocket of his" and, "So, I came across a piece of paper in his pocket that had a user name and a password ID."

## SMALL CONFRONTATIONS

"And I told him that it wasn't allowed."

Some women periodically confronted their husbands with proof of computer explorations. Early in the cycle, these confrontations were tentative. Occasionally, these confrontations happened immediately upon making the discovery while other times, confrontations occurred after finding several pieces of evidence. "There is something I want to ask you." Wives often requested that husbands give up this type of pornography or activity. However, they did not always believe it was their right to request outright that husbands discard all media. "After all, I knew he had pornography when we got married."

Confrontation did not always include asking husbands to abandon activities. Sometimes, it included demanding to know what was happening. "Why did you do this?" "Has this happened before?" and, "Where have you been and why?" Despite these confrontations, in this category, wives did not persevere. They appeared to give up interrogations without much of a struggle.

Some women chose a more passive form of confrontation. Without explanation, many women asked their husbands to relocate the computer, discontinued the Internet service, or moved the computer out of the house. Several women simply discarded the media (i.e., videos, CD-ROM's, magazines) and did not mention it to the husbands. "I remember he had been on a business trip and I think there was a magazine that was—whether it was *Playboy* or something or whether it was *Penthouse*—and I just threw it out." Other women would leave literature condemning use of pornography in hopes that husbands would understand the message and voluntarily give up sexually related pursuits.

During confrontations, some women provided their husbands with a way out. They would assume a teenage or preteen age child had been on the computer and then would ask their husbands about this possibility. "What if it was one of the kids coming to play computer games?" Others asked if the e-mails accidentally made it into their husbands' e-mail baskets.

Included in these small confrontations were minor attempts at convincing husbands they should abandon their activities. Most women emphasized damage to children. Others approached it from the aspect of morality while some women tried to reason that it was just "a bad idea," or wasn't "appropriate for on the computer."

No consequences were promised in this category and no threats were made. These confrontations appear to be fact-finding missions and initial attempts to stop the behaviors.

## EXCUSES

"I was just curious"

After initial confrontation by women, men invented excuses for the presence of evidence. Some men readily owned up to their activities. However, they minimized the extent of usage or the frequency. "It was just this one time," or "I was lonely and missing you" were two common responses. Men who admitted to viewing porn responded by saying, "it was no big deal." However, men also gave these same excuses on the second or third time their wives discovered objectionable material.

Men who pursued more than just viewing Web pages, such as exchanging e-mails or entering chat rooms, also gave explanations that "it was nothing." Other behavior wives perceived as troublesome, such as being caught with hotel receipts, generated excuses. "His reasoning was that he was going to just go watch a pornography film and go back to work." Suspicious credit card statements charging for 1–900 phone sex lines also produced excuses. "Oh they screwed up the mailing and it was only one minute." When wives questioned their spouses about inordinate amounts of time on the computer, responses had to do with, "something is loose in here" or "it takes awhile to shut this down."

Most men cited curiosity as their reason for navigating Web sites. They claimed it was a first time occurrence. Some stated that they had overheard other men discussing Web pages and wanted to see them for themselves. Flipping through, scrolling Web pages, and taking a break from acceptable computer behavior were also cited as reasons for the behaviors. Men claimed the activity was really nothing. "He just makes excuse after excuse for everything, for all of it, 'I was just taking a break.'"

Husbands would justify their activities. "He sees it that if it gives him pleasure, it is ok." They appeared not to understand why their wives found the activities objectionable. "He doesn't see the big deal why it's a bad destructive behavior." According to wives, this comment felt denigrating to their concerns.

Many times excuses took the form of blaming; men blamed wives or children. "I have no idea how that got on there." Men frequently used their sex life to justify their behaviors. "Well, if we would be having sex more often, I wouldn't have to do this." Several of the wives were pregnant at the time of discovery. This too provided convenient reasons for surfing the Web or even visiting prostitutes. Other men offered justifications that they wanted to see what was out there that could entice their children. "I went on those places because M's going through puberty and people have been making fun, you know kids love to say hey, 'you're gay, you're gay, you're gay.'"

Not only did men make excuses, wives also provided rationales. However, the women were more creative with their explanations. "Perhaps a repairman came into the apartment and left evidence." These justifications included telling themselves that it probably was one time, it was possible to stumble on Web pages, and all men were a bit curious. Not knowing much about the computer, there were some women who even believed it was possible that the pornography pages had organized themselves into file folders.

## "IT'S MY FAULT"

> "I didn't do the correct thing at the correct time.
> It was my fault."

These were the most common words heard throughout all the interviews. Upon finding the material and after confrontation, women would begin to wonder about themselves. Most of the women began by scrutinizing their own physical attributes. "Am I too fat?" "Am I not pretty enough?" "Are my breasts too small?" Other women asked themselves if they just did not, "look right." "I had gotten my hair cut, and I was heavier." They searched for causes for the rejection and wondered if they needed to change somehow. Should they lose weight, get breast implants, and somehow make themselves more attractive?

Women perceived men's preoccupation with pornography as an injury to self-esteem. They responded with feelings of inadequacy and a sense of "I'm not good enough." Some wives wondered if their activities had precipitated their husbands' behaviors. "Was I not attentive enough?" "Was I too busy at work and traveling too much last fall?" They examined not only their work habits, but also their volunteer efforts and time spent with children and friends. Wives asked themselves if time used pursuing these activities distracted them from attending to their husbands. Perhaps they had put too much stress on the husband or made too many demands of him. The "it's my fault" covered every conceivable category as women struggled to figure out how or what they might have done wrong. "If I'd been a better wife, if I'd paid more attention, if I'd been more loving … I hadn't been so wrapped up with the kids." Women wondered why their husbands lied to them about their activities. "Was I not worth the truth?" Is there something written on my forehead that says, 'I will accept any story or fabrication?'

Women's tendencies to blame themselves and take on the responsibility were regularly reinforced by the culture. Many of them focused on societal values placed on attractiveness, youth, thinness, and sex appeal. Culture's preoccupation with sex was difficult for some women. Women were aware of media's emphasis on sex. They saw it infiltrating television programs as well as commercials, movies, magazines, books, advertisements, and music. "Football commercials are the worst. And I have to sit there with him and watch them. The last one with the two women fighting in the pool taking each other's clothes off." These factored in as to how the women viewed themselves in relation to cultural expectations for them.

Several men criticized their wives' physical attributes, commenting on the small size of breasts or criticizing other parts that were too large. "And, he has said to me before that I was not sexually attractive for him." This too was experienced as a wound to self-esteem.

Blame attributed by others outside the relationship affected women and reinforced their beliefs that somehow they were responsible. Mothers-in-law, counselors, friends, and many Christian self-help books blatantly or obliquely assigned culpability to wives. Did they provide enough sexual stimulation? Did they work too many hours? Were they guilty of nagging or failing to maintain a harmonious home? "She [mother-in-law] said that, 'I knew this was going to happen in that household with what you and how you work.'"

Many women, encouraged by self-help books or self-help groups, began to examine their participation in the cycle. After reading these books, women began to wonder how they contributed to the problem. "I realized that I had some part of it." "I had a role in this ... whole reason why this occurred. And I was blaming myself more than him?" They came to believe that somewhere they had failed their spouses, and by failing them, "enabled" them to turn to pornography. Often, after exploring their part in the cycle, women began to once again take on responsibility. In many cases, therapists reinforced this sense of responsibility.

The "it's my fault" took the form of severe self-talk. Women had to become their own cheerleaders. "You are a good person. You are a good mother. You have been a good wife. You have given all to this man." Women had to remind themselves they were attractive and sexy and could not compete with images on the screen. "He's viewing perfection, almost. And, and no woman ... I could never compare to that. Or never look like that." Men who viewed gay pornography posed additional problems for women. They did not know how to compete and wondered what was wrong with them as women that their husbands could view pornographic pictures of men. "I can't tell you how this makes me feel. You know, the fact that he was looking at men scared the daylights out of me. How does he feel about me sexually?"

However, there were also women who perceived their sex life to be exciting and fulfilling. These women took initiative in the sexual relationship. They instigated sexual activity and were more aggressive during sexual intercourse. Some of these wives reported that their husbands had a lower sex drive. The women who took the initiative in the sexual relationship were also comfortable with nudity, their bodies, with experimenting in different positions, or using implements to spice up the bedroom. "In fact, I'm the one that suggested maybe, 'hey, why not a little device here, with batteries, you know, let's try it.' Put some spice into our marriage." Frequently, wives wondered if they had emasculated their husbands by their aggressiveness and desires for sex. "I feel kind of responsible for it accelerating because I told him if our life was going to be without sex, I would rather us be separated."

## "ALLURING POWER"

"Why did the pictures get the attention and I don't?"

After discovering evidence, many women wondered if they had lost something they had once had with their husbands. These women said that they believed the sexual relationship had once been satisfying. There was a quality women had early on, an ability to seduce. Women enjoyed being desired by their husbands. They were able to entice their husbands, to hold their attention. Some women termed it "control." They liked having this control. "There was a time in my marriage to D, I've always, never, ever had a problem keeping attention from the opposite sex." When husbands turned to other sources, it was a narcissistic injury to these women. "Why is he choosing that over me?" was the question repeatedly asked. "I was willing to have sex with him whenever he wanted." They did not understand the allure of pornography.

Alluring power was described by women as a physical attractiveness the spouse had for his wife. Husbands might notice that other women were better looking, but their wives were "the whole package deal," not just a body. The pornographic image may "look good or fun," but the "whole package deal is what would be the most alluring." These women wanted to be the priority, the number one choice, and the one their husbands would choose over all others.

Women feared that men preferred the fantasy of pornography to reality and that they were in competition with these fantasies. Women described this as hurtful and rejecting. They believed they could not compete with fantasy. "His whole, his whole fantasy was about the model. And their perfect bodies." Women were aware their own bodies were not perfect. They were tall, short, underweight, overweight, small and large breasted, but not perfect. "And I feel like that he would have rather have been with those people than he would want to be with me."

Participants related that pornography attacked their confidence in their sexuality. "You know, what does that do to me? How does he feel about me sexually? Um, why is he looking at any porn anyway?" Because the nature of their husbands' preoccupation was with sexual matters, women wondered about their sexual performance. "It's just that I haven't had enough sex, I don't look right." "Immediately you think, what have I done wrong? What didn't I do? Didn't I have enough sex with him?" These women believed that if they had been more sexual, more innovative and more adventurous, husbands would not have been perusing other offensive activities.

## DEALING WITH IT

> "I can grin and bear it and pretend it is not happening."

Participants struggled to find methods to cope with their husbands' use of pornography. They gave the impression that they were attempting to make sense of what was out of their control. Initially, many women blamed themselves believing it was somehow their fault. Dealing with it encompassed a variety of coping mechanisms. Some women chose to be silent and not share this with anyone. According to these women, it was too shameful and others would not understand. Other women talked to their mothers or to very close friends. However, none of these women told a large number of people. Most all women were reluctant to reach out to other people in the early stages. Fear of embarrassment was too great. Rather than telling others, women found other ways to cope. Several women relied on their religion and prayed a great deal while others attempted to push the knowledge away.

Some women chose to believe pornography was not the issue; rather, something else was the problem. Perhaps husbands were depressed, stressed at work, or going through a rough emotional time. "The depression was linked with him wanting him to do a very, um, an acting out, a very risky behavior like gambling or whatever."

Women also had to find ways to deal with the affront to their sex lives. They either avoided sex completely or indulged in sex in an effort to seduce their husbands. "We have sex less often" was a common theme that was often attributed to tiredness, rejection, sadness, or another range of emotions. Lack of sex could also be attributed to the separate lives the couples were leading. If men were spending large amounts of time on the computer and not coming to bed, the opportunities for intercourse were limited. After viewing pornography, many men were not interested in sex with their wives.

> Sometimes it's because I'm tired, sometimes it's because I don't want to and sometimes, because he doesn't want to. It's not a mutual, because maybe he's already been satisfied that day.

Other men were having affairs and thus, were not inclined to have sex with their wives. When their husbands' attention was focused elsewhere, the sex life was compromised. It was also compromised by women's withdrawal from sexual activities. Women who indulged in sexual activity hoped it would be a solution to the issue. "I guess I thought the answer then was to have a lot of sex with him and he won't want her. So, we had a lot of sex then."

## FORGIVENESS AND HOPE

> "I guess I forgave him at that time."

The final two properties in this category, forgiveness and hope, are continuing themes throughout the "cycle that keeps happening." They are intertwined. After each cycle of discovery of evidence, tentative confrontations, excuses, and realization of the loss of alluring power, wives forgave husbands. "I guess I forgave him at that time and I said, 'you know, I don't want this to happen again' I probably didn't even threaten him with divorce at the time because he promised he wouldn't and I believed him."

Forgiveness was not necessarily a conscious and verbal decision; oftentimes, it was unspoken. Only in retrospect did women realize that they unconsciously forgave their husbands and believed the justifications. "I guess I forgave him at that time because he promised he wouldn't, and I believed him." Other times, forgiveness was highly conscious. "I'd be kind and forgiving him, then be mad for a couple of days." Whether the forgiveness was an unconscious or conscious decision, wives would eventually feel more hopeful about the future and continue with their everyday lives.

In this stage of the cycle, forgiveness came more easily for women. The repeated discoveries of evidence and all the excuses were still new. Hope was there that this really was a one-time occurrence and that there really would be lasting and substantive changes. Women were ready to believe all the excuses provided by their spouses. They wanted to trust that their alluring power was not gone and that their husbands really preferred them to pornography, phone sex, chat rooms, interactive CD-ROMs, and magazines. "I thought there was no way he would do anything again." "He was very convincing and I believed him." At this point in the cycle, women accepted that the husband loved and respected them. They were certain he would not lie nor, "disrespect me."

No outside help was sought because this was not seen as an ongoing problem. Women saw it as an event and managed to push it away from their awareness. They did not want this to happen again. These women had entered marriage not considering that preoccupation with pornography would be a point of discussion. They had dreams of how the relationship would develop and goals for the marriage. Some women had had previous relationships or marriages that were disastrous and painful. They entered this marriage with high hopes and dreams.

## SUMMARY

*In the Beginning* is the first category in the "cycle that keeps happening." Many women wanted to tell their stories by starting with the beginning of the relationship or marriage. Included in the early history was family of origin information of both wives and husbands, histories which indicated interference in normative psychosexual development. Pornography and other related behaviors deemed offensive by women were not new experiences for either husbands or wives. Retrospectively, wives could trace the marital distance. The couple was engaged in individual activities that promoted separate lives. In this category, the property of collecting evidence was not a concrete intentional act. Women believed that they just stumbled onto material that caught them by surprise. They were not aware of looking for confirmation of their husbands' objectionable behaviors. Once discoveries were made, women tentatively confronted their spouses offering the evidence.

There were a number of men who admitted outright that the material belonged to them. Other men denied any knowledge of the evidence. In both cases, findings were minimized, ignored, attempts were made to sidetrack the women, and promises were given that this would not happen again.

Feelings of, "it's my fault" and somehow, "I am to blame" followed each confrontation and excuse. These feelings were rather diffuse and vague at the time. The wives tried to examine what they had done that pushed husbands into pornography use.

Associated with, "it's my fault" was the sense that their alluring power had somehow failed. Something they valued was lost. A major dilemma for the women was how to cope with husbands' behavior and with a myriad of feelings. At this point the coping mechanisms were not well defined, but consisted of trying out several alternatives to either win the husbands' attention or manage feelings. Interwoven through this particular stage was forgiveness and hope. Participants hoped each piece of evidence was truly the last and that the couple would find marital happiness.

# CHAPTER SIX

# TEMPORARY PEACE

## INTRODUCTION

> "We celebrated our first anniversary and it looked like
> things were going back to normal."

In the second category of *Temporary Peace*, there appeared to be
harmony in the household. No one spoke about the problem. Wives
had discovered evidence that husbands had downloaded pornography
or participated in other sexual activities. They had confronted their
husbands and reluctantly accepted their excuses. Wives attempted
to cope by forgetting the problem, immersing themselves in their
children and / or careers, and forgiving husbands for indiscretions.
For the moment the issue disappeared and there was a temporary, but
uneasy peace. There was no overt fighting and no major confrontations. However, under the surface, a tremendous amount of tension
existed both intrapsychically for women and interpersonally for
the couple. It was a temporary peace because there was no active

confrontation and no intense arguing even though there was underlying tension.

The properties in this category are: Collecting Evidence, Covering for Him, Keep Talking, Tolerance, and Vigilance. The properties of Forgiveness and Hope are also present in this category. Although wives reported they were not actively collecting evidence, they eventually found more material. The discovery provided them with the impetus to turn a passive search into an active search. Women then became investigators, searching, snooping, and learning how to use the computer.

Wives worked diligently to prevent husbands from accessing more pornography, visiting strip joints or prostitutes, e-mailing other women or men, and / or visiting chat rooms. They searched for answers that might be the cause of observed behaviors and reported that they found themselves covering for their husbands with family, friends, co-workers, and children. In the category of *Temporary Peace*, wives desired to keep the lines of communication open, continuing discussions about the issue. Wives also exhibited an increased ability to tolerate more awareness of husbands' activities. As they discovered additional obvious evidence, they continued to manage and deal with it. Throughout this category, wives remained vigilant, watching, and waiting. During the time of relative peace, wives had increased hope and amplified capabilities for forgiveness.

## COLLECTING EVIDENCE

"I can't prove that he's continuing in the activity."

In the earlier category, *In the Beginning*, wives reported that they discovered indications that husbands were using the Internet for some sort of sexual activity. After confrontations, excuses, and forgiveness, women could not really, "forgive and forget" and thus, remained vigilant. They did not truly trust husbands in spite of the protestations that "this was just the first time." "Honestly, I am suspicious of a lot of things that he does." It is at this point that wives clandestinely increased their search efforts and intentionally looked for proof.

They began closely watching husbands' behaviors in relation to computer use, paying particular attention to the amount of time husbands spent on the computer. Most women reported that husbands' computer activities generally took place late in the evening or in the early hours of the morning. "He'd be on and the computer always faced away from where I entered the room." Initially, women reported that they passively stumbled on evidence when they approached their husbands to inquire about bedtime. Wives did not admit to actually spying. "So, coming back down to see when he was coming to bed, I would catch him now and then looking at pornography on the Internet." As evidence mounted, women readily admitted to "pretending" they simply wanted to talk to husbands, but were in fact actively monitoring behavior. "He hadn't realized I had left the room. I had gone up three steps … and decided to come back and I looked around the corner and he had porno on there." "I approached it [looking for evidence] from a sneaking down and catching him."

Frequently, husbands moved computers to an inaccessible room. This made it more difficult for wives to track computer activity. Women also realized that their husbands were locking doors to the computer room. After knocking, it often took men inordinate amounts of time to open doors. "And then, went to, you know, turn the door knob and it was locked. So then I knocked on the door, and I had a sinking feeling when that happened."

In order to collect more proof, women educated themselves on the computer. Some had prior experience with computers, but initially, most women knew far less about computers than their husbands. "He's not super, super, super computer literate, but he is light years ahead of me." Women launched a self-education program. They read literature, talked to friends, and experimented with the computer. At some point, all women discovered they could track husbands' navigations by searching the history section. Heretofore, women did not realize there was a "history" button or that it was possible to locate Temporary Internet files. Many stumbled on this function accidentally, while others heard about it from friends. "But it never came to my mind to do it. Never. To look up the history. Or to look up recent, Internet files. Or how Temporary Internet files worked."

As women began exploring the computer, they discovered many sites husbands had visited. "I saw that there were cookies of what looked like porn sites to me." This was a whole new world for them. "It was always a trick to find out, but eventually you can find out what he's been looking at."

Not only were women able to track Internet sites, but many women also obtained husbands' e-mail accounts or followed them into chat rooms. "But I did get in and find his uh password and everything." They became quite creative in guessing what the password might be. They contacted the ISP (Internet Service Provider) and claimed they had lost their own password. The ISP would prompt the client with a particular phrase only the account holder would know. "My stupid husband, when he got his password the question was, I think, 'what is your wife's nickname?'" Thus, women obtained secret passwords in order to access account information and e-mail.

Several husbands realized their wives could trace their activities and deleted the history. This too, was information for women. "I mean, you can delete it from what you see, but there's an index file that always keeps it." Women found methods to defeat their husbands' attempts to erase files. "But he showed me on XP an area where K [the husband] wouldn't know to clear it."

## COVERING FOR HIM

> "You know I think he has business. I covered for him
> on the computer."

Women reported they did not want other people to know their husbands were engaging in activities they perceived as objectionable. They found it shameful. "It's almost like you felt shame too." Rather than tell family or friends, most women kept the information secret. However, several women confided to family members, and for many of these women, mothers were their first choice. These women expressed a need to talk to another person. "And, I, I had to call my mother and I had to have, we had to pray over the telephone." Most women felt guilty after telling their mothers as if they had betrayed their husbands. "I've told my mom. My husband doesn't know that. And I feel sort as if I've done something wrong, but at the same time, I know, hey, it's my life also."

Some women chose to not disclose any information to their families in order to protect their husbands from relatives' disapproving attitudes. They did not want others to have negative thoughts. "I never told anyone. I talked to my mother every morning and she never guessed a thing." These women felt shame for themselves as well as for their husbands. "I wouldn't have told anybody. That'd be embarrassing." In addition to shame, they also feared their husbands would experience negative consequences if others were aware. "And I didn't want to talk to many people about it. Just because of shame. I didn't want to reveal it on his part because I knew how it would affect him, his career, and people's opinions about him."

Most women continued in their daily activities, feigning normalcy. Some were aware of the pretense, "Am I just pretending? Living a little fake life?" but continued with everyday lives, not allowing children, family, friends, or co-workers to suspect there were difficulties. The women even pretended with their spouses.

Women also covered for themselves. This covering took the form of excusing husbands' behaviors to themselves and children. "I know that I've tried as best as I can to not have arguments when they're home, to do it when they are at school." Most wives wanted to protect children from knowledge of their fathers' activities. They feared the knowledge would negatively affect the children's view of their fathers. "My son loves him, absolutely loves him."

Women would also extol their husbands' virtues to me, "And he's very good to me." Men were seen as good providers, good fathers, and good husbands, except for this flaw. "Oh, he's wonderful. Besides this, he's funny; he has fun hobbies and is great with the kids. He's a hard worker. He does work around the house that very few people in this neighborhood do themselves." The pattern of seeing husbands as decent men was true even when the men engaged in actions beyond viewing pornography on the Internet. Women whose husbands had visited "gentlemen's clubs," entered chat rooms, engaged in phone sex, or visited prostitutes were able to say, "He really is such a wonderful guy." "But I adored him [he was the] sun, moon and air." Often, women wanted to maintain a belief that the behavior was not a deliberate, planned activity on the part of the husband. "I just knew in my heart, knowing him that he didn't, that he didn't want to do that either."

In contrast, women who divorced their husbands were able to identify negative aspects of his personality. "He's an addict, a narcissistic guy." However, these women professed to still love their ex-husbands and found them, "irresistible." "He's got this persona and he's really outgoing. He's good-looking." "I really believe it's the devil." In attempts to cover for their husbands, women searched for answers that explained his aberrant behavior. Women gave names to their husbands' objectionable behaviors. They called these depression, alcoholism, sexual difficulties, addiction, sin, or a narcissistic personality disorder. Depression was one of the most common explanations. "Well this psychologist says he really felt that the depression was linked with him wanting him to do an acting out, a very risky behavior like gambling or whatever." Many couples were experiencing sexual difficulties which wives would later attribute to their husbands' acting out behaviors. "We were having sex and he couldn't reach an orgasm. And I just said, 'we knew this day would come, and it's really okay.'"

Frequently women believed an outside force was in control of their husbands' behaviors. They called it an addiction. "For reasons more than porn, just sheer addiction to the computer or Internet in general. He had a computer addiction." Many of these women had contact with addiction counselors who provided them with this diagnosis.

The religious women believed Satan was in charge. "He's letting evil in his life in this way. This was just a form of like Satan is exploiting his weakness." Some women believed husbands had a character defect. "E [therapist] thinks he might be narcissistic." Other causes women attributed to the problematic behaviors were hormonal problems. "He just had too much testosterone. Scorpios are ruled by their sex organs."

## KEEP TALKING

"I ask a lot of questions. We talked about it often."

Without exception, all women decided it was of utmost importance to continue talking to their husbands in an effort to influence them to abandon their Internet activities. If they kept the lines of communication open, women had hope for change. "If I say you're totally wrong, then that breaks off any communication and I don't have any choices, that limits my options a lot." As long as there was conversation, something was happening.

The function of the communication was to convince men to relinquish their activities. All women used persuasion techniques specifically designed to appeal to their husbands. They challenged husbands using arguments based on needs of the children, theology, morality, values, or logic. If the couple was religious, women exhorted their husbands using religious terms. If husbands were scientific, women used their analytic skills. Other women attempted to frighten their husbands into stopping by invoking legal authorities. Women who had young children still at home did not hesitate to emphasize the harmful effects on the children. Although wives used a variety of techniques in their persuasion attempts, there was usually one favorite method they believed would work to their advantage.

Fear for children and the effects of pornography on children were predominant worries for women. They hoped their husbands would have enough concern for the needs of their children, not wanting them exposed to Internet activities. "And I said what if it was one of the kids coming to play computer games. They would have pushed the screen and it would have popped up." Because many husbands were exposed to pornography before they were adults, women attempted to dissuade husbands from continuing their Internet activities by emphasizing the possibility of children's premature exposure. "I've tried from the children's point of view ... do you think it would be right for you to give our son his first porn magazine when he turns 12?"

Several women were apprehensive about the authorities. "I look at him and say, 'do you realize because it's on the Internet you could have been talking to a 12-year-old girl? The reality is you could have caused us both to never be employed again.'" Women had some awareness the Internet could be used for illegal activities. "You could have been talking to a police officer." Other women feared the family could be exposed to unsavory characters that might cause harm. "What would happen if her husband found the letters on the Internet and he got really upset and he was coming to find you and the kids were home alone. And something happened to them."

Some women invited their spouses to read or view programs that addressed the effects of pornography on individuals, families, and society. "I had probably ten self-help books I had been reading through this time. And I would always throughout the years underline things and um, ask him to read it, but he wouldn't." Women hoped experts would persuade their husbands since it appeared husbands were not accommodating their concerns. These women found magazine and newspaper articles that addressed the subject of Internet pornography. Some women openly gave articles or self-help books to the husbands while others covertly left them in obvious places for their husbands to find. "I did get books on proper touching and appropriate teaching. And I read it to the kids first, and then I insisted he read them."

There were also some women who referred their husbands to an article in the local Catholic newspaper discussing my project. "The article that was written about you, hmm, it gave me something specific to do, it gave me a number to call and another avenue to open the conversation." Other women urged their husbands to watch television programs that dealt with the subject. "The story was horrible. He watched most of it with me and I was hoping it would open his eyes."

Women who believed the computer viewing was an addiction talked to their husbands using the addiction model. "We sat down one time and talked a long time about it being an addiction. I compared it to alcohol and gambling." These women encouraged their husbands to read more about addictions. Several women approached the problem by telling husbands the behavior was hurtful for them. "I can come up with arguments that say why this is a destructive bad behavior. It is hurting me." "Why are you doing this? Why are you hurting me?" Many husbands claimed to not understand why it was hurtful.

As women negotiated with their spouses, a majority of them monitored the emotion they displayed. "I try and keep my voice calm." They did not want to yell and scream, fearing this emotion would effectively terminate the conversations. Other women made no efforts to control the emotion. They admitted to screaming, yelling, pleading, and crying. "I was asking him a lot of things and I was crying desperately." Women who had not previously expressed much anger in their marital relationship discovered they were filled with rage. "And I learned a whole new vocabulary. Words that began with F. Bastard. Slut. Things that never came out of my mouth."

Some women approached their husbands in a calm manner. These wives were quite gentle in their attempts to negotiate. "So I said, 'wow, you know, that's—I don't want you to do that any more. I mean, I can't have those things on our computer.'" These women realized screaming might close off communication. Regardless of the emotion and method used in the confrontations with husbands, a consistent theme running through all women's stories was that women made numerous attempts to negotiate. "You know, so we had a talk again." If one method did not work, the women continued trying. "I tried to present it differently to him as maybe a way to try and bring him back into my circle. Not push him out of it." "I've tried from different perspectives."

A few husbands brought up the problem for discussion. "We talked in depth. He brought it up first. It is a good sign." However, in most cases it was the women who initiated conversation. "I was like, do you think about this stuff? Do you think about that at all?" Women perceived that their husbands preferred to forget the entire matter and wished their wives would also forget. "It never gets dealt with. He just puts it on a shelf for awhile and it comes back and something worse happens." Wives reported they knew they would have to initiate all conversations if the subject was to be addressed. Women took on responsibility of broaching the subject with husbands because they realized their husbands were not going to discuss the situation.

They believed husbands wanted the issue to just disappear. "Talking, I mean, I'd bring it up. Can't say we discussed it because it would be me bringing it up and he would be defensive." This pattern was the norm for many women in their communication attempts.

## TOLERANCE

"So the longer I can put up with it the longer I can stay home with them."

Most women admitted their husbands had engaged in behaviors they found objectionable from the beginning of their marriages. Simultaneously, women would deny the existence of early use of pornography. Many women were able to keep knowledge of the existence of such behaviors out of their awareness for many years. As time went by and women discovered more and more evidence of sexually related activities, they were no longer as successful maintaining ignorance. With this diminished capacity to ignore evidence, women became increasingly more able to accommodate additional knowledge of their husbands' activities.

In describing the intensification of conduct, participants stated that men progressed from viewing pornographic magazines to viewing various other kinds of media and engaging in sexually related activities. "Slowly, as the years go by" husbands began participating in what women believed were more objectionable activities. They reported that husbands' activities extended to extramarital affairs, entering chat rooms, and engaging in phone sex. "Everything, other than physically seeing him with another woman, I, I've gone through with the pornography, the chat sites." Women believed that men's use of pornography and related issues took a turn for the worse at various points in the marriage. "During the pregnancy it got a lot worse."

Women reported that they were surprised when they first discovered that husbands had been engaged in other sexual activities for the duration of their marriage. "Because at the time of the first counseling, he was talking to women on the Internet and on the phone. He met women in chat rooms and I had no clue." Men had only disclosed small pieces to their wives. In some cases, it was not until years later that women discovered the full extent of husbands' activities. "I said 'I want to know everything,' so he told me about the other two affairs and I guess, periodically through our marriage he had visited prostitutes."

Although all women claimed to not tolerate lying, most women reported that husbands were dishonest. "I mean he was lying so completely about what was really happening that she [therapist] was even, you know, taken in." Many men had histories of deceiving their wives. "But he lied about all that–lied about–he had girls' phone numbers in his wallet after trips overseas." "So he had been lying to me about that all along." Some women could not tolerate the secrecy of their husbands' actions and behaviors; they experienced the secrecy as injury. "And I think a lot would depend that he'd be more honest with me and say, 'I'm going to do this.' Maybe I could have tolerated it, but in secrecy, no."

Women had different thresholds for activities they permitted in the marriage. Some women tolerated a little pornography while others tolerated none. "He could have *Playboy* or whatever, but I didn't want any of the hard core stuff in the house." Some of these women did not view pornographic magazines as offensive material. "Because I said, I don't have an objection if you need to or like to look at women, you know, naked women or whatever." These women believed viewing nude women was a healthy desire. However, they objected to violent pornography, gay male pornography sites, or pornography involving children. "The other stuff just disturbs me."

It had not occurred to several women that masturbation was a component of pornography viewing, phone sex, and chat rooms, etc. "I didn't think about it [masturbation] until I started reading about all this after I knew he was a sex addict." The issue of masturbation was very problematic for women. Although they were unhappy with the use of pornography, the thought of husbands' masturbating really caused turmoil. "There was sometimes that he did [masturbate] after he'd read it. It really bothered me; it really upset me a lot. Because it's one thing I guess to look at it. But it's a second thing to really get excited by it." Several women attempted to convince themselves it was just masturbation, and not a problem. "You're nuts … I'll never be okay with that. But now, when I start having anxiety, I'll say to myself, it's only masturbation."

Many women professed to be unfamiliar with preoccupations with pornography and sexually related activities. However, many were familiar with alcohol abuse after growing up in alcoholic households. These women often claimed that if their husbands had been alcoholics and they had known they drank too much or used illegal drugs, they would never have married the man. "Had he been an alcoholic, I think I would have been gone. I would not live with a man who drank. Because my father drank." Some women were even conscious of searching for men who did not drink. "There wasn't addiction to drugs, alcohol, and [I saw] no physical abuse going on."

Several women admitted to being recovering alcoholics. These women confessed to overlooking behaviors they found offensive. "But, [it] probably made it easier for me to overlook his addiction because, okay, he's a recovering addict." Because these women were in recovery themselves, or divorced from a spouse who had an addiction, they believed they were searching for a spouse who did not drink or use illegal drugs. "I was searching for somebody totally different from the environment I lived in. There were drugs involved in my family … he didn't do drugs. There was alcohol involved in my family … he didn't do alcohol."

## VIGILANCE

According to all women, there was continually a sense of, "I think I'll always be on guard." Women remained vigilant throughout the cycle. This vigilance was very subtle and often outside the awareness of participants. It was only retrospectively that women could describe their watchfulness. During the time of actual vigilance, women were only vaguely aware of their heightened sense of awareness. "You know, those worries were always in my head." It was as though something was always present in the back of their minds. "So that was always in my head. That always worried me." There was always the wonder where the husband was and what was he engaged in. "Because I'm wondering where he is and what he's doing. I try to explain that more of my time is focused on him than anything else."

General feelings of uneasiness were common. "I can't prove that he's continuing in the activity. Honestly I am suspicious of a lot of things that he does." Women could not sit down at the computer without having suspicions. However, the nature of the vigilance was more passive than active. Unlike in the earlier category of *In the Beginning*, women did not admit to consciously looking for more activity. They were not searching trouser pockets, examining Internet activity, looking for phone bills, or deliberately checking cell phone records. Nor did women perceive that they were deliberately searching the computer for evidence; it would just happen. "I'd occasionally find it in his history and I'd notice the computer history."

Remaining vigilant had effects on the women. "If he's sitting out at the computer, I'm like so tense and worried about what he's doing." In the category of *Temporary Peace*, there was no relaxing. "I'm always on the lookout, on the lookout for signs." They did not like having to be alert. "I'm still uncomfortable about what he's doing. I'm hoping time helps." The inability to relax at home extended into the work environment. Many women had difficulty concentrating at work because of the tension at home. As a result, some women altered their work habits to accommodate their anxiety. "I worked sometimes late hours, so I changed a lot of that, and started coming home." Worrying about their husbands was a constant presence. "I call him at home on my break ... he's supposed to be working at home ... and he's not there, well then I have trouble focusing on studying."

In the property of vigilance, some women became adept at noticing signs of husbands' return to the behaviors they found objectionable. Initially, these signs were out of their awareness. However, as time progressed, women were able to track changes in their husbands' affect and behaviors that aroused suspicion. "All the signs were there that he started to slip into what I thought at that point was more of the depression again." As the cycle continued, women began to understand their husbands' behaviors that indicated they were continuing in sexually related activities. They closely observed their husbands for indications of their outside interests. "In fact, to the point, where, you know, we'd be somewhere, and he'd look over at a guy and I'd think 'is he looking over at him 'cause he's good looking?'" Going to bed alone was another area of uneasiness for women. They discovered it was difficult to retire if husbands remained in another room alone with the computer. "But now I can't go to bed without him, almost." Several women resolved the problem by insisting their husbands retire with them. "So now he goes to bed with me all the time, which I don't want it to be like that." For some participants, it was not easy for them to allow their husbands out of sight. "I need him to be with me." Again, several women resolved this dilemma by remaining at their husbands' sides. "And we're together a great deal now, it would be much more difficult for him."

Anxiety increased when husbands came home late, the door to the bedroom was locked, or when the husbands were spending a great deal of time on the computer. "I told him that I couldn't trust him as long as it was there [the computer]. So he got a laptop." Women could not stop worrying about the men's activities or behaviors. Frequently, wives would attempt to use the phone and find themselves perusing the redial history. "I picked up our cell phone and I just pressed the last number called and I thought, 'who does that number belong to? I don't recognize it.' This added to the anxiety. And that's not a number that I called. So, it goes through my mind; it gets tiring." Many women echoed this feeling of being tired from the constant heightened states of alert and vigilance.

## FORGIVENESS AND HOPE

Hope and forgiveness were prevalent in this category. Due to the temporary peace, wives found it easier to forgive their husbands. In fact, women could almost forget there had ever been an issue. "I can forgive this because that was the way that I was raised."

Hope was elevated because of husbands' relative inactivity in other sexual behaviors. On the surface, life appeared to be calm. There was no overt tension and wives did not notice men engaging in perceived egregious activities. Although wives remained vigilant, they retained hope that perhaps their spouses had truly abandoned their activities. They wanted to believe their exhortations and arguments finally convinced their husbands to cease behaviors they found objectionable. "I'm hoping time helps."

## SUMMARY

In this part of the cycle, a temporary peace was present in the home. There was no open warfare, no overt conflicts. Women were still collecting evidence, but in a less intentional manner than in other categories. They became more computer literate as they found new information. In order to prevent other people from knowing about their husbands' sexually related behaviors, wives covered for their husbands. They made excuses for their husbands' behaviors to family, friends, and even to themselves. Wives also hoped to convince their husbands to abandon activities. Thus, they continued conversations using communication tactics designed specifically to appeal to individual husbands. In this category, women were reluctant to draw firm boundaries or directly confront their husbands with evidence or threats. Participants' capacity to maintain ignorance of their husbands' behaviors was disintegrating. They tolerated increased knowledge but remained vigilant, constantly worrying and covertly watching for signs of behaviors they found offensive. Forgiveness and hope were prevalent in this category. Due to relative inactivity, wives were increasingly hopeful that substantive changes had occurred in their husbands' behaviors.

# CHAPTER SEVEN

# SOMETHING IS DEFINITELY UP

## INTRODUCTION

"You come to the realization."

Women could not maintain *Temporary Peace* for an extended period of time. Eventually, they discovered too many indicators that *Something Is Definitely Up*. Thus, they could no longer ignore the blatant evidence of their husbands' sexual activities. The properties of this category are: the Big Confrontation, Idle Threats, Babysitter, Desperate Solutions, Consequences, Seeking Help, and Forgiveness and Hope.

In the previous category, *Temporary Peace*, women had surreptitiously collected evidence. After mounting evidence, something unidentified spurred women to present their husbands with evidence in this category, *Something is Definitely Up*, and a major confrontation resulted. Women issued ultimatums to husbands; ultimatums they did not carry out. However, the idle threats concerned husbands enough to give in to some of their wives' demands. For example, husbands allowed wives to take charge and become babysitters. But babysitting was only one solution wives undertook in efforts to deal with new discoveries; they also devised desperate solutions, such as buying sexy lingerie or setting up romantic weekends. These desperate solutions provided some hope for change.

There were consequences associated with *Something is Definitely Up*. These included loss of trust in the relationship and adverse impact on sex lives. It was also in this category that many (but not all) women sought outside help. This assistance came at a high cost for all women, either monetarily or emotionally. The properties of Forgiveness and Hope were evident in this category as women continued to struggle with these concepts. However, there were slight variations from this property in prior categories.

## BIG CONFRONTATION

> "When I brought him in the room to confront him, we got into an argument."

After a period of collecting evidence, wives decided they had enough proof of sexual activities to confront husbands. In previous categories, women found indicators of husbands' behaviors, but did not confront them directly. In this category women took action. Not only did they confront, but also most produced concrete evidence. A few women, lacking solid evidence, relied on intuition. "I said [recalling past times], 'Well, did you take a towel in there with you?'" In this category they were not distracted by husbands' excuses. "He'd say, 'they screwed up the mailing, the billing and you are not supposed to get billed for it.'" The women were too wise to accept their husbands' excuses, arguments, justifications, and reasons. "And I just told him at that point. These are hotel receipts that happened to pop up, too ... from the local area."

For all women, evidence of husbands' sexual activities continued to mount. Searching the computer history, wives discovered the extent of visits to pornography sites. The sites appeared too frequently to be accidental. Thus, the excuse, "I accidentally opened that Web page" was no longer accepted. Wives now understood computer technology.

"The one time, when I went in to do homework and I turned the computer on and there was porn right on the screen. It didn't just happen." Women also found numerous and highly personal pop up messages. Wives realized these pop up messages were part of ongoing conversations between husbands and another person. "I was on the computer and it [instant message from a woman] just popped up." Wives encountered evidence that husbands were communicating with same sex and / or opposite sex people on the Internet. "She [instant message partner] was still on there when I got on the computer. She said something like, 'I'll see you later.' I said, 'Where are you going?' And she said ... 'who is this?'"

Repeatedly, wives found hotel bills, video rental receipts, and odd phone numbers on scrap pieces of paper. They discovered videos stashed under car seats and peculiar long distance phone bills. At some point, wives realized these were not random occurrences, but strong indicators that *Something is Definitely Up.* "I got a phone bill that was $125 for one call." Their ability to believe husbands' responses had diminished. This recognition of unusual behaviors resulted in wives challenging husbands. "I said, 'I'm going to call this number right now, are you sure this is a computer help line?' I'd call and find it was an adult entertainment line." "This kind of tied in with the whole escort service ... when I confronted him, who called was this girl, K."

Many women admitted they were reluctant to confront husbands without hard evidence. They wanted proof in the form of e-mail copies, phone bills, computer history, and other hard data. "So, I took that, um, the disk that I formatted, and went into the living room where he sat on the couch and threw all of the material at him and said, 'I want every bit of it and I want to know the truth.'"

If women failed to immediately locate incriminating material, they waited patiently as they continued their close investigations. "So once I pinned down the time ... one night we were sitting down [and] I said, 'I'm really upset about something on the Internet, on the computer.'" Women wanted to be organized, to have a strategy to counter the expected denials. "I didn't confront him right away. I didn't have a lot to confront him with."

Women did not always have hard evidence. In these cases, women relied on intuition or "hunches," which they believed were not precipitated by one incident, but based on experience. "I had a sinking feeling. I asked, 'so did you relapse?'"

When they discovered proof, most women were angry and the resulting confrontations were charged with emotion. "But I noticed it when I would find out stuff, there would be a big blow up." Women reported feeling hurt, angry, confused, and wanted husbands to know they had all these feelings. "Of course, I just blasted him away, and we were back to step one." However, not all women acted immediately, some women planned their approach. "But, when he came home from work, I confronted him with the e-mail and he confessed that he had had an affair with this woman." Women who did not immediately react tended to be calmer during their confrontations with their husbands than women who immediately confronted the men. "And I told him, 'there's something that I want to ask you. Something that I've seen on the computer. And something that made me really sad.'"

For some women, the confrontation with husbands was provoked by children's discovery of evidence. "She [child] came to me and said he [father] opened the porn e-mail that came to him." If children were aware of fathers' activities, mothers enlisted their help in confronting the men. "I said to my husband, 'you call the children and you tell them to come over this evening and you are going to tell them everything. Because if you don't I will.'" However, for the most part, women attempted to protect children from knowledge of husbands' activities, especially if women thought children were unaware of the situation. "My children are my most important thing [sic] to consider."

Many women expressed discomfort with the confrontations because they had been raised to avoid anger and arguments. "I didn't want to be confrontational and I knew that T [husband] is not a confrontational person." However, other women admitted they had no difficulty facing husbands. "I don't avoid confrontation, I said, 'Where have you been and why?' And so he couldn't think fast enough to lie to me. Then, he told me where he'd been."

After presenting husbands with evidence of Internet activities, many women demanded their husbands end all behaviors. Some women whose husbands had been having extramarital affairs confronted the "other" men or women. "And I said we will call her [other woman] right now and you'll tell her you won't see her again or it's over with me." "In fact, I had my husband confront her, but really her husband, and [I] made him [my husband] tell him [other woman's husband] what he was doing and apologize to him." Confronting the other person in front of spouses was a common occurrence. "I called him [other man] up right in front of him."

During the encounters, women demanded answers to their suspicions. Women who were unafraid to confront pressed for more detailed information. "So, I had to really confront him and ask him that thing. 'Did you look at child porn on our home computer?'" At some point, women realized husbands were usually masturbating while viewing pornography. "I never ever thought about masturbation until after he told me." Once women realized men were masturbating to sexual material, they wanted additional information. "It's natural that when you look at those things that you also, uhh, satisfy yourself through masturbating." For the most part, men were not forthcoming with information. Often it took several intense arguments before the truth would emerge. "He could come up with none [reasons] and I gave him several opportunities, and he could come up with none." Women knew their husbands' habits and behaviors and could decipher lying behaviors immediately.

> And at the time, you know, I didn't, I could tell that he was lying or anything's going on. I said 'something's going on here, and I need to know who's going on these places because we can't have that happen at our house.'

Wives were relentless in pursuing answers concerning husbands' suspicious activities. "And I kept asking questions. I don't remember exactly what I asked. How long have you been doing this? Did you have a blood test?"

## IDLE THREATS

> "I told him if he wanted any love or respect from me,
> he had to get rid of the porno."

As women uncovered additional evidence, tentative requests to abandon sexual activities evolved into more vociferous demands. These demands were usually accompanied by threats or ultimatums. "And I told him that I needed him and that I wasn't going to live with this and he would be going to get help." These threats held no muscle and thus, became "idle threats." Threats consisted of warning of impending separation or divorce or disclosing information to family, friends, employers, employees, police, and parents. "And I had told him that wasn't allowed, that he could keep doing it behind my back. He stopped doing that when I told him I'd tell his ex-wife."

Some women did not immediately declare their intention to divorce, but started with the idea of a separation. "I said, 'consider this a trial separation.' And that is what got him. He had a glimpse of his family not being with him." Over time though, they eventually relented, and husbands returned home. In some cases wives forced husbands to move out of the bedroom. "He'll sleep on the couch for a while." However, without further dialogue, the men gradually returned to the marital bed.

Threatening divorce was a common warning given by women. "It's over. I don't care what you're doing; you're cheating on me. It's over." Women admitted they were usually completely distraught when resorting to this ultimatum. "When I found out, I walked in the bedroom, he was in bed and I said I wanted a divorce." Several women admitted they made too frequent threats to end the marriage. "Because I think it was huge mistake this last time not forcing the issue to make him move out. Because I think that would have made him deal with his problems more." In the hopes of following through on threats, several women confided in other people, asking them for their strength in carrying through the promises.

> "And I have told them since, if anything ever happens
> again, do not listen to one word I say, I want to be
> separated and divorced. Even if I say 'no, leave him,
> let him stay. Do not believe me. Take over.' And,
> I don't want to be with him."

Overall, almost all the women had an inability to follow through on consequences whether they were mild or serious. If ultimatums involved divorce, the women confessed to me they did not truly wish to exercise this option. They retained hope that husbands would respect requests and do something about, "his problem." "I wish he'd get it fixed. Because I don't really want a divorce." Wives proclaimed to still love husbands in spite of difficulties. They loved the man they married, but not necessarily the man they thought he had become. "If I had had the guy back I married." Many wives wanted to make the marriage work for their children. "I still don't want to be single again, and I want my kids to have a father." Other women readily admitted they did not want to be alone; they wanted to be a couple. "And uh, so many people have said, you don't want to be alone. It's not good to be alone." Marriage provided something for women they did not want to lose. "And I know exactly what she's [other women in same situation] holding on to, she's holding on to comfort and security."

Despite realizations that their threats held no power, some husbands apparently believed wives. "All the way home from school, he was thinking, 'this is it. This is the end of our marriage. She's kicking me out.'" After the big discovery and confrontation, most men expressed profound regret and promised to never engage in forbidden behaviors again. "I guess I forgave him at that time and I said, 'I don't want this to happen again' and at the time because he promised he wouldn't and I believed him."

## BABYSITTER

> "I didn't want to be his babysitter all the time. That's
> not my role."

In spite of reluctance to be babysitters, women adopted this responsibility. For the most part, men agreed to wives' requests and instituted minor alterations that essentially placed women in control. Women became babysitters, and their situations temporarily improved. However, the role of babysitter was time consuming and draining as wives spent more time with husbands, monitored computer use, placed the computer in a central location, and made sure husbands were not alone with the computer.

> I tried spending more time, being exhausted, but not going up to bed. Being a babysitter. All these things that you know you watch on TV and swore you would never do but you don't know what else to do.

Women recognized that computer activity frequently occurred when they were absent from home, running errands, attending children's activities, or out of town. Therefore, women modified their own activities. "I would go to bed at 9:30; he would go to bed at 10:30. Or I would be out grocery shopping on a Saturday, doing all types of stuff, and he had to be doing it then."

As wives' computer literacy grew, they discovered software that monitored husbands' activities. With their new computer skills, they installed "spyware." "You can get a program called *Covenant Eyes.*" There are numerous spy software programs available. "One of the guys had come up to me, telling me about another program called *Web Tracker.*" Wives also placed parental controls on the computer that put wives in control of passwords.

In taking on the responsibility of babysitter, many women ultimately denied themselves certain privileges or conveniences. They altered sleep and work patterns and relinquished recreational pleasures such as reading or watching movies. The most common form of babysitting was modifying nighttime routines. "I would try and stay up and outlast him on the computer, he would keep telling me to go to bed. I would say, 'no you should be in bed with me.'" The women had cell phones, cable service for television, and Internet service disconnected even though this meant other family members were unable to use these services. In some cases women eliminated the computer altogether. "I insisted that we had to get rid of the computer. I told him that I couldn't trust him as long as it was there." Thus, women surrendered their own freedoms. "Oh, no. I need him to be with me. I can't go to bed without him, almost." "I worry when he isn't with me."

In their role as babysitter, many wives demanded husbands to be accountable. Accountability often took the form of activity reports. "He told me that he didn't turn on HBO because he was worried about finding out what was on and, and stuff. And he said he had some trouble."

Taking over management of computers was no different than other methods women used to manage their husbands. Some women closely managed finances, only dispensing money as needed. "I was in control of the money, the phones. We've gotten rid of the computer. I changed our phone number, all this stuff." Other women monitored the amount of alcohol consumed by husbands.

Maintaining computer passwords was another frequent form of babysitting. "I figured out how on the computer, where he has to put a password in to get onto any Internet sites." However, this method eventually broke down as husbands either overrode parental controls or convinced wives to disclose passwords. "He called me one time and he said he needed to get on the computer just to look at sport sites and just give him the password." Inevitably, wives delivered passwords and later discovered that husbands had not just used them for sports' sites. "He said that he just couldn't stop himself. That it just kept going, leading on to these harder porn sites." After discovering husbands were again visiting porn sites, women again altered passwords. "And then I changed the password again."

Most women were distressed by the task of babysitting. "It gets tiring, and I told him. It's almost like I was his keeper, and he could do whatever he wanted, and I just kept working." As men got cleverer with efforts to override controls placed on them, women tried to stay one step in front. "I didn't know how to lock him out of it, so I took the keyboard with me to school." Some women were aware of their own bizarre behavior. "I was like, this is so ridiculous that I have to be … I feel like I'm his parent." These women realized they were engaging in crazy activities. "It's like this game that you are playing, to see if you can get into trouble or not get into trouble." Other women accepted this new babysitter role without reservation. They viewed the role as their responsibility. "But as his wife, I am his best connection to work through this." They did not describe their monitoring efforts as problematic.

Several women realized they could not maintain the role of guardian. As husbands continually found new ways to override controls, some women began to understand the scope of the issue. Efforts to discontinue cable access or phone privileges did not work. "But I also don't think it will solve the problem, if we disconnected the Internet." These women understood there were a variety of other avenues available if husbands wanted to engage in sexual activities. "I know that he could also go to a video rental place and pick up a movie. Even if we don't have an Internet at home he could go and watch a movie, or go to a Borders magazine section and look at some magazines." These women realized control of the Internet was not the solution. "So I mean, Internet itself [disconnection] would never solve it."

## DESPERATE SOLUTIONS

> "I was trying desperately to be more attractive to him
> and somewhere along the line I crossed over."

In addition to issuing threats and taking on responsibility of babysitting, many women resorted to desperate solutions. Many of these solutions were intended to exact revenge on husbands, including physical attacks on spouses, contemplation of affairs, or actual engagement in extramarital affairs. However, not all solutions were motivated by revenge. Some were meant to convince themselves of their own "alluring power" over husbands, an attempt to achieve the intimacy of early years. These women perceived they had lost their ability to seduce and gratify husbands. In response, these women bought sex toys and / or sexy lingerie, increased sexual activity, took nude pictures of themselves, and attempted to add some spice to sex lives. Some women reported they had "talked dirty," set up romantic weekends, and rented pornographic videos. Often, women were consciously aware they were seeking frantic remedies in an attempt to manage what was happening at home. But for other women, the knowledge of coping efforts only could be seen retrospectively.

Drastically increasing sexual activity was a common solution for women. "And, so therefore, I would use sex to reattach him to me." These women decided lack of sex was the reason men were engaged in other sexual activities. Therefore, more sex would solve the problem. "On average his sexual appetite ... he would want sex two or three times a week and I would never deny him." These women hoped if husbands were satisfied in the bedroom, they would no longer want to view pornography or engage in other sexual activities. "I thought the answer then was to have a lot of sex with him and he won't want her." Various women initiated viewing pornographic material with their husbands. "I said, 'We haven't seen any sexy videos, why don't we get some.' I thought, well, if this is what he wants to do and look at it together."

Many women expressed surprise at the solutions they considered. "I find myself contemplating things that I never in my wildest dreams would have contemplated." Some considered affairs. "I find myself wondering what it would be like to be with someone besides my husband." Prior to this, these women had never contemplated extramarital affairs.

The desperate nature of solutions seemed to be in direct proportion to the perceived severity of husbands' actions. Women whose husbands were having phone sex, chatting with other women or men, visiting prostitutes, or engaging in extramarital affairs were more likely to consider their own revenge affairs. "And that night her brother came and sat next to me [and said] that he couldn't believe that R treated me that way. I ended up sleeping with him."

For some women, revenge provided them with some satisfaction. "But I want it to destroy him more than it destroys me and the kids' lives.

How do I do that? It is kind of [a] vengeful thing." However, other women experienced guilt. "I like to think if I had more faith I wouldn't have gone down that road. I would have been a little stronger." Sometimes, the feelings were mixed. "Guilty. Something I could never say I would never do. I could never say that again. But I did feel vindicated." Many women did not like themselves as a result of their own perceived objectionable behavior. "I went from this person to this person trying to be sexy to whatever he deemed sexy. Whatever it was he was looking for I was trying to be. The biggest regret of my entire life."

Women who did not seek revenge through affairs sought retaliation in a variety of other ways. In anger some eliminated the material they found offensive. "I walked around that house like an idiot, every time I went somewhere, I picked those magazines up and took them with me." Others destroyed the contraband. "Then I, broke the CD in half and threw all the material at him." Some women informed other family members of husbands' behaviors. "The stepdaughter asked me. So I told her. Without going into the gory details, I told her that he was having an affair on the Internet."

Several women chose to confront the "other woman." They phoned them or visited in person. "I wanted to go meet her. I just wanted to see what she—I have this insatiable desire to see who this woman looks like." This was the reason most cited by wives when they chose to confront the other woman; they wanted to meet the competition. "I confronted the women that he had met. We drove to their houses and announced 'I just want to see what a woman like you looks like.'" For most women, this interaction with the other women served to temporarily assuage self-esteem. "I mean, they were ugly. Very ugly. And one of them was a very obese woman." Wives felt good after discovering the other women were ordinary or even ugly. "After meeting the women I felt great. Cause I thought I looked a lot better. And I knew I did." The fact that the other women were unattractive (in the wives' eyes) served to reinforce to the wives that they themselves were still attractive and had allure.

Many women considered notifying authorities because they were so concerned about the nature of their husbands' activities. "If I thought he really would do that to a young child I would go to the police, wear the bug. That's too dangerous [involving a child in a ménage a trois]." Other women wanted authorities to actually examine the computer for evidence of illegal activities. These women contemplated requesting police forensic units to examine the computer hard drive for evidence of husbands' illegal activities. "I even called the crimes division of police because I wanted to make sure he was not doing that [illegal activities]."

## CONSEQUENCES

> "I could just tell it was like, the worst possible news.
> But it wasn't the worst possible news that day. It got
> worse."

In this category, the consequences were limited in comparison to consequences experienced in other categories. Wives reported a profound loss of trust in their husbands. "Regardless of how he is doing [what he tells me he is doing] that I just don't trust him. I can't shake it." Inability to trust their husbands was not just confined to worries about sexually related behaviors, but permeated the whole relationship. "It permeated other areas of domestic life. I'm so mad at him and I don't trust him and I just think that everything about what he does is secretive and behind my back."

Several women lost more than trust in their husbands. Many women believed their marriage was based on truthfulness. Thus, for these women, they had lost the basis of their whole marriage. "I thought at that point that we had that honesty between us."

Faith in husbands was so shaken that many wives did not know if they could ever regain trust. They wondered if they would be suspicious all their lives, forever vigilant about husbands' behaviors. "So I just understood that there's so many ways that he can do it and I can have no clue about it. I can ask him and he can look at me and say everything is fine. So it's hard to believe in words now." "I wonder if I can be confident and trusting in him not doing this anymore, which I can't be." A few women wondered if they could ever even love their husbands again since trust was a basic component of love. "I certainly, I will never love again like I did the other him [before I found out his behaviors]."

Loss of trust was not the only consequence of husbands' activities; sex lives were impacted, usually in a negative way. Women who had actually viewed pornographic material reported that the images were imprinted in their memories and were recalled during sexual intercourse. "They're permanently etched. They do not ever go away." The knowledge of husbands' activities, such as viewing pornography, masturbating, online chatting, phone sex, and sexual intercourse outside the marriage, was very disturbing for wives and affected their desire for sex with their husbands. "Oh my God, the thought of sex with him just made me sick, sick to my stomach." During sexual intercourse, wives worried that husbands were fantasizing about people. "He grabbed me from behind and took me to bed. It was not me that he was making, having sex with." After discovering husbands' activities, wives had difficulty viewing their husbands in the same light. "I couldn't even look at him the same."

Life changed for women in this category. They began to understand their husbands' sexually related behaviors were a problem in the marriage. "It's not fair the way we're living right now, the way I'm living, I'm living right now." Women realized the problem would not only continue, but could possibly get worse. "Because I'm constantly worried about when the next episode is going to happen. And how far is he going to go this time."

## SEEKING HELP

> "I think I feel better talking to someone I know that hasn't had the experience than I would talking to someone I don't know that's had the experience. Because I'm more comfortable talking to people I know."

After making concerted efforts on their own to convince husbands to relinquish behaviors, many women sought outside assistance. However, most women had no idea where to begin their search efforts.

Some began with their minister or priest. Several of these clergymen directed women to psychiatrists or psychologists while other clergymen counseled women and encouraged husbands to come in for help. Other women turned to self-help groups, literature, doctors, prayer, and the Internet. For a few women, talking to me was the first step. Often, women made many outreach attempts before actually finding a qualified person who appeared to understand. With each failed attempt, women felt great disappointment. Despite their disappointment with failed attempts, all women found some comfort in their pursuit of help. It offered hope that answers and solutions existed. They learned there were other women who were experiencing similar problems, helping mitigate their feelings of isolation and shame.

For women who self-defined as religious, the first course of action was to seek help from a parish priest or pastor. "We both went out to get some help for him and talk to our priest." "I even talked to a priest, the priest that married us." Women who sought clergy for assistance inevitably took spouses with them. "And we went back to our priest again." For the most part, clergy saw the problem as serious and facilitated a course of action. Some clergy referred the couple to a psychiatrist or psychologist. "He mentioned a guy at church that is actually an addiction specialist." Many clergy members had helpful advice and provided comfort for women. "When the priest said that, I burst into tears. Finally we're going to figure this out together."

However, there were clergy that were unable to provide comfort or advice. Their inability to help was due to ignorance of the issue, lack of education, personal failing, or pursuit of an agenda contrary to that of the wives. "I went to a friend's pastor and he's just a Christian pastor, and he was really into [being] saved and born again." In spite of the clergy's inability to help, women persisted in seeking help. "The second time, he said if we weren't going to be saved, then he couldn't see us anymore."

Other clergy offered assistance that was more distressing for wives than hopeful. "He [the priest] told me he felt that something was wrong and that M was never meant to be married." This type of advice caused despair. "I went home crying and thinking, you know, I failed in one of the major things in my life." The women who proclaimed to have a strong faith and were connected with their church had great expectations for assistance and were quite disappointed to discover that clergy were human and unable to offer assistance. "Then we found out that the priest from our church that tried to help us get past this ran away with the music director at church."

Many women turned to other Christian resources in addition to clergy for assistance. Several Christian organizations offered couples' retreats that helped couples improve their marriages. "We went to a retreat on reconciliation." "Then we went to Retrovaille [marriage retreat]." However, most women found that these retreats did not adequately address the source of the problem. "It did help us express our feelings better to each other. But it never got deeper, never got to any problem solving."

Women also found other Christian organizations that provided resources to educate and assist individuals coping with Internet pornography. Women who self-identified as Christian sought out these services. "The Focus on the Family, they have a Web site for the thousands that are addicted to sex and pornography." In addition, Christian organizations gave instructions on how to track Internet activity. "It [Focus on the Family Web site] talks about on there how to search the file." Often, Christian Internet sites directed women to Internet pornography educational literature. "I read this book, too, this *Every Man's Battle*. And I read a couple other ones, too, that were very helpful." Once women discovered Christian self-help books, they urged husbands to read them. "He has this book that he reads and it's a great book for men who are open to dealing with it, called *Every Man's Battle*." Although self-help books seemed to offer some women hope, they also moved other women to hopelessness. "I mean, it said 90% of all men have a problem to some degree." This statistic was not optimistic. "But they said that only 10% of all men have no problem with it, that it's not even an issue for them."

Women who did not turn to religious sources often began with counseling. "We started with a psychiatrist." Initially, multiple mental health professionals diagnosed the problem as depression in husbands.

"He went to see the psychiatrist again. Did he [psychiatrist] think it [viewing pornography] was related to his depression? He [psychiatrist] said, yes." In several cases, doctors also diagnosed wives with depression and encouraged them to take medication. "My therapist today suggested that I go on a drug Medication." Several women found the diagnosis of husbands' depression helpful and hopeful. If husbands' problem was depression, then there was a solution. Depression could be treated with medication and therapy. If husbands were not diagnosed with depression, wives were once again disappointed. "I demanded to see a psychiatrist that morning because I was so angry with him. That he, you know, had never helped us with this." Often, the actual assistance provided by heath professionals was not helpful, and in some cases, hurtful to the couple. "We talked to a psychiatrist who was absolutely worthless. Um, I mean he couldn't, he said, 'well, yeah, this is probably an addiction.' He couldn't refer to us to anybody." Health professionals sent men to in-patient or outpatient programs as a way of addressing the issue. "We went for intensive outpatient therapy. And I went to work, because I thought he's getting help and I was extremely upset." This proved to be time and money lost when depression was discovered not to be the answer.

Psychiatrists were not the only mental health professionals who were consulted. Some women found addiction therapists or EAP counselors. "We called employee assistance here." "And [we] went through employee assistance and then that's where all of the addiction came out, was in the counseling." Other women went to addiction counselors. "I had been going to a counselor that specialized in addictions." In some cases, women sought addiction counselors because friends or other professionals advised it. "A friend of mine read her articles every Sunday and she had some on sexual addiction. So, we chose her as our marriage counselor." The addiction therapists appeared to be most useful for women. They provided information and direction to other resources, including self-help groups, addiction literature, individual therapy, couple's therapy, and group therapy. "And then, she, after I saw her, we saw her a few times, she suggested I see someone on my own." Pursuing individual counseling proved to be a comfort and support for wives. "With the help of the counselor … I could start thinking about myself in a different light."

About half the women sought out a self-help group called COSA. Many husbands, on counselors' advice, attended SAA first and encouraged wives to follow suit. "My husband first went to SAA meeting and he told me that there are also meetings for codependents, or co-addicts." Other women found the COSA group first and convinced their husbands to join SAA. "With me at him all the time telling him he needs to find a counselor, and I wanted him to go to SAA." Attending these self-help groups was often another avenue for locating a therapist. "He finally went to an SAA meeting and learned from someone there, a counselor, and um, started going to her." Attending COSA meetings offered women more resources. This included literature, education, access to addiction counselors, and other self-help groups. "We go to Recovering Couple programs, to keep our relationship healthy and improve it."

Many women discovered they could search the Internet for information on Pornography. The goal was to learn about husbands and their behaviors. "I went online. I looked at a bunch of her [Jennifer Schneider] stuff. I wanted to make a big order from Amazon." The Internet presented women with strategies to grasp the scope of the issue. "I got some things about codependence and some other things I wanted to order. So I actually ordered that book." Many women read every book they could find in an effort to find solutions. "I've read every book on betrayal. I've read Gary Zukov's books on love and soul and I tried to research this because it frightened me."

Several women who decided the problem must be sexual problem pursued sex therapy with a sex therapist in efforts to improve their sex lives. "We went to sex therapist five or six years into the marriage. We went through all that and nothing was working. And she suggested that we try some pornography." The pursuit of help was associated with both financial and emotional costs. "I haven't even seen E. [the therapist] yet. It's so expensive. It is $98 a session, and for us, that is an incredible amount of money." Women were resentful because they saw this as their husbands' problem and yet, they (the women), were incurring the financial cost. "He's supposed to go to group therapy with the idea that once he goes to group, I will go to group. It is like six or seven hundred dollars for a session." Women spent large amounts of money visiting therapists, buying literature, and using outpatient and in-patient therapy services. "It's just way too expensive."

A commonality for all women was their determination to find answers and resolve the issue. Women were persistent in their efforts; if one avenue was not productive, they kept searching. Each step helped a little, but nothing actually solved the problem as defined by women. "That's why I, we're still looking for help. The thing is, financially, we don't have the money to just go find any therapist or counselor."

A small number of women had not talked to anyone else concerning this disruption in their lives, not priests, counselors, or friends. I was the first person with whom wives spoke. "The article [in the local Catholic paper featuring me] that was written gave me something specific to do, it gave me a number to call and another avenue to open the conversation." I was presented as a safe person as well as someone who appeared to understand. "We both could relate to you. Your article said you were specifically interested in this so that made you safer than just opening up the phone book."

## FORGIVENESS AND HOPE

> "To forgive means that I'm not bitter. To, to forgive means that, that I, I am keeping him in my heart. To be forgiving meant ultimately that I would be forgiven."

Forgiveness and hope were active in this category. Most women struggled with the concept of forgiveness, yet they appeared to forgive numerous times. Often, forgiveness was an unconscious process that women, only retrospectively, realized had happened. "I guess I forgave him at that time and I said, 'you know. I don't want this to happen again.'" As long as men made some concessions or promises, wives were ready to believe. "I probably didn't even threaten him with divorce at the time because he promised he wouldn't and I believed him." Forgiveness was sometimes a conscious decision. "I want to make it work. So, I decided I was going to forgive him." If wives believed their husbands were not engaging in sexually related activities, the women were able to forgive. "I could just say, God says let's be forgiving, I'm going to stay with this man."

All women came into marriage with high expectations for a fulfilling life. "I entered the marriage, it was going to be like my mother and father. We were going to be a team here. We have goals that are similar, that is why we got married." Wives were reluctant to let go of those dreams. They believed their efforts and machinations would finally solve this major disruption in their lives. The big confrontation helped provide women with some sense of relief as husbands were obedient temporarily. Furthermore, wives believed they were doing something useful by taking on the role of babysitter. Husbands seemed to be managing to behave themselves, at least in the short term. The search for assistance also provided optimism and hope for women. With each pursuit in a new direction, women anticipated a final resolution.

The most common form of hope was the intense desire to believe husbands when they proclaimed they were no longer engaging in such activities. "Because I believed him when he said, I mean, I thought everything was … that he wasn't really going to have a problem with it anymore." Many wives lived with hope that one day their husbands would not only abandon sexually related activities, but would also apologize. "But every single day [he would say,] 'I am so sorry that I did this. And I can hardly stand to live with the fact that I know that I did this, and this is what it did to you.'" They longed for husbands to completely comprehend the level of hurt and pain they felt. They expressed a desire to hear words of comprehension and regret. "[I want him to say,] 'I can see the effects on your face, and I can see how badly it hurt you and I am soooo sorry. And I know there's nothing that I can do, nothing that I can ever say. But I love you and I want to make it right.'"

Wives expressed a strong desire to be able to let go of the pain and truly forgive. "Well, we can't let it go because it's our very being, it's who we are, it's our whole life. Women are so, emotional and so invested in, and we don't just cut those parts of [ourselves] off." Nevertheless, women continued to hope, and this hope was connected to the anticipation that perhaps husbands would finally change. "I actually, I guess I just hope that he hits rock bottom thinking about it and not just having to go through it." According to most women, rock bottom meant losing the marriage and family. "To lose his family. He truly loves us. And he said, 'I can't imagine losing you.'"

Some women were anxious to hear other wives' stories, especially those women who remained in the marriage. These stories offered them hope. "I know women who did work it out. They are still married. It gives me hope." For other women, evidence that husbands were actively trying to give up behaviors offered hope. "I think he, maybe, is in tune with his feelings, in touch with them. It gives me hope." If husbands continued on the right path, the marriage could and would survive. "I think we'll stay together and just do what we're doing and he's taking care of, pretty good care of me right now."

## SUMMARY

In the category of *Something is Definitely Up*, women gathered enough evidence to prepare for a big confrontation with husbands. In the process of confronting, wives made many threats: separation, divorce, informing other family members, or informing the police. Invariably, wives were unable to completely follow through on the threats and eventually relented on their enforcement. In this category wives became babysitters, taking on the role of monitoring husbands' activities. In efforts to recapture their husbands' attention, wives relied on desperate solutions and attempted to reassure themselves of their own "alluring power." These solutions included increasing sexual activity, agreeing to participate in bedroom fantasy scenarios, contemplating adulterous affairs, and in some cases, actually engaging in extramarital sexual activity. In this category, there were also severe consequences for the marriage, as women lost trust in their husbands and the desire to have sex, as pornographic images or thoughts of husbands' betrayals entered their minds. In order to deal with the perceived betrayal and the negative consequences that resulted from this betrayal, many women sought assistance from ministers, priests, therapists, self-help literature, and for some women, joined 12-Step groups.

CHAPTER EIGHT

# THE BIG DISCOVERY

## INTRODUCTION

"It came to a head"

Approximately half of the women began their stories with a narration of "the crisis." In the previous category, *Something is Definitely Up*, wives continued collecting evidence and conflict eventually erupted. Women noted that being on guard was fatiguing; and over time, they could not maintain the stance of, "I know and I don't know." Eventually, wives discovered evidence, which was experienced as so overwhelming that it was both internally and externally disruptive.

> The properties of this category are: Major Betrayal, Raw Emotions, "I Don't Know Him: He Doesn't Know Me," Confrontation, Cyber Detectives, Consequences, "I Know: I Don't Know," Dealing with It, and Forgiveness and Hope.

Without exception, women related the particulars of the major betrayal: the exact day, time, and location, any individuals who were involved, and other minutiae. This big discovery was very traumatic for women and evoked intense emotions. Following the big discovery, wives confronted their husbands and became cyber detectives, collecting information in earnest. They were on a mission to obtain information.

Women reported that they were not the only ones to experience consequences associated with betrayal. Often, consequences spread beyond the disrupted marital relationship and affected both children and external family members. For women themselves, consequences of betrayal influenced their awareness of the ability to both know and not know simultaneously. The various methods women used to deal with the discovery are explored in this category. The final property, the small cycle of Hope and Forgiveness, had some variations as women wrestled with this large betrayal.

## MAJOR BETRAYAL

"I won't ever forget."

Eventually, the diligent work of collecting evidence provided women with concrete evidence. "I found some information dates on my bank card that I certainly didn't recognize and some outstanding hotel receipts." These discoveries ranged from uncovering pornographic Web pages, to finding proof of the following: visits to "gentlemen's clubs" and prostitutes, pornographic video rentals, viewing of male and child pornography online, exchanging e-mails with other men or women, and actual extramarital affairs. "Six years ago, I found an e-mail from a woman to my husband." Although most women discovered the evidence themselves, there were cases where other sources provided information. "My son came over to our house and confronted his father with facts." Moments of discovery appeared to be permanently etched in women's minds, as they vividly recalled the exact date, precise location, circumstances connected to the situation, other individuals who were present, and raw emotions that emerged.

For most women, the date was so significant it became a turning point for them in their experiences. "It was January 13th," "It was January 30th," "It was February of last year," "And the day after Christmas, December 26," "It was a Wednesday, I will never forget it." Variations of the refrain, "I will never forget it" are consistent with careful attention paid to detail.

All women could recall their precise location in the home. "And the day after Christmas, December 26, I went up to go to bed and there were these little pieces of paper floating in the toilet." They were aware of the absence or presence of children. "When I found this out, he [husband] was upstairs sleeping. It was in the morning. The kids were at school." Furthermore, wives knew the whereabouts of husbands. "But the next morning, when I woke up, and he was still sleeping, I was looking at his history at what he had been looking at." "We were sitting in the hot tub talking."

For women whose children began realizing there was a problem, this was a defining moment. "The kids are sitting on the couch and he's got the office door locked right next to them. You realize that there is a problem. He's doing it while the kids are awake." The realization that the children were aware of the husbands' activities was distressing for women, and something they could not tolerate. "It was two o'clock and I got a call on my cell phone by my son. The police were looking for me [and had phoned my son to find me]." "One time, my oldest daughter [12 years old] and her friend were cleaning up the house I had a panic attack thinking they could have seen the magazines in the closet." "I don't want that for my children."

## RAW EMOTIONS

> "So, when, when the bottom fell out, I guess that's how
> I refer to it because I really felt like that was, that was
> what happened ... the bottom completely fell out."

Exposure of husbands' sexually related activities was devastating for wives. They spoke of shock, betrayal, disappointment, sadness, depression, agitation, confusion, fear, isolation, resentment, devastation,

disgust, and overwhelming anger. "I would just be like, disgusted."
In response to these raw emotions, some women took immediate action
and confronted their husbands. "Well, I had the paper and I handed
it to him. The minute he got home." Others took time to contemplate
the ultimate confrontation. "I didn't go and wake him up. I just started
ironing clothes. And two hours later, he woke up." This lag time offered
an opportunity to plan the approach. "And I told him, 'Well, there's
something that I want to ask you.'"

Some women experienced a sense of shock, not wanting to believe the
evidence they had uncovered. "I was in shock." "And at first I thought
it was, you know, a joke, an advertisement or something." This state
of shock was often so overwhelming for women they felt incapacitated,
unable to take immediate action. "I remembered. I didn't even cry.
I didn't do anything." Often the shock was a result of material wives
perceived as disturbing. "He said, 'considering you always had a penchant for young boys, you think there is any way that you could get
this young boy to our house and I could get off on you getting off on
him.'"

If activities were deviant or illegal, women felt significant fear.
"I noticed that there were sites that really kind of scared me." Men who
viewed child pornography caused the most consternation for wives.
"At the same time I'm frightened for the kids." What did it mean that
their husbands were interested in child pornography? "If he is willing
to involve a minor in sexual pleasure. I was expecting it to come up
again, but never in that direction. Never. I mean I'm numb just thinking
about it again." Women also expressed horror over their husband's
viewing of teen sites, gay male porn sites, and sadomasochistic Web
pages. "They had pierced nipples and they were being led around by
a strap. Or they were being flagellated with like a horse or a whip."
These images were troubling. "I thought, 'Oh my God, what is this,
is this his fantasy?'"

Wives had a broad range of emotional responses. Many women were
angry. "I hyperventilated so bad." "I'm resentful." "Well I was totally
floored" "I was never so angry." "It feels like I've just had my heart
ripped out." "I'm so mad at him and I'm so un-understanding and I'm

so angry." But often, angry and mad were not strong enough words to describe emotions. "I hated him. And I wished at that point, he would die." Some women noted they experienced depression for the first time in their lives. "I would spend a lot of time just, I guess, crying." "The depression, feeling like there is no point to a lot of things." Eventually, some women went on anti-depressants in order to cope. "I started on anti-depressants yesterday. I was trying to make it through without anything, but I decided I needed something."

While some women expressed anger and others experienced depression or both, every woman recounted strong feelings of betrayal. "I felt that it was a huge betrayal." "I was really unaware of the degree to which I felt betrayed. I was really unaware of how hurt I was deeply, deeply hurt." This sense of betrayal stemmed from the conviction their husbands' behavior was like an affair. "Because I do feel like this is a whole um, an affair, sort of thing." "He went into chat rooms with other people. That was like having sex with them, I believe it was an affair." Whether the behavior was viewing pornography or actually inter- acting with live women, women felt betrayed. "I feel like he cheated on me. And I feel like that he would have rather have been with those people than he would want to be with me."

## "I DON'T KNOW HIM: HE DOESN'T KNOW ME"

> "The first thing that hit me was he doesn't know me at all and I don't know him at all."

Exposure of husbands' activities was often so traumatic it precipitated intense confusion for women as they as began to question the identities of husbands. "It scared me, you know, who was I with." Many women believed they had actively searched for a partner who possessed certain positive characteristics. In some cases, women intentionally chose men who appeared to have qualities opposite those of their own fathers. For example, women who came from alcoholic families searched for men who did not have addictions, while women whose fathers had had extramarital affairs searched for husbands they believed would remain faithful. "I honestly thought that being a Catholic he [husband] would be less inclined to stray. I had hoped." Once wives discovered the betrayals, they experienced their husbands as men completely different from the ones they had married. "He just gets that look that you just can't deny it. He is not present. I don't know him at all."

Although women considered female pornographic sites to be disgusting, they perceived gay and child pornographic Web pages as truly appalling. Women who assumed their husbands to be heterosexual were dismayed and perplexed to discover husbands viewing gay male pornography Web sites. "That was his porno. He also said that it wasn't just always guys. He would sexualize women too and masturbate." Many women did not know how to process this information; husbands viewed gay pornography in addition to or instead of heterosexual pornography. "That's the first time bisexual came up, but I didn't believe it." A few men were not only viewing gay male pornography, but also corresponding via e-mail with men. "He had already been in chat rooms and porn sites, but that was when he met someone in a chat room and went off and it was a guy." Women who discovered husbands entering child pornography sites were horrified. "Oh my God, you know, what is this? And is this really my husband anymore? I mean, who is this horrible person that, would be doing all these things. [It was] not only sex, but boys! That made it worse."

A corresponding feeling to "I don't know him" was "he doesn't know me." This thought was both frightening and confusing for women. "Well I was totally floored. I never had a penchant for little boys; I had no idea why he would think that. Obviously, he doesn't know me and I don't know him." The idea, "he doesn't know me" evoked confusion in wives as to self-knowledge. Some women were amazed at their own reactions. "My husband brought out a person in me that I didn't know was in me. I mean I didn't know that I could be so angry." Reports of powerful unknown self-anger were common; women believed they had never experienced such intense rage before. "I yelled like I had never yelled in my life."

Not only did women question their own identities, but they also questioned the roles they occupied in marriage. "I was at a loss what role he saw, what role I was through his eyes in the marriage?" They described a sense of no longer knowing how to behave, how to act, or who they were in this marriage. "Was I just there for kids? I obviously wasn't fulfilling every aspect that I should have. Was I just the housekeeper? It felt I wasn't there for any of the sexual stuff at all." They also began to doubt the meaning of marriage. "Which then I felt like, it made me a three quarter person. It feels like you are not whole and the marriage is not whole." Moreover, many women expressed insecurity about whether their husbands truly loved them. "They can't love you and betray you like, they can't truly love you and respect you."

## CONFRONTATION

> "I don't avoid confrontation." I said, "Where have you been and why?"

Armed with evidence, women confronted their husbands. These confrontations occurred at various times and in various locations. Some women took immediate action. "And then um, I called him even from work the next day and made him come in because I just was not okay with the whole thing." While these confrontations contained some of the same characteristics from previous categories, there were also variations. Women did not rely on gut intuition as in the category, *Something is Definitely Up*. In this category, women had concrete proof. They were absolutely convinced their husbands were engaging in activities they perceived to be offensive. Major affects accompanied the confrontations, especially more tears and more anger. However, the outcomes women desired were never achieved. As in the previous category, wives confronted and husbands instituted changes. These changes were a bit more substantial than in the previous category.

After confrontation, women seemed more determined than ever to prevent their husbands from distracting them from accusations and questions. Women were less likely to accept any excuse. "It just hit me then that this is a big problem." They believed they were more educated and understood the dynamics of the activities better than their husbands. "You can't tell me you have never masturbated." Women also reported continuing, persistent interrogation of their husbands.

"I always, and I would even say to him, are you not doing anything on the computer, like porn?" "That's usually how he handles thing. Just trying to skirt it. But I noticed it. Sometimes I don't notice it right away. But I noticed it and I asked, so did you relapse?" Thus, women were persistent with interrogations. However, responses from husbands in this category varied slightly from responses in previous categories. In this category, many men attempted to avoid the topic with their wives rather than give excuses.

Another distinct feature of this category was that women were armed with significant amounts of information and much more confrontational. They appeared both more determined to get to the source of the problem and less likely to accept any excuses. "I said, 'Stop it, tell me straight out. You know stop sitting here trying to beat around the bush. Just tell me what's going on instead of giving me little pieces of information.'" This determination was manifested in persistent questioning by wives and / or insistence that their husbands receive outside help. "I told him that he needed help and that I wasn't going to live with this and he would be going to get help."

Confrontation in the previous category, *Something is Definitely Up*, resulted in some minor changes in men's behaviors, and appeased wives temporarily. However, in this category, it took much longer for husbands to assuage their wives, and this only occurred after husbands appeared to have made substantive changes. Women required men to demonstrate their willingness to obtain help. Some men joined SAA and found sponsors while others read self-help literature. "He has this book that he reads and it's a great book for men who are open to dealing with it." Some women requested changes in computer use; the computer had to be moved to a central location or removed altogether. "I insisted that we had to get rid of the computer." Although women required different types of changes from husbands, all wives retained anger for a significant period of time and many expressed their anger directly. "[There was] more anger and dissension between him and I [sic]."

Women in *The Big Discovery* category were suspicious of everything. E-mails, phone calls, computer time, and receipts were no longer considered innocuous; all were grounds for questioning their husbands. "I found an e-mail that he had sent to a woman that he obviously worked with and it was really nothing, it was somebody he had just worked with."

In previous categories, women accepted that husbands were making changes and retreated from being on guard. In this category, women remained on guard for a more extended period of time. However, as before, women eventually retreated. "But he convinced me—I was stupid—that he no longer needed counseling ... that everything was okay. We were getting along good. Everything was fine."

## CYBER DETECTIVE

> "I became snoopy in my own right by seeking out
> ways to figure out exactly what he was up to."

The big discovery can occur at any point in the cycle. In fact, there may be several "big discoveries" that hit with a huge emotional impact. Women continued to collect evidence throughout and became more sophisticated in their investigative work over time. If it was the computer that absorbed their husbands' interests, women became cyber detectives. Taking on the role of cyber detective was similar to the property of babysitting in the category *Something is Definitely Up*; however, cyber detective work required additional energy and increased computer knowledge. Some women installed computer software that tracks user history. If the husbands' were involved in additional sexually related activities, women adopted the role of "super sleuth." With increased frequency, women monitored men's activities both on and off the computer. They accessed e-mail accounts, rummaged through pockets and automobiles, retrieved phone messages, and explored cell phone numbers. Several women waited until their husbands had retired before beginning their investigations.

If the men engaged in activities other than viewing online pornography, women had to find more covert methods of spying. "[I'd] find women's room numbers and stuff on the back of cards and in his wallet when he'd been gone for awhile." Unlike earlier categories of the cycle, wives were no longer inclined to believe excuses after finding numerous indications of husbands' infidelities. "You don't believe it. If he hadn't lied before I'd probably believe it. But I don't." In pursuit of truth, women often invented covers in order to pursue their investigations. "I acted as if I was the one who called for my brother. I said, 'Are you an escort service?' and she said, 'yeah.' I said, 'Oh, Good! Because my brother called one last night.'" Women explored any mildly suspicious aberrations. "I decided to check that backpack to see if I could find anything else, and there was diskette in there and all it said was 'S. Sands.'"

Some women attributed their ability to uncover evidence to something or someone other than their own ingenuity. "I just thank God for revealing everything that I needed to know for him to, to give me the strength, to give me what I need to know. God says all secrets would be revealed and I've always believed that." With this perceived assistance, women found necessary information that would provide them with ammunition when they confronted their husbands. "I found his user name and his password and God just poured these things on me … I have found his user name and his password, so I go into this account and, and I read his profile."

Accessing e-mail accounts was the most common form of collecting evidence. "So, I came across a piece of paper in his pocket that had a user name and a password ID." Once they had the e-mail account, wives began probing further. "I started searching to see what he was doing. I found the second e-mail address. He thought he had erased everything, but he didn't erase the trash bin."

Women were very creative in their attempts to locate passwords. By trial and error on the computer, they could guess the password. Men commonly used birthdays, nicknames, or favorite sports teams. "Well, he's always called me 'pudding' my whole life. So that was his password." Other women did not search for codes because they asked their husbands for them outright. "I asked him what the code was and he gave it to me. In his mind, he thought he was safe. And he used my name as his code." Once women were able to access passwords and secret accounts, they examined all information available on the computer. "I found [something] it was a memo to him saying that his profile had been accepted for this Web site called Adult Friend Finder and it's called World's Largest Sex Personals." Several women collected information they found and maintained files for future ammunition. "I have a whole folder of all this stuff. Of letters that he's written me. And uh, one of the women wrote me two or three letters."

As wives learned more and accessed additional material, husbands reacted by attempting to out maneuver their wives. "He tried to do the porn sites but he realized that it could be traced too easily to a credit card. Because he had to use a credit card online." Once husbands discovered their wives knew how to research the computer history, they attempted to erase evidence. "He had of course had deleted history. I know the IT people at work pretty well. And I knew it's on 2000 where you can't delete history at all. I mean, you can delete it from what you see, but there's an index file that always keeps it." Thus, women figured out how to recreate the history.

Often, there was doubt as to who was wandering into pornography sites on the computer. In these instances, women became skilled at knowing how to pinpoint the culprit. "So, I figured out. I would check a day and then I would go back, maybe a few days later and sometimes I'd see it. Sometimes there wouldn't be anything." In this manner, wives were able to ascertain exactly who was on the computer at the time the pornography sites were being entered. "I figured out the time periods that I knew that J [son] wasn't home to use the computer."

In their capacity as cyber detectives, women taught themselves a great deal about the computer. Every woman discovered the history button at some point in her investigative work. Some women enlisted computer savvy friends while others educated themselves by playing around with the computer. "My friend is very good with computers, so he told me, just ask me and I can tell you how you can find things if you have any doubts and you want to find out things." Computer expert friends knew a variety of ways to investigate the computer. "He said there are so many different ways you can find about it. Look up the history, or look up recently, Internet files, or Temporary Internet files. Where you can see all the pictures that have been visited." If women did not have computer knowledgeable friends or felt too much shame to ask someone, they discovered how to navigate the history on their own. Women located the dropdown bar that accessed the computer history. "I knew that in that one little bar that you could pull it down and you could go to something that you had recently gone to." Some realized simply by typing in a few letters, they could access sites. "Sometimes you type something in and it would be something that you had never been to, but they'd be pop-ups." In addition, all women discovered how easily they could access the history. "They have icons across the top and I clicked that on and what pops up is a little window on the side, Monday, Tuesday, Wednesday, and you can go into the history."

Women who were unable to figure out how to use the computer and wanted more high-tech computing skills contacted their ISP to learn more about accessing the Internet. "I actually went online with the AOL which is our Internet provider and I asked him, how can you see the history more fully, and they told me." Once wives had computer-navigating information, they could follow their spouse's activities. "And I was really able to see a lot of these, you know, cookies, it was. It was Internet history."

Some women tried to refrain from investigating. "I try not to spy because that just gets to me, it doesn't get to him." Yet, these women reported they were unable to stop themselves. "I became more and more suspicious and would sneak down the steps and spy on my husband." For the most part however, women admitted to spying "I was spying on my husband. It was a kind of subterfuge, you know? It was a kind of covert operation on my part."

Women interrupted social activities and work and home responsibilities in order to try and "catch" their husbands in the act. "I drove over here and he didn't hear the garage door and he didn't hear anything. I went down the steps and he had just finished masturbating to the pornography on the Internet." Spying was taxing for women. "It wears you out to be a detective. Because you have to do so many things." They expended large amounts of energy attempting to collect evidence and entrap their husbands. "One day I had to go upstairs, and I knew something. I had gone up three steps and decided to come back and I looked around the corner and he had porno on there."

The women became devious. "I found out he had a post office box. And so I got the key for it. So one day, I was zooming to the post office, so I could fit the key. And I got a speeding ticket for that." A common strategy for wives was to wait until their husbands were occupied at other places in the house. It was a widespread occurrence to engage in spy activities while husbands were in the shower. "So the next day while he's taking a shower, I'm checking again and sure enough there was another card."

Several women considered going to the police in order to gain concrete proof. I said 'this is that stuff where I go to the police station and they put a bug on me and I make you say it again and you are in jail.' Some women not only considered this action, but also actively sought out police and had them examine the computer's hard drive for evidence of illegal pornography. "When I found out this was going on I even called the crimes division of police because I wanted to make sure he was not doing that." Some women did not contact the police; the police contacted them. "It was the police and they had a search warrant for our house, for our computer."

## CONSEQUENCES

> "Because I had to face people. And then we lost our friendship with our best friends."

The consequences experienced by wives extended beyond the disrupted marital relationship. Some of the women experienced loss of friends, status, and in some cases, financial security. Some were subjected to invasion by legal authorities. This not only brought shame for the family, but dread as well, as women did not know what would follow. "Then they told me the very worst was that he was also going to be arrested and they had a warrant out for his arrest." A few husbands had engaged in illegal Internet use and were caught by authorities. "And the police were looking for me. And I was like, you know, I thought I was going to die."

The shame of extended family members and community having knowledge of husbands' activities was traumatic for several women. "It's horrible for alcoholics. But, it's more accepted now. It's not as much as stigmatized as this. This is, the worst possible thing I could think of. As far as stigma." Some women lost friends when it was discovered husbands were using the Internet for pornography. "Then we lost our friendship with our best friends. The wife told me that if I stayed with my husband, she could no longer be my friend." Women reported feelings of distress after noticing children had lost respect for their fathers with knowledge of sexually related activities. "I don't think they [the children] respect him now. They see him and they're good to him and everything, but I think if they ever had to make a choice [they would choose me]."

In several cases, husbands were caught using pornography in their work place, which resulted in termination of employment. This placed financial hardship on the families as well a loss of social standing. "In October he was fired. When he came home he had to tell me that he had lots of pornography on his computer. He had been using their 1-800 number for phone sex and all."

Depression was the most common complaint from the women. "I think part of it is all of the stress in my life … the depression … feeling like there is no point to a lot of things." In addition to reported depression, some women sustained physical ailments they attributed to stress of dealing with the issue. "I have high blood pressure now. I have high cholesterol. I'm on tons of medications; I have a blood disorder. And, I didn't have any of this until this started."

"His whole sexuality really hurt our sex life, my sex life." The quality and quantity of the sex life was negatively impacted by the husband's activities. "You know … him and sex … Oh my God … the thought of sex with him just made me sick to my stomach." For some couples, sex activities decreased. "We didn't have sex, I mean, twice a year maybe." Many women no longer wanted to have sexual intercourse with their husbands. "[Lack of] desiring sex with him." "We haven't slept in the same bed in over three years." If the women chose to have sex, they unintentionally focused on the husbands' other sexual activities. "I didn't like my husband lusting after another woman when he was with me. I felt like a vehicle in which, physical vehicle only." Many women expressed emotional disconnection from their spouses. "You are not making love to your husband you are simply having all and out sex."

Furthermore, women reported their husbands' pornographic activities interfered with sexual intercourse when it did take place. "If it's something I knew that he did recently, then it invades [love making] a lot." Their perceptions of their husbands' fantasies often became engrained in their head during sex. "He would always, and this creeped me out. He probably would love to see me with another woman, actually watch me have sex with somebody else, another man." Invasive images of the husband's behaviors stirred up anger.

> I have a lot of anger still. My husband and I are not sexually active, because every time I think about having sex with him, I see all of these other things in my head, the pornography, the other women. The phone. Everything.

Some women knew their husbands had been viewing pornography by their attitudes toward them. "And he grabbed me from behind and took me to bed. And, it was, not me that he was making—having sex with." Many husbands made requests in the bedroom that were unusual. "The one thing that really scared me one time was [when we were] having oral sex. He said one time, 'you know, you haven't done that in a long time.' And he's never been really directive in sex like that." This prompted the women to question his previous activities. "He was looking at men. So ever since then, I'm thinking, does he really like women or does he really like men more?"

It was not always wives who withdrew from sexual activity. "I'd say around the same time he started having trouble coming to fruition through normal ways, in the normal way." According to participants, numerous husbands had difficulty with intercourse. "We are still intimate but not necessarily the typical intercourse way."

For some women, husbands' sexually related activities interfered in the marriage to a great degree. In fact, it was cited as the reason for seeking dissolution of the marriage. "The divorce is almost final and he's going to move out soon." Divorce meant loss of financial security, trepidation about the future, and disruption for the family. "But, the house, the equity, and the house is joined. So I have to give him half that." Since many women had not worked outside the home after having children, they were scared to reenter the workforce. "Because I didn't know if I could ever make it on my own. I had been off of work for so long." The competitive nature of the wage labor force was also intimidating for women. "Gosh, could I get back out there? Could I be competitive again?" Women not only had fears about reentering the workforce; they had concerns over being single parents. "You know, could I raise my children even with his help, without him being there physically?"

All women contemplated a divorce at some point during the cycle. They considered the extent to which a divorce would disrupt family life. "It would take a lot of selling of the house. Getting rid of everything we've collected 44 years and starting over. And that would not be easy." Although all women considered divorce, only a few exercised this option. These women claimed it was not a choice they desired, but a last resort.

## "I KNOW: I DON'T KNOW"

"I never knew really it was bad. I knew it was bad."

By this point, many women allowed themselves to acknowledge the existence of their husband's sexual behaviors. "I thought he would lie basically and I chose to believe those lies for many, many years in this marriage." They attributed their previous denial of activities to numerous sources including the women's own youth / gullibility and bad influences on the husband. "I was pretty gullible at the time. I was 26. I did believe him, but not at all, really. It all added up." Other women cited the negative influence of other people on their husbands. "This one guy is a huge catalyst to him disappearing, the last step out of my life." Wives did not want to concede to the idea that their spouses could have initiated the offensive behavior. "I'm pretty sure it was never his idea to go, he's not really a strip club kind of person. He's not a really yucky porn kind of person."

Many women conceded they knew pledges to change were empty promises. "I thought that was his goal. He told me that was his goal even though I knew his behavior didn't show it." "We were married 13 years; he had an affair with a girl that worked for him. I found out about that, and he swore that it would never happen again ... and promises galore. Well, I believed him." Women believed their husbands even though they knew behaviors were unlikely to change despite the promises. "But I wanted to believe him [even though] he had lied pretty much all along."

The women acknowledged they deliberately ignored the facts. "It may be the blinders that I chose to use." "Part of me put up with it and I think ... in weakness." There was some apparent recognition their husbands' behaviors were not new to the marriage. "I think I, throughout the course of marriage, I always knew it was a thing, you know, that he liked." "All the signs were there." Some women acknowledged they really wanted to believe their husbands, because if they admitted their husbands' behaviors would not change, they would be forced to alter their current situations. "[Believing him] allowed me [to stay in the marriage] because I was afraid of being on my own with three children. At that point, I didn't know if I could do it."

Several women admitted to a previous awareness of an uninspiring and unsatisfactory sex life. Retrospectively, they wondered if this was an indication of husbands' outside sexual activities. "As a lover it was pretty cut and dry, not very adventuresome. It was very routine from the beginning. I probably initiated sex more than he did." Husbands' lack of sexual interest in their wives was a common theme. "He is not very sexually aggressive. I'm more the person to initiate sex."

Many women knew their husbands exhibited addictive-like behavior in other areas of their lives. "He has one of those personalities where he can give up one addiction just fine, he can stop. But another one slides into it." Women reported their husbands compulsively gambled, spent money, ate, dieted, exercised, and abused alcohol, and drugs. "He's fought that [alcoholism] and eating disorders too. He and I talked about the sex addiction in his family." Several women believed their marriages were "shams" and they were participants. "I became somewhat of an actress over the last year and a half. I was trying to act normal in spite of everything ... pretending." Some questioned how long they could maintain these pretenses. "So the longer I can put up with it, the longer I can stay home with them. Can I do it until they're in college? It's a lot of years to pretend."

Initially, some women claimed to have no awareness of the availability of Internet pornography. However, in further discussions many of these women acknowledged some awareness of it. "Yeah, [I had an idea] that pornography was available on the Internet." Even though some women installed anti-pornography software at work, some of these women denied knowledge of Internet pornography availability. After in-depth discussion, these same women eventually admitted their awareness. "In my business life I installed all kinds of maintenance applications that we would check once a week [for pornography] and you know, we knew." Wives were hesitant to purchase home computers due to the accessibility of Internet pornography. "I just knew that I never wanted to get a computer because of the Internet. I just knew that would just bring up a whole new bag of worms." After acquiring home computers, women were cautious. "I think I had suspicions. The day we got the computer, we talked about why I really didn't want it in our house ... because of his pornography use at home, the magazines, the movies, and the 1-900 calls."

## DEALING WITH IT

> "Well, I don't make any sense of it [his behavior].
> I just accept it I guess."

Dealing with husbands' sexual behaviors in *The Big Discovery* category was slightly different from dealing with behaviors in previous categories. The nature of the major betrayal was so devastating that women found new methods to cope. Many women turned to their faith, using available spiritual resources. Prayer was a common source of solace. "Oh, God, I prayed so much. Prayer, too, is what has gotten me through." Prayers were the expression of their self-professed important personal relationships with God. "I know that prayer is my answer. I've had a very strong prayer relationship with God. And I always believed that He would take care of me." Additionally, religious self-help books gave hope to these women. "I have a book called, *The Power of the Praying Woman*. And I've been praying for me to be able to control my mind." Other women found comfort in familiar spiritual rituals, such as confession. "I know that when I went to confession to Father K, Father said that this has been a problem for R since before, since as soon as it could be a problem." Women also took comfort in husbands' use of prayers and religious rituals. "Because, I know, right now, he's doing rosary, once, sometimes twice every day. His spiritual life has—just at full exposure right now." Even simple acts, such as service attendance, consoled women. "I don't think we could do this battle if it weren't for him [pastor]. He just has that courage to go and stand up at that pulpit and talk about this stuff."

Women who attended COSA meetings relied on the 12-Step program for comfort. "I am in my own recovery journey." The program kept them focused. "That's just part of the 12 steps. I was powerless over his sexual addiction, and I'm powerless over my codependence." COSA encouraged women to concentrate on their own behaviors rather than their husbands. The 12-Step program also provided women with methods to manage their pain. "It empowered me in that there is something I can do about this. I can't take a pill, but there is something I can do about this." Managing their own pain gave women a sense they were actually doing something. "Instead of being scared to death. Feeling hopeless and helpless. And you know, maybe I can find something here that's going to help me."

Several women dealt with the problem by admitting they could no longer fight the battle with their spouses. They had to accept their life situations. "Well, I don't make any sense of [his behavior]. I just accept it I guess." Some women attempted to reassure themselves the sexual behaviors were not things their husbands really wanted to do. "I know, I just knew in my heart, knowing him, that he didn't want to do [Internet pornography] either."

Dealing With It for some women meant talking to me. Several divorced women agreed to talk in an attempt to understand what happened in their marriages. "I guess I called you because I [want to] go back and try to figure out what happened wrong so it doesn't happen again." Some expressed they wanted to help other women in similar circumstances. "I just want to help other women who go through this same thing." Some wives hoped their stories would offer other women solace. "I feel that it is important because it is such a huge issue to me. I want other women to know that they are not alone, and if I can help her to have a glimmer of hope." For some women, talking to me was addressing the problem. "I am starting the process of doing something. I am not one to sit around and it feels like I am doing something."

### FORGIVENESS AND HOPE

> "And I actually, I guess I just hope that he hits rock bottom thinking about it and not just having to go through it."

The small cycle of Forgiveness and Hope took on small variations in this category. The nature of the big discovery dampened the ability and desire to forgive and hope for change. There was a direct relationship between the number of major betrayals and the likelihood of forgiveness and hope: the fewer the number of major betrayals, the more likely the women would forgive and have hope.

If it was the first major betrayal, women experienced a more conscious degree of hope than women who had moved through the cycle numerous times. Women who were experiencing major betrayals for the first time had not yet encountered the disappointment of failed outside help. Therefore, they were able to remain hopeful. In this category hope is directly connected to finding assistance. Each time wives encountered big discoveries; they were unyielding in their pursuits for continued professional assistance. By pursuing outside sources for help, wives admitted that professionals were needed for permanent changes in men's sexual behaviors.

## SUMMARY

*The Big Discovery* began with the property, Major Betrayal. This big discovery brought about a crisis in the life of women. It appeared to be the moment in which wives admitted there was a huge problem that would not just disappear. Emotions that were evoked by this discovery included shock, betrayal, disappointment, sadness, depression, agitation, confusion, fear, isolation, resentment, devastation, disgust, and overwhelming anger. Women wondered if they could recover from the effects of *The Big Discovery* findings. The major betrayal left women confused about the identities of men they had married. In addition, wives began to question if their husbands really understood them. In the wake of the major disappointment, disillusionment, and rupture of the relationship, women experienced identity crises. They questioned their roles and functions in their marriages. The discovery of the betrayal led to another confrontation, which appeared to be larger and have more impact than in previous categories. The perceptions of the betrayals had consequences that affected not only wives and husbands both individually and collectively, but also children, extended family, and friends. The consequences were financial, social, physical, and emotional. The wives struggled to find coping methods.

No substantive changes emerged from this category of *The Big Discovery*. Women were unable to permanently disrupt the cycle. After a period of time, wives relented on their demands, calmed down, and once again the couple created a temporary peace together. However, the temporary peace could not last and the cycle continued.

# Chapter Nine

# COSA Women

## Introduction

In the category of *Something is Definitely Up*, all participants sought outside assistance in dealing with the issue of husbands' sexually related activities on and off the Internet. At this point in the cycle, two separate types of women emerged. One group of women sought assistance from clergy, medical doctors, or therapists. The other group of women joined a 12-Step self-help group, COSA, while most of their husbands attended SAA.

There were several variations between COSA and non-COSA women. These variations form the properties of the COSA category: a New Language, COSA as Ritual, Work Your Own Program, "I'm No Longer Isolated," Abundance of Information, Marriage Enrichment, and Forgiveness and Hope.

COSA women described a cycle that was highly similar to the cycle described by non-COSA women. Both groups of women were aware of problems early in the relationship and hesitantly confronted their husbands with suspicions. As with non-COSA couples, COSA husbands made excuses and wives retreated. A *Temporary Peace* was established. Although wives retreated from direct confrontation, they continued to talk about the issue with husbands. Moreover, COSA wives, like non-COSA wives, wished to believe they were not really seeing evidence of behavior they found objectionable. However, evidence continued to mount until they realized *Something is Definitely Up*. Eventually, wives discovered irrefutable proof of husbands' activities. This resulted in a major confrontation in which wives issued threats they were unable to enforce. Their trust had been violated. Thus, wives took on babysitter roles, continually monitoring their spouse's activities. Both COSA and non-COSA women sought professional assistance. However, COSA women's search efforts led them to the 12-Step program. Despite using this 12 step-program, their coping mechanisms were very similar to the non-COSA women. The properties address these variations.

## COSA

> "He told me that there are also meetings for codependents, or Co-addicts."

COSA is a 12-Step group devoted to individuals who are in relationships with sex addicts. Women learned about COSA from a variety of sources: husbands, therapists, and / or media. Some wives discovered COSA through their husbands. These men attended SAA and often encouraged their wives to join the Co-addicts program. "I [found out] about the meetings when my husband first went to SAA meeting, and when he came back home he told me that there are also meetings for codependents, or Co-addicts." Initially, some women were reluctant to attend, not understanding how a self-help group could be of assistance. In addition, shame of sharing prevented a few women from attending. "He told me that, there's a possibility also for me to attend the meetings if I wanted to share with somebody. I didn't want to talk to many people about it. Just because of shame." Some women acknowledged they were not ready to admit there was a problem in the marriage.

"But, I also didn't want to admit that, we were supposedly that very happily married couple."

Therapists were the primary sources for information on COSA and SAA. "When we went to the theological seminary, she [therapist] told us that he probably was a sex addict and she told us about the open meeting out on the east side." However, there were several women who learned about addictions through other resources, particularly the media. "I had been listening to a program on the Internet, but it's on a Christian station. And they talk about sex addiction all the time." Some read about addictions in the newspaper. "A friend of mine read her [addiction counselor's] articles every Sunday and she had some on sexual addiction."

If husbands were not already attending SAA, this group of women encouraged them to find a SAA meeting. "[I was] at him all the time telling him he needs to find a counselor and I wanted him to go to SAA. And he finally went to an SAA meeting." Men responded in a variety of ways to women's requests. Some were hesitant to attend. "I don't know how a bunch of sex addicts can get together and help each other." Other men were willing to go. "I asked him a long time ago if [he would go] so he decided that maybe he should go. He started working the program."

Initially, several women expressed apprehension regarding their spouse's attendance at SAA. They worried it could be another forum for husbands to indulge in their compulsions. "I knew there were a couple of women in his group. It seems to me that it could almost be a fantasy for them to sit and listen to these women talk about what these women do in their addictions." Despite these concerns, women attempted to convince themselves SAA was helpful. Yet, the concerns remained. "I think they run a very serious risk of listening to all those people and getting ideas. Of things to try or even that … causing them to have a fantasy." This concern was not restricted to COSA women; even non-COSA women often cited this concern as a reason for discouraging their spouses from attending SAA. "I don't know how a bunch of sex addicts can get together and help each other."

## A NEW LANGUAGE

"Because I am codependent."

Once in COSA, women learned a new language that aided them in making sense of their husbands' behaviors and their own thoughts, feelings, and behaviors. They spoke of "codependency," "enabling," "addiction," "accountability," "acting out," "working the program," and "recovery." COSA women articulated their cycles using the new language. "I want to say work the program." "He's acting out with people all of the time." "I was powerless over his sexual addiction, and I'm powerless over my codependence." Some of this new language provided comfort for women, particularly the word "recovery." "I think one part is after you find out about the addiction and once you are in recovery, it is good to have abstinence for maybe 80 or 90 days." "But now, when I work in the steps, I can see that it's something that I had already had."

However, other words in this new language were not initially comforting for the women. Labeling the issue an addiction was difficult for several wives. "I didn't understand the whole addiction thing. Still don't." Addiction counselors were often the first individuals to assign the addiction label to the dilemma. "I had counseling with a counselor who knows about all these addictions." Once introduced to the concept, women struggled to grasp how it applied to their husbands. "I became more and more aware that [addiction] was probably his problem." Prior to this, many admitted to knowing very little about addictions. "At that point, none of us knew about sex addicts." "I did not realize at the time that the Internet could be an addiction. For me the addictions were alcohol and drugs." "But I didn't realize that there was an addiction at the time." Over time, addiction became a label women could apply to a variety of areas in which one overindulged: religion, love, bodybuilding, health, and nutrition. "I'm pretty sure she's a love addict." "I didn't understand that there was such a thing as an addiction with that [religion]."

Women believed labeling the problem an addiction was a non-pejorative way to discuss their husbands' problems. The sexual behaviors were not misconducts but addictions. "To use addiction, puts it into the realm of a disease rather than a misbehavior." The husbands were not perverts; they had a disease. "I didn't know people had sex addictions or what it was like. Society thinks that a sex addict is a pervert and some of them are stalkers, voyeurs, exhibitionists, and that they are trying to harm someone." Labeling the behaviors an addiction was reassuring for women. "They are involved in addictions." "But, part of this has to do with his addictions." In contrast, non-COSA women labeled their husbands sick or perverted. "I kind of think of him as a pervert." COSA women no longer considered their husbands to be simply weak men, but men caught in the grips of an addiction. "He's got a weakness for that, that's for sure." For other women, labeling their husbands' activities as addictions helped them to view these activities as part of an illness rather than a morality issue. "It's the whole religious thing and it kind of makes me a little uneasy because what he was doing was wrong. I don't think of it as being immoral because that was his addiction." This non-immoral viewpoint was distinctly different from the non-COSA women who believed their husbands' sexual behaviors were immoral and evil. "I just remember over the course of time, it became obvious to me that this was a form of evil." If women labeled husbands' sexual activities an addiction, the problem was categorized and fear was reduced. Initially, some wives had worried that their husbands could possibly hurt other people with their peccadilloes. "It doesn't really have anything to do with wanting to harm someone, it's just about them getting their fix."

## COSA AS RITUAL

"It's the whole religious thing."

The 12-Step program functioned in a similar way for the COSA women as religion functioned for some non-COSA women. It became a ritual for wives. "I try to go every week, I've only missed this past week. We've been every Wednesday." The meetings occurred at the same time and in the same location each week. The format of the meeting was consistent; focus was on the women and not on their husbands. Each meeting opened with a spiritual address to a higher power. Then, the 12 steps were read aloud and the group concentrated on one of the 12 steps each week. Much like the non-COSA women who turned to prayer and familiar ritual in their faith background to find comfort and encouragement, these women turned to the 12-Steps. Wives were encouraged to read daily from a 12-Step book, although several women confessed to having difficulty with this. "I have been working on that but I don't necessarily do my devotional reading each day or do something with the program each day which I should do."

After attending the first meeting, women were encouraged to read the book, *Out of the Shadows* as a basic primer for understanding the disease of sexual addiction. Other books on addictions and codependency were also recommended. "We always recommend that at our meeting. We recommend they read that [*Out of the Shadows*], and then read *Co-dependent No More* by Melody Beatty." "I read *Out of the Shadows*. Everybody starts with that ... and then, *Addicted To Love*. I have a whole library of them."

## WORK YOUR OWN PROGRAM

"That was very codependent, I realize now."

COSA women believed they could extract themselves from pain by working the program. "I think the ones that do well are the ones who really want to be out of the pain, be free from the pain, and to be able to have a better life." Part of choosing this better life entailed realizing they participated in the husbands' addictions. "They [COSA women] are able to recognize that they had a part in this. Not that they helped contribute to the addiction, but there was parts of them that they needed to work on for themselves because they relied on them [husbands]." The language of codependency and enabling were used liberally. "We were about as codependent as two people can be." "Codependent, that also implied to me that I had a part in this." Anytime women found themselves experiencing strong emotions as a result of their husbands' activities, they considered themselves as being codependent. "Cause I was feeling angry, and frightened. And all the stuff that goes with being a codependent." The new language not only described their husbands, but how the women related to their husbands. "I've been in an enabling situation all of my life. I've developed a codependent relationship with any male relationship that I've had. It has always been an enabling love addiction."

Women wanted to be certain they were working their own program and not their husbands' program. They also worried constantly about being "codependent" or "enabling" of their husbands. Despite these worries and understandings, many women engaged in behaviors they knew were not right: snooping, checking up on husbands, and taking responsibility for husbands' actions. "I had found C's [his] address and I decided to send him a note. That was very codependent, I realize now. But I was very angry then." According to women, enabling meant aiding men in their addictive behaviors. "You know, but somewhere along the line I enabled him." "I learned why is it that I enabled him to do [the porn]. My lack of knowledge about myself, my voice."

The precise meanings of enabling and codependency were not consistent among all COSA women. Some women believed codependency meant ignoring behaviors. "I don't feel that I was a total codependent because I didn't ignore things. I would always meet them, the minute they came up, and I met them head on." Other women described codependency as needing to be in a relationship no matter the cost. "I just needed to feel important. I needed to feel loved. I needed to have someone, I needed to have that feeling that their life would not be complete without me in it."

## "I'M NO LONGER ISOLATED"

"I was no longer so isolated, so alone."

All non-COSA women experienced a strong feeling of isolation. They were ashamed and humiliated to have others know about their personal lives. "I am isolated. First, you can't say anything to people about. People who would never understand." They feared the stigma associated with other people knowing about their husbands' behaviors. "I feel like there is no one to talk to about it. Even friends, when people found out what was going on in our marriage, you get one friend telling you to leave and another telling you to work it out." They were also hesitant to speak to family members. One of the biggest concerns for me was that I could not talk to anybody about it. Of course, I didn't want to talk to my family." The COSA women were also reluctant to talk to friends and relatives. "I couldn't really go out and talk to my best friend that I had growing up and saying my husband is a sex addict." Talking to others would reveal their husbands' shame and their own shame. "I couldn't talk about [it even] to a family member because I felt I was violating my husband's trust if I was releasing something that was his problems, the addiction. Mine was the codependency issue."

Weekly meetings provided COSA wives with an opportunity to share with other women who had similar experiences. "And you know, maybe I can find something here that's, you know, going to help me. Help me in this situation ... to find my way on what to do with the situation." The weekly meetings helped ease the sense of isolation. "It made me feel like I'm not alone. And now, I know I'm not alone. There are millions of us." Some women became leaders in COSA and found this to be grounding. "By talking to the other women and I am the contact person for COSA, women call me and talk to me and tell me their stories."

The COSA women were very private about their attendance at the 12-Step group and uncomfortable discussing sex addictions in public. "A COSA member mentioned [COSA] at a Christmas party and some-one asked what group she was talking about and she told them it was sex addiction." Women were aware of the stigma associated with sex addiction and wanted the group to remain anonymous. "I and several other people said they really didn't want anyone else knowing what our particular addiction was."

## ABUNDANCE OF INFORMATION

> "His counselor felt that it was a good idea to tell me about it, and they wanted him to really be descriptive with me and tell me everything."

COSA women had far more knowledge of their husbands' behaviors than did non-COSA women. One reason for this knowledge was because husbands shared more information with the wives. "He told me he was talking to his sponsor and his sponsor was saying 'what have you been doing about your program work?' [My husband] said, 'Well, I do something each day, some program.'" Communication between the couple allowed for more exchanges of information.

Since SAA and COSA meetings were on the same evenings in adjacent rooms, SAA husbands and COSA wives accompanied each other to their respective meetings. Often, wives actively sought information from their husbands. "And sometimes I'm willing to know what he's been talking at the meetings about or what he's been talking with the sponsor." Moreover, in several cases, sponsors or therapists suggested husbands confess everything to their wives. "His counselor felt that it was a good idea to tell me about it, and they wanted [my husband] to really be descriptive with me and tell me everything." Several men provided comprehensive details about their activities. "[The therapist] said, 'Well did you hear that your husband had sex with animals, how do you feel about that?' I'm like, 'when?'" COSA women also shared information with each other about the nature of husbands' addictions. "We talked about the addictions that our husbands have."

Wives understood the 12-Step programs and due to their familiarity with SAA, COSA women had an understanding of progression through the 12 steps. They knew the appropriate questions to ask husbands in hopes of gathering information. Wives also had a better comprehension of their husbands' dynamics. They learned to detect subtle changes in their husbands' affects and behaviors. "I told my dad, I said, 'I hope that [my husband] doesn't act out as a result of this because he is really upset.' When I got home, I found out that he had acted out."

The increased knowledge of husbands' sexual behaviors augmented the uneasiness for some COSA women. "I've read all the stuff on addictions. I think those are very depressing because you read that it's you and your life." They expressed apprehension about their husbands' sexually related behaviors.

> The more research I got into, and I'm like, why is it so critical what they look like? You know, to me, an addict will have sex with anybody so, they don't care … is the person is heavy? Or, you know, they aren't attracted to me.

Not only did women have language to express the anxiety, but they also had large amounts of information about sex addictions. "I learned that many times it is progressive. I learned how it begins. If it then becomes an escape … to alter whatever is going on at the moment." Based on this increased knowledge and understanding of addictions, the COSA wives lived with concern their husbands' behaviors would escalate. "[Internet pornography] was anonymous. And it was certainly available. That it would escalate to the point it did where he just got crazy." The knowledge and understanding of addictions also brought a realization the addiction would never fully disappear. "Well, I think I don't worry because it's going to happen if it's going to happen, no matter what I do."

## MARRIAGE ENHANCEMENT

> "Several of us go to RCA, which is Recovering Couples Anonymous. It's open to any recovering couples."

COSA women recognized their marital relationships were in crisis and needed some attention. Although their husbands were very involved in SAA, many women did not always feel that their husbands were attending appropriately to the marriage. "I think that I try harder to put the marriage back together, I really do. I mean he's busy working his program and everything, but not especially working at the marriage." This was a familiar refrain. If the couple did not pursue marriage counseling while attending the 12-Step programs, they found other outlets to concentrate on the couple relationship. Several COSA women and their SAA husbands joined a group called Recovering Couples. This group was also a 12-Step group, but it was designed to help the couple relationship. "And we go to recovering couple thing ... to keep our relationship healthy and improve it. And get past some past issues."

## FORGIVENESS AND HOPE

"Maybe I can find something here that's going to help me. Help me in this situation."

Hope persisted in this category and centered on COSA, a 12-Step program, as it offered women a way out of their dilemma. Even though some women experienced anxiety over their husbands' participation in SAA, most believed as long as both the husbands and wives worked their respective programs, the couple could continue in the marriage and potentially reach relative peace. "When they get into recovery, it works." COSA women believed viewing their husbands' behaviors as addictions gave them a sense of hope. "It empowered me in that, there is something I can do about this instead of being scared to death and feeling hopeless and helpless. If I come to these meetings and watch what these other women are saying to me maybe I can find something here that's going to help me."

"The 12 steps are steps to recovery, but I don't think they are a cure." None of the women believed their husbands would ever be "cured" of their addictions. "There was no one saying, 'Okay he can be fixed, this addiction can be fixed.' You know, we can work with this, and we can talk about this. But I can't give you any guarantees that he is going to change." For these women, hope resided in the 12-Step program. They realized SAA would ease the problem and provide comfort. "I'm supposed to trust him? So, I think that as long as he's going to his meetings, I feel that his acting out is going to be cut to a minimum."

Hope for the future was also connected to the relationship itself. Women reflected on good times and positive aspects of the marital relationships. "So we had a good history. We had a basic appreciation of each other and liked and respected the other person. And so that

I think is the basis for remaining [in the marriage]." Women placed hope not only in recovery programs, but also in marital counseling. "We go to [counseling] to keep our relationship healthy and improve it and get past some past issues." Whether through counseling or recovery programs, women believed facing the issue was, "empowering." "That was truly empowering because it said to me 'Okay, you've met the devil, you looked it in the face.' And for some reason, it's not so scary anymore."

Like non-COSA women, COSA women also wanted to forgive their husbands. "I try to put what he's done in the past in the past, and not let it affect me today." The women knew "making amends" was a crucial part of the 12-Step program and wanted husbands to ask for forgiveness. "Six years ago [he made amends]. He hasn't this time. I'm still waiting for it." Other women admitted they had forgiven their husbands numerous times. "Even though he's been forgiven, you know, two or three times." These women appeared to be more conscious of times they had pardoned their spouse. "I guess I forgave him at that time and I said 'you know. I don't want this to happen again.'"

## SUMMARY

Two distinct groups of women emerged from this particular study. While all the women sought assistance at some point in the cycle, half of the women found help through clergy and therapy while the other half sought help primarily from a 12-Step self-help group called COSA. These women attended weekly meetings that aided them in staying focused and coping with their husbands' sexually related activities. Although there were variations between non-COSA and COSA women, the cycle itself was virtually the same. However, women who joined the COSA group varied in the methods in which they coped. There were seven variations between this group and the non-COSA women. These variations form the properties of the COSA category a New Vocabulary, COSA as Ritual, Work Your Own Program, "I'm No Longer Isolated," Abundance of Information, Marriage Enhancement, and Forgiveness and Hope.

COSA women learned a new vocabulary to articulate the dilemmas they encountered in their marital relationships. Women spoke of "enabling behavior," "codependency," and "sex and love addictions." COSA meetings functioned in much the same way as religion for non-COSA women. It provided comfort and a format for remaining focused. The women credited the COSA program in helping them remain focused on themselves and not "working the program" of their husbands. Unlike non-COSA women who often felt isolated, these women reported the support of other 12-Step members decreased their sense of solitude. COSA women exhibited greater knowledge and understanding of their husbands' activities than did non-COSA women. COSA wives were also more aware of the negative impacts on their marital relationships, and they concentrated on improving that relationship.

Forgiveness and hope varied slightly in this category. One of the 12 steps in an addictions group is making amends. These women were cognizant of the necessity of this step in moving toward forgiveness of their husbands. In this category, the hope for a more peaceful life resided in attendance at COSA for the women and SAA for the men. As long as men appeared to be "working their programs" women felt increased hope.

CHAPTER TEN

# SUMMARY OF THE RESULTS

Husbands' activities with the Internet were a major disruption in the marriage and caused intrapsychic distress for wives. Moreover, participants saw the activities as out of everyone's control. In recounting their experiences, women described a repetitive cycle of husbands' use of pornography and their own efforts to manage and cope with this knowledge. Although there were small variations in the cycle throughout the marriage, it essentially remained constant. The category, *In the Beginning*, recounted the origins of pornography use. This category introduced the cycle that "keeps happening." Three categories comprised this cycle: *Something is Definitely Up*, *Temporary Peace*, and *The Big Discovery*. The fifth category, *COSA Women*, described variations between two groups of women in the study, those women who attended 12-Step COSA and those who did not.

The first category, *In the Beginning*, remained a constant, as it was the start of the story and established the foundation for the following categories. *Something is Definitely Up*, *Temporary Peace*, and *The*

*Big Discovery* were the actual categories in the cycle. These categories were not necessarily in sequential order, but ran a circuitous course. The fifth category, *COSA Women* described wives caught in the same cycle as non-COSA women with some variations in how they managed.

Each category consists of several properties. Some properties are unique to the category while other properties are consistent in all categories. The properties that are consistent are: Collecting Evidence, Dealing with It, Confrontations, and Forgiveness and Hope. These properties have variations within the categories. Forgiveness and Hope are intertwined and are a small circuit unto itself. Hope feeds forgiveness and forgiveness feeds the hope.

## IN THE BEGINNING

All women were aware of husbands' use of pornography from the beginning of the relationship. Because the Internet was not readily available in the early days of the relationship, men relied on magazines, videos, strip clubs, and / or peep shows. Most women cited that their husbands' preferred choice of pornography was *Playboy Magazine*. Although women found this magazine objectionable, they did not believe it was their prerogative to demand that husbands discard it. Therefore, women tolerated its presence in the home. Over time, and as technology expanded, men introduced new media and expanded their repertoire of behaviors.

The properties in this category of *In the Beginning* are: Family of Origin, Experience of Pornography prior to the marriage, Separate Lives that couples began living at some point in the marriage, Collecting Evidence of husbands' activities, Small Confrontations followed by spousal Excuses, the sense that husbands' activities were somehow "It's My Fault," the belief that they, the wives, had loss their "Alluring Power," Dealing With It, and Forgiveness and Hope.

Women discussed family of origin histories of boundary violations, infidelity, divorce, alcohol, and drug abuse. They brought individual experiences and previous exposure to pornography into the relationships. These experiences affected their reactions to husbands' sexual behaviors. Some women tolerated what other women viewed as offensive. Retrospectively, women realized that they had been living separate lives from their husbands for months, if not years, prior to discovering abundant evidence. Periodically, women confronted husbands with their suspicions, sometimes with proof of husbands' sexually related activities. Husbands offered excuses, which women tended to accept early in the cycle. All women struggled with the beliefs that their husbands' behaviors were somehow their own fault and that they had lost their "alluring power," that quality they had to seduce husbands and maintain happiness. Women struggled to find coping methods to deal with the behaviors of men. Interwoven through this category was the ability to forgive husbands and to continue hoping that they would completely abandon activities women judged to be offensive.

## TEMPORARY PEACE

In the second category, *Temporary Peace*, home life appeared to be harmonious. There were no overt confrontations between husbands and wives. Although domestic life seemed to be peaceful, there was a great deal of intrapsychic and interpersonal activity taking place just beneath the surface, and tension existed in the household. The properties of this category are: Collecting Evidence, Covering for Him, Keep Talking, Tolerance, Vigilance, and Forgiveness and Hope.

Wives continued collecting evidence, albeit in a more covert way, and did not openly admit to having strong suspicions. Women became computer literate in their endeavors to locate signs of undesirable behaviors and adopted the role of expert investigator. However, even as they collected proof of sexually related activities, women covered for husbands with family, friends, and ultimately, with themselves. They sought to maintain the belief their husbands were truly decent men in spite of behaviors they found to be unacceptable. Women kept husbands engaged in discussions with hope that they would ultimately convince their spouses to abandon unwanted behaviors. As time progressed, women were increasingly able to tolerate more awareness of the conduct. However, women eventually expressed awareness of the problem when husbands intensified their offensive activities. Forgiveness was easier to grant in this category due to the temporary peace. Women also had more hope in this category that husbands had truly abandoned most, if not all, forbidden activities.

## SOMETHING IS DEFINITELY UP

The temporary peace was truly temporary. There were too many indicators that men had not terminated suspicious conduct and were continuing to access Web sites women found offensive and / or participating in other behaviors wives perceived as inappropriate. Eventually, wives realized *Something is Definitely Up*. The properties in this category are: the Big Confrontation, Idle Threats, Babysitter, Desperate Solutions, Consequences, Seeking Help, and Forgiveness and Hope.

Something unidentified provided the impetus for wives to approach husbands with evidence, resulting in a big confrontation. Women collected evidence over a period of time before confronting husbands. For some women, there was eventually a piece of evidence so suspicious that it could not be ignored. Other times, the tension just became unbearable. During confrontation, women issued threats or ultimatums. Husbands temporarily appeased wives by expressing regret, promising to discontinue behaviors and instituting small changes. Small modifications temporarily pacified wives, and they relented on threats. Thus, threats appeared to be idle, lacking potency. However, in order to prevent husbands from reneging on promises, wives established themselves as babysitters, taking on responsibilities of preventing access to inappropriate Internet sites and forcing husbands to be accountable to them. In establishing themselves as watchdogs, wives often denied themselves certain privileges and conveniences.

In addition to issuing threats and taking on the role of babysitter, many women sought out desperate solutions in seeking solid coping methods. These solutions seemed to be designed to either enact revenge or to convince themselves of their "alluring power." As a result of exposing evidence of husbands' activities, many women experienced major negative consequences in their own lives, including their marital relationships, family lives, social lives, and intrapersonal lives. Sex lives were also profoundly affected.

At this juncture, a majority of women decided it was an opportune moment to seek outside assistance. Women turned to clergy, self-help groups, literature, doctors, prayer, and the Internet for help. Seeking help offered the most hope for women. They believed that with help, husbands would eventually recognize problems and begin to deal with them. This hope made it easier to forgive husbands for perceived transgressions. Once help was sought, a temporary peace once again resumed.

## THE BIG DISCOVERY

The fourth category, *The Big Discovery*, follows the disquieting peace. Throughout the course of the cycle, wives never really abandoned their efforts at collecting evidence. Although some women were not actively searching, most women were continuously on guard, and eventually, they stumbled on a significant discovery that caused a personal and marital crisis. This big discovery was not necessarily new evidence. The properties in this category are: Major Betrayal, Raw Emotions, "I Don't Know Him: He Doesn't Know Me," Confrontation, Cyber Detective, Consequences, "I Know: I Don't Know," Dealing With It, and Forgiveness and Hope.

Wives experienced the discovery of significant evidence as a major betrayal, a betrayal they vowed never to forget. This betrayal was so devastating that women could recall minute details associated with exposure of the major betrayal. Moreover, women remembered the range of raw emotions the betrayal evoked. Women reported feelings of intense anger, hate, shock, betrayal, disappointment, sadness, depression, confusion, fear, disgust, and resentment.

Often, evidence was so traumatic that it precipitated intense confusion and fear. Wives discovered men were viewing gay and child pornography, sadomasochistic pornography, and / or engaging in what appeared to be homosexual activity. These behaviors prompted wives to question the identity of husbands. "I don't know him" was a common refrain. If men encouraged their wives to participate in activities women claimed to find distasteful, wives began to wonder if husbands really knew who they were. The statement frequently repeated was, "he doesn't know me."

Armed with evidence, women confronted their husbands. In this category, they were more persistent in their confrontations. If women previously had been computer illiterate, they began educating themselves, essentially becoming "cyber detectives" on a mission to obtain information. They earnestly spied on husbands.

There were consequences associated with the major betrayal. The consequences went beyond the disrupted marital relationship and often affected children and extended family members. Women lost friends, men were fired from their places of employment, and the legal system was often involved. All women reported their sex lives were negatively impacted by spouses' activities.

It was also in this category that women began to admit they both, "knew" and, "did not know" simultaneously. They started to explore their own patterns of deliberately ignoring signs, signs that had been present early in the relationships and in the months and years preceding *The Big Discovery*. The property of Dealing With It took on new significance as women struggled to find new coping methods. If women had not sought outside help earlier, they found some type of help now through religion, pop psychology books, therapists, addiction's specialists, self-help groups, doctors, clergy, and myself as a researcher.

Although forgiveness and hope persisted in this category, there were less of both. Women hoped husbands would hit rock bottom and make substantive changes. Their ability to forgive depended on the number of times the couple had cycled through the problem.

## COSA WOMEN

All women sought assistance of some form after *The Big Discovery*. Two distinct groups of women emerged in the final category. About half of the women learned about a 12-Step group called COSA and began attending meetings. Most of their husbands joined SAA. The properties in this category are: A New Language, COSA as Ritual, Work Your Own Program, "I'm No Longer Isolated," Abundance of Information, Marriage Enhancement, and Forgiveness and Hope.

COSA women experienced the same continuous cycle, as did non-COSA women. However, although women's overall experiences were highly similar in both groups, variations occurred in how COSA women dealt with their experiences. Addiction counselors and husbands who attended SAA referred women to self-help groups. The COSA experience taught women a new language, one they used to articulate their sense of entrapment in the cycle. Women spoke of "addictions," "codependence," "enabling," and discovered other phrases to express their experiences. This language appeared to help them understand their predicaments in new ways.

Like non-COSA women who turned to religion and religious rituals in order to cope, COSA women relied on the 12-Step program to perform a similar function. The COSA program encouraged women to "work your own program" and avoid focusing on spouses. Many women acknowledged they had difficulty adhering to this step. The most important function COSA served was providing women with support. Unlike non-COSA women, COSA wives no longer felt isolated from others. In addition, they also appeared to know more about husbands' activities and the dynamics surrounding these activities than did non-COSA women. This knowledge came from husbands who shared information with their wives or from weekly attendance at COSA meetings.

COSA women were cognizant of the disruption in the marital relationship as a result of husbands' behaviors. These women addressed this disruption in therapy or through a group called Recovering Couples Anonymous. The final properties in this category, Forgiveness and Hope, were slightly different from forgiveness and hope in other categories. COSA women, unlike non-COSA women, had different understandings of forgiveness. They were not as ready to forgive their husbands until the men had, "worked their programs" and "made amends." Hope for the future resided in both partners attending SAA / COSA.

In the narrations of their stories, women described a cycle of men's use of pornography and their own efforts to manage and cope with this knowledge. The cycle was a repetitious one. Each round was essentially the same; however, there were slight variations. The cycle commenced with the category "In the Beginning." The remaining three categories, *Temporary Peace*, *Something is Definitely Up*, and *The Big Discovery*, have the capacity of occurring at various points in the cycle and are not necessarily sequential. Two separate groups of women emerged in this cycle; women who attended COSA and women who did not.

The cycle of It Keeps Happening was a part of marital relationship almost from the origins of the relationship. None of the women in the study experienced permanent and / or substantive changes as they attempted to cope with knowledge of spouses' objectionable activities. The cycle had small variations, but remained constant through the life of the marriage.

# CHAPTER ELEVEN

# THEORETICAL IMPLICATIONS

## INTRODUCTION

The following chapter presents considerations of the findings and theoretical implications of "Women's Experiences of Husbands' Use of The Internet for Sexual Activity." After a brief summary of the findings, the theoretical implications will be discussed in view of the Background. This will be followed by clinical and social implications. The final section addresses topics for future research.

## BRIEF SUMMARY OF FINDINGS

This research began as a focus on women who reported that their husbands used the Internet for viewing pornography. As more information was gathered, it became apparent that pornography viewing was the tip of the iceberg for 94% of women. Men were not only viewing pornography, but also engaging in activities of a sexual nature women believed to be objectionable and highly offensive. Activities included viewing Web sites featuring gay males, children, sadomasochism, and bestiality. Many men did not confine their activities to viewing pornography, but visited chat rooms, e-mailed women and men, arranged assignations with women and men via the Internet, visited strip bars and prostitutes, engaged in online sex, and called 1-900 numbers that featured phone sex. Men confessed to having sexual intercourse with members of the same sex, opposite sex, and with animals. The viewing of pornography turned out to be only one of the sexual behaviors wives found objectionable. However, for as yet unexplained reasons, pornography viewing was identified as the problem in the marriage. Pornography viewing and other Internet related activities will be grouped under one heading and referred to as sexually oriented behaviors or activities. Women in the study claimed to find these sexually oriented activities offensive and objectionable.

## FINDINGS

The results of this study demonstrated nine discrete yet related findings. All findings related to dynamics that maintain what is called the "cycle that keeps happening." Each individual's psychodynamics contributed to and perpetuated the cycle. Various theoretical contributions to psychosexual development will advance a deeper understanding of the experiences of study participants. Many theorists concentrate on normative maturational processes. However, study participants did not develop in normative ways; most had traumatic psychosexual developmental interference. When discussing the results, it will be difficult to separate the second finding of early childhood trauma from participants' inability to interrupt the unhappy cycle. The third finding, overlooking evidence, is interwoven with women's significant psychosexual development. The findings of sexual desire, happy marriages versus unhappy marriages, and compulsive behaviors on the part of men, will be discussed in light of the previous three findings. Several findings, such as repeated references to forgiveness and hope and COSA women and SAA men, are able to stand alone. However, the latter two findings correlate with the finding of childhood trauma and are certainly impacted by it. The last finding, the corresponding vertical splits can be understood in relation to early childhood trauma.

*Finding #1 Reoccurring Cycle*

Women reported their experiences consisted of a large cycle that was repetitive and appeared to be a permanent fixture in their relationship. They related that they were unable to break the cycle or affect permanent change. Their efforts produced minor changes on the part of husbands, but nothing substantive. Women repeatedly used the word "cycle" to describe the experiences (Chapter Four, Introduction). The category, *In the Beginning*, explains the role of pornography in the early years of the relationship. This category is followed by three categories that form a continuous loop, *Temporary Peace*, *Something Is Definitely Up*, and *The Big Discovery*. Two groups of women emerged from this study, women who attended COSA and women who did not join the 12-Step group, non-COSA women. Although the cycle was highly similar for both groups of women, there were several variations. The most important finding to emerge from this study is that wives appeared not to have the capacity to achieve substantive results, which they identified as behavioral changes on the part of husbands. Thus they felt caught in a repetitive cycle that "Just Keeps Happening."

*Finding #2 Childhood Trauma*

All women reported experiences of childhood trauma. These histories included physical, sexual, and emotional boundary violations and resulted in compromised psychosexual development (Chapter Five). In addition to early childhood sexual violations, many women experienced additional sexual trauma in adolescence or young adulthood (Chapter Five).

Participants' parents, due to their own deficits, were unable to establish optimal conditions necessary for normative development. Parents were emotionally or physically absent, over-involved in daughters' lives, abused alcohol or drugs, had extramarital affairs, and exhibited violent behavior. Careers, divorce, mental illness, and death were sources of parental absences. Although participants described both parents as possessing major limitations, they seemed to focus more on fathers than on mothers as sources of disappointment.

Yet these families adopted a middle class veneer and presented themselves as highly functional. Fathers held responsible jobs and were leaders in the community. Mothers were either homemakers or had careers outside the home. From the outside, most of these families seemed to be "normal."

Several women in the sample had children out of wedlock like their mothers before them. Many women demonstrated a history of involvement with men who treated them with disrespect and brought into the relationship their own difficulties. Several women reported divorcing men that were significantly similar to subsequent husbands. Second marriages were strikingly similar to first marriages in terms of marital problems.

### Finding #3 Overlooking Evidence

Early on in the relationship, women noticed that something was not quite right. Many husbands had dubious histories that included difficulties with the legal system, alcohol and drug abuse, conflictual previous marriages, patterns of treating women with disdain, and unregulated family backgrounds (Chapter Five). As the relationship progressed, women either failed to notice abnormalities and potential problems or recognized and minimized the signs; in both cases, they consistently overlooked crucial evidence. Odd behaviors exhibited by men were rationalized. Wives sensed something was wrong, but overlooked pertinent information. Only in retrospect were women able to identify signs and symptoms that originally had been present. This information extended beyond the use of pornography to include other types of behaviors that women found objectionable (Chapter Five). Many women were cognizant of problems in men's family of origin. In-laws violated physical boundaries with the women, family members abused alcohol, and many parental relationships appeared to be conflictual. Wives desired to view husbands as decent, honorable men so they pushed negative information out of awareness (Chapter Six).

## *Finding #4 Sexual Desire*

I expected to hear women relating diminished libido, sexual inhibitions, and lack of sexual desire. However, a majority claimed they were the initiators in the sexual relationship (Chapter Five) and capable of robust sexual lives. Women reported dissatisfaction with their spouses' desires to explore novel sexual practices with them (Appendix C, question 35) and indicated concerns about husbands' lack of sexual interest in them. In attempts to reclaim attention from husbands, many women resorted to desperate solutions that included initiating novel sexual practices and requesting frequent sex. There were several women who reported little interest in sex, but that was not the norm (Chapter Seven).

## *Finding #5 Survey Results vs. Interview Data*

Listening to narratives, it appeared that COSA and non-COSA women were unhappy in their marriages. They described complex situations in which they lacked potency to affect substantive change, identified intense emotions of anger, fear, confusion, devastation, disappointment, sadness, and depression (Chapter Eight, Big Discovery), reported chaotic behavior on the part of husbands, and disrupted lives. However, questions extracted from the General Social Survey (Appendix A) addressing marital happiness, indicated that over half the women were generally happy in their marriages and 80% were happy with their lives. This means that just slightly under half the women were unhappy in the marriage. One hundred percent of the women disagreed with the statement "it is better to have a bad marriage than no marriage at all" (Appendix A, question 27). The subjective information seemed to be contradictory to the objective information. A split existed between what women indicated on the survey portion versus what they related in their narratives.

In addition, a large percentage of women agreed that pornography should be accessible to individuals over the age of 18. Yet, none of the women believed their husbands should have access to such material.

The disparity in the quantitative versus the qualitative findings suggests that quantitative research may not work with people who have vertical splits as it can skew the data.

### Finding #6 Men's Sexual Conduct

The women focused on Internet pornography as a source of marital discord and intrapsychic distress. Yet, for most women, Internet pornography was the most benign sexual behavior in which men were engaged. Men were engaging in a variety of sexually related activities that far exceeded pornography viewing. For most men, viewing pornography was only one type of compulsive behavior that was problematic for wives. Wives reported men were compulsively involved in gambling, alcohol and drug abuse, bodybuilding, and religion (Chapter Five). Pornography was only one source of disappointment and rage for women in this study. However, viewing pornography and other sexual behaviors became the focus for women. Men's other compulsions failed to elicit the wide range of intense emotions (Chapter Eight, Big Discovery). Wives experienced behaviors related to sexuality as major betrayals (Chapter Eight, Big Discovery). Pornography appeared to be the portal that broke down disavowal. There was something about the intimacy of sexuality that made this issue far more unsettling for women than other compulsive behaviors.

### Finding #7 COSA Women and SAA Men

There was a particular group of women who sought assistance by joining COSA, a 12-Step program. Their husbands attended SAA. COSA women struggled with exactly the same issues as non-COSA women. They found themselves repeatedly circling through the dilemma. However, COSA women learned a new language, which assisted them in articulating their conflict (Chapter Nine). The COSA women were able to talk about their problem as an "addictive cycle." Their version of "its my fault" was "work your own program" (Chapter Nine). The language fostered additional understanding of the "disease." COSA women felt less isolated due to the sharing of experiences with other women. However, COSA women, like their non-COSA counterparts, professed feeling powerless. Ultimately, they reported a lack of success in a permanent disruption of the cycle.

## *Finding #8 Repeated References to Forgiveness and Hope*

Initially, research focused on Roman Catholic women. These women did not seem to recognize a connection between their sex education in the Catholic Church and difficulties they encountered in their relationships. Thus, the study expanded to include other women who were not Roman Catholic. These women came from diverse Judeo-Christian backgrounds. No matter the religious background, all women in the study made repeated references to a need to forgive (see Hope and Forgiveness in every category). Women appeared to struggle both consciously and unconsciously with this concept. The property of forgiveness appeared in every category and took on slight variations. Retrospectively, women could identify that as the cycle continued they repeatedly forgave husbands.

Several women identified this need to forgive as emanating from their religious background. The women from COSA articulated their struggles with forgiveness using references to the 12-Step program (Chapter Nine).

The concept of forgiveness cannot be discussed without the inclusion of hope. These two properties were intricately woven together. Each time women forgave husbands, they experienced a bit of hope. In turn, this hope enabled wives to continually forgive husbands. Thus, forgiveness and hope was a small cycle unto itself.

## *Finding #9 Corresponding Vertical Splits*

The research suggests that not only does the wife have a vertical split, but also it appears there is a corresponding split in the husband. Thus, husband and wife participated in each other's vertical split. This mutual participation served to reinforce the reoccurring cycle in which the women reported feelings of "stuckness." In efforts to maintain self-cohesion and avoid intense affect, participants periodically confronted their spouses regarding the husbands' sexually related activities. Husbands responded in various ways to the confrontations.

These confrontations offered the couples opportunities for continued disavowal and maintained what appeared to be a cohesive marital enmeshment.

## DISCUSSION OF SURVEY RESULTS

The quantitative portion of the results consisted of questions extracted from the General Social Survey (Appendix A) concerning attitudes toward religion, marriage and personal happiness, and pornography and questions amended from the Indiana Happiness Inventory and Marital Satisfaction Inventory (Zillmann & Bryant, 1988). Tabulated results of the survey can be found in Appendix A.

The focus of the study changed when it was discovered that participants were not making connections between their religious upbringing in the Catholic Church and sexuality. In addition, the study expanded to include a group of women who attended COSA meetings. Although all women had some religious affiliation, information concerning religious attitudes was no longer the focus and thus, irrelevant in the findings.

Attitudes toward marriage, personal happiness, and pornography offered some interesting results. Of intrigue was the finding of Happy Marriages versus Unhappy Marriages (Finding #5). Results of the survey indicated that 80% of the women were pretty happy or very happy today. Fifty-three percent of women were pretty happy or very happy in the marriages. This meant that 47% were unhappy in the marriage. However, listening to the audio taped interviews and reading the transcriptions produced the opposite understanding. None of the women appeared happy in their marriages and many seemed miserable with their lives.

A large percentage of women (66%) believed that marriage was very important to extremely important. However, they appeared ambivalent about personal freedom versus companionship in marriage and ambivalent about the happiness of married people in general. Almost all women did not agree with the statement that "the main advantage of marriage is that it gives financial security," yet many cited financial concerns as a reason to remain in the marriage.

Attitudes toward pornography were consistent with the qualitative results, 93% believed it led to a breakdown of morals. Yet, only 57% wanted laws forbidding the distribution of pornography to everyone while 42% were willing to make it illegal to those under 18. None believed it should be completely legal. However, the qualitative findings demonstrated that none of the women thought their husbands should have access to pornography as it was viewed as causing marital conflict. These findings showed some ambivalence toward the use of pornography.

## COMPARISON TO EXISTING THEORY FROM THE BACKGROUND REVIEW

The findings demonstrated that wives had difficulty claiming self-agency and interrupting the cycle they reported to be distressing. Several questions are raised as a result of the finding. Why was it problematic for wives to interrupt the cycle? How did individuals' psychosexual development influence the dynamics of the cycle? No particular theory can fully explain the experiences of women in the study, as each woman is an individual. Contributions by various theorists to the study of psychosexual development will be examined in an effort to illuminate further understanding of women's experiences. These theorists offer some explanations that possibly expand the understanding.

I have chosen an object relations theoretical lens through which to examine the findings. Object relations theory accounts for the inordinately complicated adult relationships that are strongly influenced by internal representations of significant early relationships. Participants' internal relationships affect and color their present interactions with husbands. This theory, with its focus on the development of individuals within the context of a relationship, provides analysis as to the experiences of participants. Benjamin (1988, 1990, 1995), drawing on the infant research work of Stern (1985) locates difficulties in mutual recognition in the 0–18-month phase of development. Both theorists are interested in the development of the inner subjective life of the infant. Chodorow's (1980) contributions will expand upon the idea of development within the context of a relationship and difficulties in developing self-agency. Fairbairn (1943, 1949), Kernberg (1975), and Armstrong-Perlman (1994) add further clarification in their consideration of women who have patterns of choosing object relations that appear to be pathological.

Early developmental difficulties are not the only explanation for experiences of women. Individuals, who are greatly disappointed by mothers in early phases of development, turn to fathers during the Oedipal phase. Chasseguet-Smirgel (1988) focuses on a particular feminine position in the Oedipal situation.

The concept of the vertical split (Goldberg, 1999) may account for women's ability to tolerate behaviors they claim to find distasteful and offensive. Several theorists (Akhtar & Kramer, 1996; Alperin, 2000; Kernberg, 1995) discuss aspects of intimacy that may illuminate the dynamics of women in the sample. These theorists locate difficulties during separation-individuation as problematic in later adult relationships. Finally, the works of Akhtar (1999, 2003) explore dynamics of forgiveness and hope.

Object relations theory views individuals as relationship seeking rather than drive oriented (Fairbairn, 1943, 1949, 1963; Kernberg, 1975; Klein, 1937). Thus, individuals develop and mature within relationships. Children develop an interpersonal world by forming object attachments to significant others. If these others fail in their responsibilities, the integration of realistic good and bad object representations is compromised. Relational templates laid down in infancy become the foundation for future adult relationships.

## OBJECT RELATIONS THEORY

Stern's (1985) work on the infant's subjective experience provides a foundation for exploring experiences of participants who are caught in the cycle That Keeps Happening. Observation of infants led Stern to conclude that a sense of self exists in some form from birth, prior to self-awareness and language, and moves through increasingly complex modes of relatedness throughout life. If this sense of self is impaired, normal social functioning will be disrupted (Stern, 1985). Development does not occur in stages, but is a process and continues through life stages. He defines four senses of self: the emergent self, the core self, the subjective self, and a verbal self.

In these four different senses of self each define separate domains of self-experience and social relatedness. The first of these is the sense of an emergent self that forms from birth to two months. Between two and six months, a sense of core self and core other begins to consolidate. A sense of core self and core other is essential if the infant is to experience an intersubjective state with another. Stern (citing Trevarthan) believes that intersubjectivity is an "innate, emergent human capacity" (Stern, 1985, p. 134) and that the capacity for it unfolds as the infant matures. The state of intersubjectivity is the infant's realization that what is in her mind can be shared with another. The core self is a "separate, cohesive, bounded, physical unit, with a sense of her own agency, affectivity, and continuity in time" (Stern, 1985, p. 11). Between 7 and 15 months, a sense of a subjective self is formed. During these months, infants gradually come upon the momentous realization that inner subjective experiences, the "subject matter" of the mind, are potentially shareable with someone else (Stern, 1985, p. 124). The last domain is the sense of verbal self wherein the toddler between 15 and 18 months begins to imagine or represent things in her mind with language that eventually leads to a narrative self. Stern emphasizes that these senses of selves are not successive phases, but rather, each forms and remains active throughout life.

Benjamin (1990, 1995) is particularly interested in the infant's experience of a core self and core other which must be consolidated in order to experience a sharing of a subjective experience, or a "domain of intersubjective relatedness" (Stern, 1985, p. 124). She refers to this as "intersubjectivity" (Benjamin, 1990). In this phase, the infant discovers she has a mind and that other people also have minds. Recognition by a significant other allows the infant to know that she can affect others and in turn, be affected. When Benjamin (1995) speaks of recognition, she means that the "other is mentally placed in the position of a different, outside entity but shares a similar feeling or state of mind" (p. 184). Benjamin specifically focuses on one aspect of Stern's definition of core self, self-agency. Stern defines self-agency as "authorship of one's own actions and non-authorship of the actions of others; having volition, having control over self-generated action, and expecting consequences of one's actions" (Stern, 1985, p. 71).

In western culture it is the female who generally gives primary care to children of both sexes and therefore, is the first significant object. If the mother fails to provide "good enough" mothering, developmental failures occur. The major limitations of participants' mothers contributed to problematic development of the capacity for mutual recognition.

Benjamin (1995) examines development of mutual recognition, locating its origins in the mother / infant dyad. During the 0–18-month phase, infants develop a subjective experience of the self and the other (Stern, 1985; Benjamin, 1990, 1992). According to Benjamin (1995), maturational progression means the infant must build up a gradual and imperfect capacity for mutual recognition with the parent. This capacity to see both self and other as subject is crucial to normative development. The infant needs to elicit a confirming response from the mother, a response that indicates she is recognized and allows her to know she can impact her environment. "Mother's recognition is the basis for the baby's sense of agency" (Benjamin, 1995, p. 34), the ability to change one's own mental state by causing the other to be more or less stimulating. Failure of the mother to acknowledge the infant creates obstacles in the movement toward a sense of personal agency. If the mother is unable to acknowledge the infant, the infant will be unable to see her mother as a subjective other, a person in her own right. The mother remains omnipotent, the one with total control. Appreciating the other's reality and establishing a shared reality is compromised.

For the participants in this study, the mother's inability to recognize and acknowledge the infant as a subjective self resulted in the developmental failure of the infant's capacity to see mother as a subjective self. Without the capacity for mutual recognition, participants were blind to potential problems in future choices of mates. They were unable to see husbands as core others containing both good and bad attributes.

Mutual recognition is the foundation of future relationships. It is "I see you and I can make an impact on you. You see me and I am influenced by you." Parental limitations interfered with consolidation of the core self and its components, specifically self-agency for the participants. If the women did not have the preoedipal experiences of being able to influence another and in turn be impacted by significant others, they faced difficulty in adult relationships. Participants were unable to fully articulate how husbands' behaviors impacted them. In addition, they could not exert influence on husbands and expect appropriate actions. A component of self-agency is the ability to maintain the "tension between recognizing the other and asserting the self" (Benjamin, 1995, p. 38). Participants had problems relinquishing responsibility for husbands' actions. In addition, they were unable to make demands of their husbands and expect consequences.

A mother's inability to facilitate the development of mutual recognition resulted in the developing females' incapacity to relinquish the subject-object complementarity. Consequently, she continued to view her mother as omnipotent, the one with control. The internalization of the mother's omnipotence carried forward into adulthood and manifested itself in adult relationships. In this study, husbands became the "omnipotent" other who held control. In the face of this omnipotence, women experienced themselves as victims to their husbands' wishes and desires. Participants were unable to access their own self-agency and permanently disrupt the cycle. They viewed husbands as having authority, being in charge. Women experienced themselves as limited in their own efficacy.

Fairbairn's (1943) concept of the internalization of the bad object contributes additional understanding of participants' dynamics. The self develops and is structured in the context of relationships with the object (the mother) and is affected by the limitations of that relationship. The infant encounters real frustrations in the mother-infant relationship and those frustrations lead to the development of accentuated need and further frustration. The infant experiences the frustration as a lack of love from mother. This places the infant in a bind, making it problematic to express frustration in a way that leads to gratification.

Expressing frustration as anger risks further rejection. To express the need for the object risks continued humiliation and depreciation of the love and absolute need. Due to frustration, the infant develops an ambivalent attitude toward the object; she finds it both exciting and rejecting. The exciting object represents hope for need fulfillment. The rejecting object is not always able to fulfill those needs. However, the infant is completely dependent on the object for physical and psychic survival and thus, ambivalence becomes dangerous. In order to cope with the frustrations of an unsatisfying external object, the infant removes the bad object from the outer reality into a sphere of inner reality where the infant exerts control. This preserves the perception of mother as safe and good.

However, internalizing the bad object does not change the outer reality and the mother is experienced as both frustrating and exciting. The internal object continues to perform both frustrating and exciting functions with the infant's ego. In defense, the infant splits the internalized whole object into an exciting object and a frustrating object, and then represses both objects. Repression gives rise to the splitting of the ego. The libidinal ego attaches itself to the exciting object and the antilibidnal ego attaches to the rejecting object. The external reality does not change, but now the developing infant has the defense mechanisms with which to cope and protect the relationship. She does not believe that mother is bad; therefore it must be the infant who is bad. If the infant is bad, there is hope for altering or controlling the internal bad.

The infant's adaptive response to the environment, while maintaining a connection with the object, interferes in adult relationships. The endopsychic structure, laid down in infancy, is so powerful that all future relationships result in pathological suffering. For women in the study, the cathexis of ego to object made it difficult for wives to separate from the depriving and exciting other. They held on to the object, and anticipated the good it could offer. As long as the bad object remained inside, women maintained control over the bad. Thus, the repeated phrase "it's my fault" was an effort to manage the environment. However, internalizing the bad meant that the good was projected onto husbands.

This moral defense gave impetus to properties of desperate solutions, collecting evidence, babysitting, idle threats, and keep talking. In addition, employing the moral defense controlled women's aggression that threatened to annihilate the important external object.

The use of the moral defense left women with the good object external to them. Lacking the good object, they were unable to access self-agency and influence husbands. With the bad internalized, participants had a pervasive sense of unworthiness. Inability to access one's sense of goodness inhibited the ability to exert control over the environment.

Kernberg (1975) and Armstrong-Perlman (1994) also contribute to the subject of the internalization of object relationships. An infant chooses a painful attachment rather than isolation in order to avoid the anxiety of annihilation (Kernberg, 1975). This pattern often persists into adulthood, driven by the infantile need to look for the object who will help regain "the lost unity of the self" (Armstrong-Perlman, 1994, p. 224). Wives in the study remained strongly attached to husbands in spite of reported experiences of deep pain. They exhibited patterns of choosing tortuous relationships and remaining in those relationships. A painful attachment was better than isolation and the anxiety of annihilation.

Participants were preoccupied with the "bad object." Hope existed that perhaps the parents who failed them would finally come through and would rescue them. Husbands, the replacement objects for parents, continued to under perform, offering little evidence of a capacity to compensate for parental failures. However, wives maintained hope.

Like Benjamin and Stern, Chodorow (1978, 1980) maintains that development of a self occurs within the context of a relationship. She examines the role of separation-individuation, which takes place in relationship with a primary other and the development of the capacity for recognition. An essential early task of psychosexual development is to establish a separate sense of both the physical and psychological self. Adequate separation means the infant must perceive a subjective sense of the other and experience the mother as "not me." It is through the experience of continuity provided by the mother that a sense of the "central self" emerges.

Ideally, this self is able to develop a sense of self-agency or the "sense that one is able to affect others and one's environment" (Chodorow, 1980, p. 427). The sense of agency is nourished by significant others who do not project their own experiences or feelings onto the child. Optimal conditions for development of a self in connection with other were unavailable for study participants. Without optimal conditions, participants retained their preoedipal attachments to mothers, and continued to experience themselves as continuous with mothers. The inability to experience themselves as separate likely contributed to their inability to disrupt the cycle. It also contributed to participants' obsession with husbands' activities and the marital relationship. Moreover, it added to the belief held by participants that "it is my fault."

Chodorow (1980), like Benjamin (1995), is also concerned with development of self-agency. She locates the difficulty in creating self-agency during the separation-individuation phase. Mothers and fathers with developmental deficits were unable to facilitate the necessary security for a "central self" to emerge. Chodorow defines this central self as "internally, a relational ego, a sense of self-in-good relationship" (Chodorow, 1980, p. 427). According to Chodorow, the more secure an individual, the less need to define oneself as separate from another. Conversely, the more insecure, the greater the need to define oneself as completely connected to the other. The lack of security in early development made it difficult for participants to perceive themselves as individuals in relation to spouses.

The first 18 months of development are critical as the somewhat differentiated infant learns about the subjective world. During this phase of development, the infant begins to appreciate her own sense of self as well as the subjective sense of another. The mother-infant relationship takes center stage during this phase of development, as mother is key in the development of intersubjectivity. If the young female is unable to negotiate these tasks, future adult relationships may be problematic. The capacity for self-agency becomes impaired if the core self has not internalized a sense of itself as "good-in-relationship" and is susceptible to the expectation of itself as "bad-in-relationship."

Some participants were undoubtedly impacted more by preoedipal disruptions than others. These early developmental complications contributed to increased difficulty in Oedipal development, which later interfered with their adult relationships. Preoedipal development for other participants progressed in more normative fashion and disturbances occurred in the Oedipal phase. The interferences in this phase played a dominant part in conflictual adult relationships. Benjamin (1995) and Chasseguet-Smirgel's (1988) contributions on the Oedipal conflict and difficulties negotiating this phase advance the understanding of the experiences of participants in the study.

Development of the capacity for mutual recognition does not end with the preoedipal phase, but continues into the Oedipal phase where stress is now placed on father's role (Benjamin, 1995). Preoedipal children identify with both parents. However, upon entering the Oedipal phase, young girls acquire the ability to notice differences between mother and father. In the push for separation-individuation, conflict arises between the need for attachment as represented by mother and the need for independence, as represented by fathers. Father symbolizes a different kind of object than mother; he is "the mirror of desire" (Benjamin, 1995, p. 122). He is the powerful subject who is the young female's ideal; he confirms her push for independence while simultaneously acting as the subject on whom one can depend. Benjamin introduces the concept of "identificatory love," the young girl's identification with father who is different from the first object. Father must recognize this need for identification and appropriately affirm it otherwise the girl experiences disappointment. This disappointment results in an early deflation of omnipotence. "Too often such daughters wind up admiring the men who get away with their grandiosity intact" (Benjamin, 1995, p. 129).

Father's failure to recognize his daughter's needs for independence and identification compromised the success of separation and individuation. Adult women must be able to manage the tensions between independence and dependence in adult relationships. Participants encountered problems with this dialectic. How does one both assert her needs and remain dependent on the ideal other?

Chasseguet-Smirgel (1988) is also interested in the father's role in psychosexual development, specifically his role in the Oedipus complex. She puts forth the idea that developing females encounter a particular aspect of the Oedipus complex, which does not have a counterpart in the experience of males. Little girls, unlike little boys, experience a specifically feminine form of anal-sadistic guilt in the change of object. This change must take place in order to move forward developmentally. It represents both the continued effort to separate from the original primary object (mother) and achievement of triadic relations.

For the change of object to occur, a good object capable of alleviating the shortcomings of the first object must exist (Chasseguet-Smirgel, 1988). The little girl projects the good aspects of the primary object onto a secondary object. Simultaneously she maintains the projection of the bad aspects onto the original primary object. The primary object, the mother, must be capable of providing optimal frustration and the secondary object, the father, must be solid enough to receive the good projections. If these two conditions are met, the little girl will go through the change of object and establish a "non-conflictual identification" (p. 92) with the mother without undue importance given to idealization of the second object.

According to Chasseguet-Smirgel (1988), the process of turning to the father is far more complicated for young girls than for boys. In order to attach to the father, little girls must "repress and counter-cathect the aggressive instincts" (Chasseguet-Smirgel, 1988, p. 91) which exist in relation to the father. The change occurs due to the process of de-idealization of the mother and an idealization of the father. The idealization of father cannot be sustained with an awareness of the aggressive instincts. Thus, by repressing the aggressive instincts, the little girl maintains identification with the idealized father. As a result of the repression of aggression, "a specifically feminine form of guilt [arises that is] attached to the anal-sadistic component of sexuality which is radically opposed to idealization" (Chasseguet-Smirgel, 1988, p. 91).

The transition in the change of objects will heavily influence a woman's future psychosexual development. The parents must be able to smoothly facilitate the process so that the little girl does not experience inordinate amounts of guilt that interfere with the maturational process and impede success in sexual, social, and professional arenas. Mother must offer appropriate frustration and father must be able to accept the little girl's aggression and idealization.

However, if the mother is too frustrating, the father becomes the last chance for establishing a good relationship with a satisfying object. The little girl devalues the mother and turns toward the father inevitably giving disproportionate importance to the idealization of the father and the paternal phallus. In this context, the penis serves both as an organ and as a phallus that represents a "treasure of strength, integrity, magic power, or autonomy" (1988, p. 111). The phallus, something that was absent in former object relations, symbolizes both aggression and sexuality. In order to safeguard her idealization of the father, the little girl represses aggression toward her father (and toward the penis). Retention of the aggression results in guilt, as it is impossible for the little girl to experience aggression and idealization of the father (and the penis) simultaneously. Retention of the aggression also results in a regression to the anal-retentive stage and a fixation takes place at a point when, as a result of penis envy, the little girl desires the phallus.

If the father cannot contain the aggression and tolerate his daughter's idealization, the future of her achievement of a satisfactory psychosocial / psychosexual adult life is jeopardized. The little girl retains a primitive over-idealization of the penis and subsequent devaluation of the self. She establishes a conflictual identification with the devalued mother. To actually succeed in these areas means the mature female has surpassed her own mother by appropriating her father's penis and she may also have "castrated the father" (Chasseguet-Smirgel, 1988, p. 101) resulting in overwhelming guilt.

Study participants consistently spoke of major interferences in normative childhood development (Chapter Five). Mothers with deficits were neglectful, abusive, failed to appropriately gratify daughters or protect them from incestuous family members. Fathers also had major limitations due to alcoholism, boundary violations, and emotional, and / or physical absences. They could not be the good objects capable of alleviating the mothers' shortcomings. The idealization / de-idealization process was compromised and developing females were prematurely frustrated. The two conditions that needed to be present in order to establish a non-conflictual relationship with mothers and appropriate idealization of fathers were not met. Participants' fathers, due to their own difficulties, could not both encourage and contain aggression and nurture femininity.

There were other contributing factors to the development of over-idealization of fathers. In deficient home environments, young girls never really got to know their fathers with character flaws and limitations. The fathers were not always able to communicate authentic feelings of love and acceptance to their little girls. In the absence of authentic feelings of being loved, young girls had to assume they were loved. This left fathers in an idealized position and maturing girls maintained distorted images of their fathers. Mothers of the participants, caught in their own disorganized lives contributed to idealization of fathers as they elevated the fathers' positions in the family. In turn, the fantasy of loving, accepting fathers affected future adult relationships. This also may account for participants' inability to see potential problems in men. Participants idealized their husbands and attributed qualities and virtues to them that appeared based in fantasy. Just as earlier they had fantasized relationships with fathers; participants fantasized relationships with their husbands.

This absence of optimal conditions resulted in a continued identification with the devalued mother, a suppression of appropriate aggression and an over idealization of the father. In identifying with a depreciated mother, the women ultimately devalued themselves and were unable to mobilize appropriate aggression. The participants became submissive and the ideal of the father was transferred onto the husbands. Wives experienced themselves as powerless to disrupt the cycle.

Participants' inability to access self-agency was connected with their early repression of aggression and Oedipal over-idealization of husbands who represented the powerful phallus. They could not maintain idealization and tolerate aggression toward their husbands at the same time. Participants experienced a marked inability to act as the author of their own actions, to take control over self-generated actions and to expect consequences of those actions (Stern, 1985). They seemed unable to turn the repressed aggression into appropriate self-agency without experiencing guilt. They struggled with the concept of who would be in control and who had the power in the relationship.

## SELF-PSYCHOLOGY

Participants disregarded early evidence indicating their potential mates had serious flaws. Goldberg's (1999) concept of the vertical split contributes another perspective to the complex relationships between men and women and the issue of sexually related activities.

In order to manage the relationships, to carry on with daily activities of raising children, managing households, and maintaining careers, women used disavowal. This enabled them to tolerate and even participate in behaviors they reported to find objectionable. By using disavowal, women managed to maintain relationships with their husbands and seemingly tolerate sexual activity in and outside of the marriage.

Wives felt betrayed by husbands' sexual activity and they professed to hate the lying and deceit on the part of the husbands. Yet, repeatedly men engaged in sexual activities that wives disliked and continued to lie about such activities. In desperate attempts to stop their husbands, women engaged in behaviors they claimed to find disgusting. These behaviors often consisted of participation in sexual activities they claimed to dislike. In addition, many women found themselves lying and practicing deceit in their desperate attempts to stop their husbands' behaviors.

The vertical split consists of an experience, in which there are coexisting feelings that lead to different and opposite results. The split in the self leads to "the convenient practice of disowning parts of the world that one finds disagreeable" (Goldberg, 1995, p. 65).

The coexisting feelings are diametrically so opposite that the two separate structures are formed within the self.

The vertical split is a way for young children to deal with the parental inconsistencies and the accompanying emotions. It helps preserve the relationship with the caretakers and in the face of their faulty responses, their lack of responses to self-object needs, contradictory experiences, and conflicting behaviors and messages. In light of such discrepancies, children disavow aspects of the self in order to stay connected to the sustaining self-object and to guard against further pain. Disavowal maintains the vertical split and hence a tenuous state of self-cohesion.

Vertical splits are not necessarily problematic, but can become pathological when fantasy life becomes so divided from reality that it takes on a life of its own. Women in the sample demonstrated varying degrees of self-pathology and evidence of pathological use of the vertical split.

The separate structures maintained by disavowal lead to "a certain sort of blindness" (Goldberg, 1995, p. 64). This blindness allowed participants to overlook obvious signs of problems in their future choices of mates. Women reported sensing that something was not quite right with their potential mates, but nevertheless, moving forward into marriage. The vertical split continued to function in the marriage as it permitted participants to maintain idealizing feelings as well as deep disappointment and anger toward their spouses.

According to wives' reports, their husbands had unreliable caretakers and early childhood trauma. This allows for speculation that the men also came into the marriage with their own vertical splits. The genesis of this is unknown as it was not the focus of the study. The cycle in which the women felt caught had to do with two selves with separate vertical splits participating with each other's vertical splits and perpetuating the cycle. The wives' vertical split interfered with their ability to solidly assert themselves and make their husbands abandon the sexual activity. However, vertical splits allowed wives to invest their energy in husbands' and continue to disavow their own pain. Wives participating in their husbands' vertical splits helped maintain self-cohesion.

Prevalence of early sexual boundary violations of women in this study also indicates the possibility they dealt with early trauma by splitting the self. Affects related to trauma were disavowed or possibly repressed, thus the trauma remained untreated. The disavowal of the untreated trauma contributed to the continuing problem in the marriage.

Participants focused on the Internet pornography as a source of marital distress to the exclusion of overtly sexually behaviors. It is possible that the vertical split allowed for this focus. Internet pornography seemed far less offensive to women than other sexual activities. Periodically the disavowal would break down and women would confront their husbands. The study did not demonstrate what triggered this breakdown and participants could not self-identify. There may have been other crisis or disappointments in psychosexual development or even in the marriage that had been previously disavowed. The breakdown of disavowal may have brought massive earlier untreated disappointments to the surface. In the face of these disappointments wives focused on the Internet as something that was both concrete and available to comprehension.

## CAPACITY FOR INTIMACY

Frank (1996), Kernberg (1974), and Kramer (1996) contribute to understanding experiences of participants by addressing issues of intimacy and infidelity. All women experienced their husbands' Internet activity and other sexual activity as affairs. These theorists begin with the supposition that intimacy in the relationship between mother and infant affects the capacity for infidelity later in an adult's life. Difficulties that arise during the separation-individual phase can disrupt intimacy. An individual should emerge from this separation-individuation phase with a sense of clear boundaries between self and object and a sense of self and identity. This successful individuation is a prerequisite for object relatedness, closeness and intimacy. The essence of intimacy is a physical and psychical merger between two individuals. Involved in intimacy is the simultaneous experience of being both separate and merged. If early experiences of intimacy were compromised, the ability for adult intimacy can become a future problem.

There may be a question of the participants' ability to enter into intimate relationships. According to Kernberg (1974), a deep and lasting relationship requires that both people have the capacity for empathy and understanding. In addition, intimacy demands that couples maintain exclusive love relations with one another. Kernberg (1974) notes though, that there are differences between men and women in their ability to tolerate discontinuities in love and sex. Men seem to be capable of maintaining a sexual relationship even if they no longer love a particular woman. However, women need an emotional connection, they must be able to feel love and care for a man and know their feelings are reciprocated. Many women in the study no longer believed their husbands loved or cared only for them. This theory may account for women who reported little sexual interest in their husbands after discovery of evidence. Not feeling especially cared for or loved diminished their interest in sexual activity with their husbands.

According to Alperin (2000) not all individuals are capable of experiencing intimacy. He also cites a successful separation-individuation process and establishment of secure boundaries between self and other as prerequisites for intimacy. If problems occur in this important developmental step, future adult relationships are compromised. Even the act of love making as a "fully involving interpersonal event" (Stern, 1985, p. 30) can be adversely affected by complications in this process.

According to Stern (1985), making love involves:

> first the sense of the self and the other as discrete physical entities, as forms in motion-an experience in the domain of core-relatedness, as is the sense of self-agency, will, encompassed in the physical acts. At the same time it involves the experience of sensing the other's subjective state: shared desire, aligned intentions, and mutual states of simultaneously shifting arousal, which occur in the domain of intersubjective relatedness (p. 30).

Mitchell (2000) adds another dimension to problems in intimacy. Marriage seems to be a death knell for romance as individuals find it difficult to maintain romance amidst the monotony of daily living. Affairs may be the result of problems in sustaining romance in long-term relationships. Couples need both danger and attachment. Intense attachment provides safety that is desperately needed. However, safety is antithetical to danger and couples experience difficulties managing this dialectic. Many wives in the study sought out "dangerous" and exciting men to marry. While these men provided excitement and danger necessary for romance, they failed to offer safety. Like other theorists (Benjamin, 1988; Chasseguet-Smirgel, 1988; Fairbairn, 1943; & Kernberg, 1975, 1999), Mitchell locates difficulties in synthesis of danger and safety in the infant / mother dyad and establishment and maintenance of dependence / independence. Traumatic childhoods and disrupted psychosexual development left women unable to manage these necessary tensions. This difficulty manifests itself in an inability to disrupt the cycle of "it just keeps happening."

## COSA Women and SAA Men

Women who joined COSA hoped the 12-Step program would empower them to permanently disrupt the cycle of "it just keeps happening." However, they too were mired in the cycle and unable to permanently disrupt it. COSA women lacked essential tools to manage disruptions in their own homes. Joining the 12-Step program gave them additional skills unavailable to non-COSA women. When their lives felt unregulated, they could turn to sponsors, to the group, and to comfortable rituals in order to soothe and achieve self-regulation. In addition, they received support from other women and a safe place to openly discuss and process their experiences.

COSA offered a structure to those participants who chose to attend and members of the program became transference objects. The individual's sponsor became the new object, a consistently reliable one who was available during times of crisis. Thus, sponsors could offer new experiences for women, experiences of an object capable of responding to a need. The early object attachments to significant others were often painful and conflictual for participants. Due to their own character deficits, parents failed to provide appropriate responses to the developmental needs of the maturing infant. The good-enough mother of the separation-individuation phase could not tolerate her daughter's burgeoning independence and conflictual demands. Sponsors, with their ability to appropriately respond as the "good enough" object without inflicting shame, allowed participants to rework some of the original trauma. In the time of need, objects were accessible and could respond with care, consistency, and offer a holding environment. Thus, COSA women had opportunities for reworking aspects of the original trauma.

In spite of the availability of a specific type of structure and available object, the COSA women were unable to disrupt the cycle "that keeps happening." COSA programs do not address the underlying pathology that would allow women to achieve substantive change.

## FORGIVENESS AND HOPE

The properties of forgiveness and hope appeared in every category and were an integral part of the cycle "that just keeps happening." Forgiveness and hope took on different nuances in each category. This discussion will treat the phenomena of forgiveness and hope as a small cycle. The variances in the property have been examined previously in the categories. The analysis of forgiveness and hope will be based on contributions by both Akhtar (1999, 2003) and Casement (1991) and thus, will use their language.

Often forgiveness was an unconscious act recognized retrospectively. At other times it was a very conscious act articulated by participants. All participants struggled with this concept no matter what their religious affiliation. Therefore, it cannot be attributed primarily to religious upbringing and necessitates a psychodynamic understanding. The desire and ability to forgive augmented feelings of hope and increased hope allowed for a greater ability to forgive.

There is an absence of discourse about the concept of forgiveness in psychoanalytic literature. According to Akhtar (2003), Freud mentions the word "forgiveness" only five times in his entire corpus of work. The notion of forgiveness has unmistakable religious and social overtones, something with which participants were very much aware. The property of forgiveness was pervasive in participants' narratives. All spoke of the necessity to forgive and forget. Akhtar (1999, 2003) focuses on the dynamics of forgiveness from the perspective of trauma, disenfranchisement, or injustice. His discussion will illuminate this property and its importance to participants.

The online dictionary (http://dictionary.reference.com) offers the following definition of the root word "forgive":

1. To excuse for a fault or an offense; pardon
2. To renounce anger or resentment against
3. To absolve from payment of (a debt, for example)

There are two mental operations involved in forgiveness. The first part requires a change of affect or emotion and the second requires a giving up of an entitled attitude. Although Akhtar (2003) reviews both the bestowing of forgiveness as well as the dynamics of seeking forgiveness, the focus will be on the first due to its relevancy. Participants believed themselves to be victims of injustice and in mourning due to trauma. Wives were not interested in seeking forgiveness for their actions, but in granting forgiveness to husbands.

The process of forgiveness involves three separate factors, revenge, reparation, and reconsideration (Akhtar, 2003). Revenge, or getting even, is good for the development of ego narcissism; revenge turns passive into active and ironically creates empathy with the perpetrator. It puts the "victim's hitherto passive ego in an active position" (p. 214). The victim is no longer the wronged innocent, but can begin to feel a sense of mastery. In exacting revenge, the individual accesses aggression and experiences power. Participants frequently expressed desires to take revenge on errant husbands (Chapter Seven). After executing a bit of revenge, most women felt vindicated. Akhtar believes revenge allows for growth of empathy as each party now shares in the other's experience.

Reparation, the process of making amends is the second factor involved in forgiving and is important in the recovery process for the wronged individual. Participants longed for husbands to realize the harm their behaviors caused in the marital home. COSA women were keenly aware of the need for "making amends" and husbands' responsibilities in this area. Failure of others to acknowledge harm contributes to distorted perceptions of reality (Akhtar, 2003). All the participants grew up in disorganized homes where there were numerous infringements and violations of boundaries. Significant others failed to acknowledge the impact of their actions. Parental inability to recognize harmful actions induced additional trauma. Thus, the women had little experience of reparation for the original trauma. The lack of earlier reparation probably increased the need for reparation from husbands who had caused emotional harm.

Acknowledgments of responsibility for trauma inflicted and acts of reparation permit movement toward healing. This healing effect is experienced in the "shifting (of) the psychic locale of the representations of trauma from the actual to the transitional area of the mind" (Akhtar, 2003, p. 215). Once in the transitional realm, the possibility of examining the trauma from various perspectives increases. Thus, the trauma is reconsidered and the wounded individual can eventually let it go. The individual has the opportunity to separate the trauma from the past and see it for its own properties.

Many participants were able to exact some revenge, however, a very few actually received reparation. This made for diminished opportunities for reconsideration of the perceived traumas and ability to let them go. Women remained stuck in the forgiveness / hope cycle with no way to integrate the experience.

The capacity for forgiveness has both evolutionary as well as individual origins. Akhtar makes a convincing case for the "hardwired" status of forgiveness, linking it to survival based on primate studies. He relies on Klein's (*Love, Guilt, and Reparation*, 1937) contributions in understanding the ontogenetic origins of forgiveness. The mother / infant dyad is the foundation for the development of the intrinsic capacity to forgive. Both mother and infant are involved in the mutuality of forgiveness with mother's ability to forgive the infant for her aggression and the infant forgiving mother in the fantasies of her shortcomings. This mutuality of forgiveness is what Benjamin (1998) refers to as mutual recognition. These acts of forgiveness help to metabolize aggression and prevent revenge seeking patterns from being activated. Aptitude for forgiveness continues to develop through each phase of psychosexual development. However, derailment of normative development impacts forgiveness and leads to the appearance of psychopathologic syndromes. Although Akhtar discusses eight such syndromes involving forgiveness, only two are pertinent to these theoretical implications.

The first of these syndromes is "premature forgiveness" (Akhtar, 2003, p. 224). A large percentage of participants exhibited a pattern of repeatedly forgiving without appropriate internal processing. This enabled participants to bind their own anger by using compromise formation to manage aggressive impulses and superego prohibitions. Akhtar cites a more severe from of premature forgiveness, which is "defect-based" (p. 224). These individuals lack the capacity for a "healthy capacity for indignation" (Akhtar, 2003, p. 224 citing Ambassador Nathaniel Howell, personal communication, April 1996). Their object-hunger is intense. Participants with a history of severe developmental deficits were more likely to prematurely forgive in a desperate attempt to hold onto the object.

"Excessive forgiveness" (Akhtar, 2003, p. 224) is the second pathological syndrome exhibited by participants. Akhtar links excessive forgiveness with masochism and sadism claiming these individuals live in a state of "near addiction" (p. 224) to those who are sadistic. Participants absolved their husbands' multiple times, and permitted repeated activities regarded as offensive. Participants adamantly believed that forgiveness would eventually transform a terrible relationship into a good relationship. Forgiveness would make things right.

Hope, both conscious and unconscious, forms the complementary part of the forgiveness / hope cycle. Forgiveness gives rise to increased hope while hope allows for repeated attempts at forgiving perceived injuries. This small cycle is repeated in each of the five categories,

*In The Beginning, Temporary Peace, Something Is Definitely Up, The Big Discovery*, and *COSA Women*. Casement (1991) and Akhtar (1999) elucidate aspects of unconscious and conscious hope. Research findings indicate that both types of hope were present in participants. Conscious hope was articulated clearly in statements participants made concerning the future while the unconscious hope appeared more in behaviors and actions. Wives expressed strong desire to believe husbands were changing behaviors and with each discovery would profess to have hope of further change. Unconscious hope was evident in wives' desperate attempts at solutions and search for outside assistance.

Unconscious hope is the search for something that will meet the unmet needs and includes "any form of striving toward what is needed" (Casement, 1991, p. 294). Casement recognizes that sometimes behaviors can be understood as repetitive communication attempts to satisfy unmet needs and not necessarily a pathological repetition of events. Repetition compulsion indicates the presence of an unresolved conflict. Casement views attempts to resolve conflicts and generate solutions as a hopeful sign. Thus, participants' inabilities to extricate themselves from the cycle may be interpreted as an unsuccessful search for a responsive object that can fill a void. The repetition of the circle and behaviors involved can be seen as wives' hopeful attempts to find an object that will mitigate previous disappointments, meet the unmet needs, and help resolve the conflict.

Hope originates in the mother / infant dyad. When a significant other gratifies essential needs, infants anticipate and rely on those good experiences. Mother's ability to respond appropriately and timely to the infant's needs contributes to the development of hope. Not only does the infant learn to confidently expect good experiences, but also she learns to anticipate the repair of bad experiences. Furthermore, she learns to expect that significant objects will continually accommodate her needs. These expectations form the basis for a sense of security. This cycle of need, gratification, and quiescence forms the origins of hope. If needs meet frustration too frequently, hopelessness develops. Lacking verbal skills, it becomes mother's responsibility to recognize and understand the infant's needs.

Like Casement (1991), Akhtar (1999) locates the origins of hope in the satisfactory relationship of the mother / infant dyad. While hope can be a positive attribute as it contributes to meaning in life and inspiration, it can also be pathological when it serves a defensive function and impedes the executive function of the ego. Hope is "permeated with ambivalence, with conflict" (Searles, 1979, p. 479), and often devoted to destructive ends. Hope that is devoted to destructive ends, that bypasses recognition of the problems, and avoids reality is "pathological hope." Just as too little hope leads to despair, too much hopefulness can be maladaptive. Pathological hope is an attempt to hang on tenaciously to the idealized, embellished vision of one's mother, longing for symbiotic relationship of the mother-infant (Akhtar, 1999).

Akhtar distinguishes realistic from unrealistic hope. Healthy or realistic hopefulness is a source of support and gratification. It emanates from successful integration of prior disappointments. Unrealistic hope comes from repression of loss and despair and lack of successful integration of prior disappointments. It is unrealistic to have faith in an illusion that what is past or lost can ever be restored (Amati Mehler & Argentieri, 1989). As a result of disorganized family environments, participants experienced numerous disappointments that deficient parents were unable to help metabolize. The experience of preoedipal, Oedipal, and later childhood disappointments and trauma augmented unrealistic hopefulness. In adulthood, participants unconsciously hoped for a good object to relieve or repair those disappointments. In their search for a good object, participants turned to their husbands who lacked the requisite skills due to their own inadequacies. Hope became pathological as it certainly inhibited abilities to disrupt the cycle in which they felt caught.

Relinquishing hope is tantamount to admitting that the object is truly lost and the possibility of symbiotic merging with the mother will never be. Unconscious admission of the unavailability of the lost object causes absolute despair. Holding on to hope that there exists an object capable of preventing, rescuing, or transforming the original trauma keeps despair at bay. For women who experienced Oedipal interference, the sought after object representation was the father. Hence husbands were experienced as object representations of fathers. Other women who encountered preoedipal failures experienced husbands as object representations of the mother. If participants lost the hope that spouses could reform and provide the harmonious domestic life for which they longed, they would plunge into despair.

Akhtar (1999), furthermore describes two classifications of hope, the "some day" and the "if only" (p. 208). The majority of participants demonstrated the "someday" variety, while the remainder exhibited "if only." The nature of the "someday" and the "if only" in participants moved beyond realism into pathology. The "someday" fantasy is the belief that life will magically improve at some future date. The "if only" fantasy allowed participants to live in the past. Both types blocked access to self-agency.

Several mechanisms maintain the structural integrity of the "someday" (Akhtar, 1999). The first of these is the denial and negation of external reality that contradicts the hope of "someday." While abundant evidence indicated that spouses were not abandoning sexually related activities, participants denied or split off that knowledge and preferred to believe that a specific solution to the problem existed. In order to keep the "someday" alive, participants also needed to split off self and object representations capable of mobilizing aggression (Akhtar, 1999). This version of a pathological hope maintained connection with husbands as well as maintained unconscious connection to the original disappointing objects. If women could mobilize their aggression they could access efficacy or self-agency (Benjamin, 1990, 1992; Chasseguet-Smirgel, 1988). However, mobilizing self-agency would be an admission that the object was truly lost. Thus, hope was placed in the husband as the new object, capable of relieving the disappointments, frustrations and trauma associated with the original objects. Participants tolerated present conditions in hopes that there would be great rewards in the future. Wives longed incessantly for idealized object. The act of forgiving was a piece of the relentless pursuit of the idealized object. Forgiving husbands gave wives a sense of control over the situation. If they forgave enough times, they could control the outcome.

The second type of pathological hope is the "if only" fantasy. These individuals lack interest in the future and long for an idealized past. This type of hope was not as evident as the "someday" variety. Participants retrospectively idealized the path not chosen. Living in the past allowed them to tolerate the present unfulfilling situation. However, idealizing the past also kept them mired in the cycle. The idealization of the past can also be conceived as a search for the lost object. Like the "someday," the "if only" fantasy also has its origins in early childhood frustrations and disappointments. It is a product of an unconscious awareness of separation from the now idealized object and longed for joy at reunification through fantasies. "If only" can be attributed to incomplete mourning of traumatic disruption of early mother-child relationship.

Both the "someday" and "if only" are similar in the use of defenses of splitting, denial, and primitive idealization. These defenses are based in the unfinished mourning over preoedipal and Oedipal traumas. Capacity for hopelessness is part of normative development and contributes to acceptance of reality. Research participants, due to disruptive development, did not develop the capacity for realistic hopefulness or hopelessness.

Participants experienced levels of both conscious and unconscious hope. They articulated the conscious hope as a desire for harmony and peace in the relationship. They wanted to be taken seriously and respected. The unconscious hope centered on the longing to have a significant other meet the unmet needs, repair the trauma, and for an object to be there in times in crisis. The unconscious hope was represented in circuitous behaviors and activities.

The properties of forgiveness and hope appeared in each category and produced some variations. All women, regardless of their religious affiliation, unconsciously and consciously demonstrated a desire to forgive in the hope that relationships would bring happiness. The capacity for forgiveness and for hope has origins in the developing mother / infant dyad. Developmental impairments impact this small cycle.

## SUMMARY OF THEORETICAL IMPLICATIONS

Various theorists' contributions to psychosexual development produced understandings as to the experience of wives whose husbands used the Internet for sexually related activities. These women were embroiled in the cycle "that just keeps happening." The theoretical implications strongly suggest that an inability to affect change in the marital relationship is grounded in early infant caretakers' failures to meet essential needs. Furthermore, later childhood traumas caused by boundary violations negatively impacted development. Derailed development and trauma impeded self-agency, that ability to take responsibility for one's own actions, make decisions, carry out actions and expect consequences. Participants employed various defenses in their attempts to manage and cope with the marital situation. These defenses included vertical splits, and pathological hope and forgiveness. The findings also indicate that abilities to establish intimacy were also impaired by normative developmental derailment.

## CLINICAL IMPLICATIONS

The study began by investigating Internet pornography and experiences of women whose husbands used pornography on the Internet. All women self-identified as having husbands who accessed pornography via the Internet. Participants also determined that the Internet and easy access to pornography was a major source of conflict in the marriage and in many cases, the cause of progression to other sexually related activities.

Internet pornography was the tip of the iceberg; viewing pornography was only one piece of the problem. However, the women identified Internet pornography as the major issue. There is not enough information as to why women decided Internet pornography was the focus.

The data indicates the problem of Internet pornography is more complex and cannot be reduced to pornography viewing. All participants had prior untreated developmental deficits due to interferences, neglect, emotional and physical abuse, and sexual abuse. Deeper characterological issues contributed to participants' inability to interrupt the cycle. The provocative nature of Internet pornography and the media's attention to it has the potential of distracting therapists from the underlying issues and tending to the symptom instead.

Current research on Internet pornography (Carnes et al., 2001; Civin, 2000; KcKenna & Bargh, 2000; Schnarch, 1997; Schneider, 2000) focuses on the Internet as an addiction. In this model, the Internet is perceived as dangerously seductive in luring men and women into its grips. Although some individuals may use it for recreational purposes, addicted users or those with a history of intimacy and relationship concerns and previous patterns of sexual acting out (Schneider, 2000) may become addicted.

However, the Internet and the mind are two separate entities. The Internet is not the cause of sexually related activities although it may facilitate such behaviors. When a woman presents in therapy identifying the Internet as a major cause of dissatisfaction in the marriage, careful consideration must be given to the nature of the individual's underlying pathology. The data results underscore the importance of obtaining a thorough history of the individual that includes any untreated traumas associated with sexual, emotional, and physical abuse. A genogram can be useful in mapping generational patterns and the interplay of those patterns in the identification of individual pathology. A complete psychosexual developmental history must include any developmental interferences, failures, and parental deficits.

While the research examined the experiences of women, it became apparent that wives are a part of a complex marital relationship. It appears that the split of the woman meets a corresponding split in the man and together they form a complex, intertwined relationship. Naïve therapists may find themselves focusing on various aspects of wives' defenses and ignoring the important function the big cycle performs for wives and for couples. One such defense mechanism that appeared in the study was the repeated references to forgiveness and hope. These properties formed a small cycle unto itself as forgiveness increased hope and increased hope gave way to forgiveness. However, the small cycle of forgiveness and hope actually perpetuated the problem rather than functioning as actual attempts at reparation.

Clinicians should be aware of the defensive nature of forgiveness and encourage clients to examine the roles forgiveness and hope play in preserving the status quo.

It would also be erroneous for therapists to assume that divorce is the only viable option for women who claim to be in despair about husbands' use of Internet pornography. The marriage relationship is a system and as such, certain pathological ways of functioning may be the glue that binds the couple together. Therapists must encourage clients to closely examine the marital system as well as understand their own personal dynamics. In addition, therapists should assist clients in analyzing the disavowed affects, memories, or trauma. The therapeutic work is to bring these split off and separated contents together.

Although the women claimed to be in despair over their husbands' Internet use, these women also spoke about their husbands in idealizing ways. These seemingly polarized feelings are both valid. However, the disparate feelings were not integrated, but part of the disavowal and therefore, therapy should focus on mending the split.

Many therapists refer women to 12-Step programs as a supplement to psychotherapy. The data suggests that consideration should be given to the possibility that these programs may reinforce the pathological marital relationship. Although COSA offers new ways for women to articulate their problems and reduces the sense of isolation, COSA may also inadvertently reinforce the vertical split.

While the study focused on Internet pornography and the role it occupied in the marital system, the findings may be generalizable to other couples engaged in similar dynamics. What may appear to be pathological to the therapist serves an important function in the relational life of the couple. Therapists need to be cognizant of the role certain dynamics play for the couple.

Therapists should be mindful of the presentation of the preceding understanding of the marital system when working with individual women. Various participants reported that professionals fostered the belief that women were responsible for their husbands' behaviors. Therapists must time and carefully word interventions that encourage women to explore their own participation in the cycle. Premature interventions can foster resistance to such exploration.

Countertransference is always a consideration in the therapeutic relationship. Study participants did not always admit to feeling despair and hopelessness, but seemed to disown these negative affect. Consequently, the transcribers, editors, and I carried the intense emotions for the participants. Therapists must closely attend to their own feelings of despair, hopelessness, sadness, anger, and distress and use these emotions to inform the therapeutic interventions. Therapists need to guard against furthering the existing split.

## SOCIAL IMPLICATIONS

An Internet search on pornography netted numerous Christian web pages citing the Internet as a problem in the dissemination of pornography as well as contributing to increased usage. One web pages, "Probe Ministries" (http://www.leaderu.com/orgs/probe/docs/pornplag.html) claims "Pornography is tearing apart the very fabric of our society." (Anderson, 1997). Pornography is viewed as a causal factor rather than a consequence. If the focus remains on Internet pornography as the source of the problem, the larger syndrome is not addressed. Pornography is another way in which individuals can sexually act out. If successful elimination of pornography were achieved, individuals would discover new ways to act out sexuality.

## AREAS FOR FUTURE RESEARCH

Informal data suggested that there were three different types of women: (a) women who were aware of their husbands' pornography use and were not concerned, (b) women who discovered their husbands using Internet pornography and demanded they quit, and (c) participants in my study who knew their husbands were using Internet pornography and were unable to make them stop. An empirical study could be conducted to determine if there are three distinct types of women and the percentages that comprise each category. An increase in the number of selected participants would lend validity to the study and produce more data.

Another area for research could be an empirical study that examines personality characteristics of the three groups of women. What is different? What is similar? The results indicated that men were doing far more than viewing pornography. Are there men who are into pornography and do not extend their activities into other sexual realms?

The quantitative instrument used failed to provide reliable data for analyzation. The questions from the General Social Survey and the Indiana Happiness Inventory and Marital Satisfaction Inventory were often vague and subject to misinterpretation. The results of my study could be used to improve the quantitative instrument. Furthermore, other quantitative instruments exist that could yield more reliable data. The quantitative instrument, in combination with a qualitative approach may provide more interesting data and demonstrate different or additional results.

The study did not indicate any conclusions as to why the women pinpointed the Internet as the difficulty in the marital relationship when there were clearly other factors at play. These factors were present long before the inception of the Internet. One possible conclusion is that women focused on the Internet in a defensive manner. Fliers advertised for women whose husbands used the Internet for inappropriate activities. The possibility exists that women responded to the fliers as a segue to talk with a therapist about the Internet pornography and then used the opportunity to explore other concerns. Further research may offer answers to this question.

My findings suggest that the women's disavowal periodically broke down. Again, the data failed to reveal the origin of the break down of disavowal. Further study may demonstrate why the disavowal broke down, and why at that particular point.

COSA is another area for future research. The study concluded that a certain type of woman found COSA to be helpful. The findings did not determine why some women choose to go to COSA while others who had heard of it were reluctant to attend. The findings suggested that women's attendance at COSA and husbands' attendance at SAA may have reinforced the vertical split. A close examination of these phenomena would provide interesting material.

This study gathered data from a limited number of women. The only criteria were the use of the Internet for pornography. Many other factors may have been associated with the women's experiences. Future studies addressing personality characteristics, comparison of the three different types of women mentioned previously, and an in-depth examination of COSA would advance knowledge in the area of women's experiences of their husbands' use of Internet pornography.

## CHAPTER TWELVE

# POSTSCRIPT

Research on the topic of the Internet and sexually related activities proved to be a distressing endeavor for the transcribers, editors, and me. The transcribers reported on the disturbing nature of the material they were transcribing. I found myself debriefing both women. In addition, both discovered their significant others using the Internet for pornographic purposes. One chose to terminate transcribing and used disavowal to defend against the knowledge. The second transcriber was horrified to notice her actions closely resembled the behaviors of the study participants. She demanded that her significant other seek psychodynamic informed treatment and she also sought therapy. This transcriber chose to continue transcribing.

The editors also commented on the depressing nature of the study. I had to debrief the editors. I also believe that one editor was so affected by the material that it inhibited her editing style and I had to find another editor. I too, experienced the process of interviewing, transcribing, reading, and analyzing the material as often overwhelming and depressing. There were many times when I was convinced that all men act out sexually in some form and most women are powerless to improve on their life circumstances.

I was aware of the availability of pornography on the Internet, but did not fully appreciate the various forms accessible until I began talking with participants. These women shared their stories, many times not sparing the graphic details of their discoveries. Some of the stories and images remained with me for days. After listening for hours to these women, I began to wonder if perhaps the lives they lead were "normal." I doubted the relevance of even researching this topic assuming perhaps a majority of couples must live like the couples in my study.

It was painful listening to the hopeless cycle in which the women felt so caught. As I interviewed each participant and heard the same story over and over, I found myself getting depressed and feeling hopeless. My mentor, Dennis Shelby, offered reassurance that being immersed in such sexually explicit material was difficult. Early in the data collection phase, he began to observe how depressed I sounded when I checked in for debriefing sessions. My depression is many times expressed as anxiety and I needed Dennis to help organize and calm me after immersing myself in what turned out to be the craziness of the lives of the women, not just the problem of pornography.

As the interviewing and writing continued, I heard increased number of female clients introducing the subject of husbands and Internet pornography. Some of the clients were new and others had been in treatment for several years and the topic had never been mentioned. A check with other colleagues revealed that they were not hearing the same stories from their female clients. I wondered if perhaps my name was out there as a referral source for this presenting problem. However, none of the women seemed to have prior knowledge of my research topic.

The topic of this study was an icebreaker at social gatherings. Although I emphasized that I was researching women's experiences, non-academic individuals could not take the focus off the topic of pornography and men. Everyone offered advice and suggestions about the users of pornography. Men tried to persuade me that all men do "these things," "it's normal," and perhaps the "women were responsible for not providing enough sex at home." My colleagues also centered on the men's use no matter how many times I pointed out that the men's experiences were not the topic of interest.

The religious world focuses on the morality aspect of pornography and sexually related activities. Social feminist examine domination and subordination of women and civil rights, however, nowhere in the literature is the topic of depression discussed. It appears that there is a link between sexual acting out and depression, despair, and hopelessness as evidenced by study participants, transcribers, editors, and this researcher.

It is possible that Dennis and I were both experiencing countertransference during this process. We were feeling what the women and their husbands could not feel. This link between depression and sexual acting out that I encountered is of note for other researchers studying associated topics.

# APPENDIX A

## CYBERSEX SURVEY

**Would you like an opportunity to participate in a research project on Internet pornography?**

I am doing a research project on the experiences of Roman Catholic women (or women who were raised Roman Catholic) whose husbands use Internet pornography. I am seeking married women who either suspect or are sure that their husbands use the Internet to view pornography or engage in cybersex.

If you are willing to participate please e-mail me or phone me. The time commitment is about three hours. This would involve completing an optional survey questionnaire and participating in an in-depth interview. This would be completely **confidential**. I will use the results to write a study.

Sue Cebulko M.A.
10585 N. Meridian St. Ste. 340
Indianapolis, In 46290
317-580-4003
e-mail:scebulko@hotmail.com

Women needed to participate in research study:

**Is Your Husband Using the Internet for Inappropriate Purposes?**

I am conducting a study and am interested in hearing your experiences about your husbands' inappropriate use of the Internet. I am seeking Roman Catholic women or women who were raised as Roman Catholic.

If you are willing to participate please e-mail or phone me. The time commitment is about three hours. This would involve completing an optional survey and participating in an in-depth interview. This is an opportunity for you to speak with a researcher who is knowledgeable in the field. I will use the results of the research to better understand how to help and treat individuals and couples who are experiencing a disruption in their lives. Your participation is confidential.

For further information please contact me at:
scebulko@hotmail.com
317-580-4003
Your inquiry and participation is completely confidential.

Sue Cebulko M.A. LMFT
10585 N. Meridian St. Ste. 340
Indianapolis, In 46290

# APPENDIX B

## PARTICIPANT'S INFORMED CONSENT FORM

### INSTITUTE FOR CLINICAL SOCIAL WORK
Individual Consent for Participation in Research

I, _____, acting for myself, agree to take part in the research entitled: The experiences of women whose husbands are preoccupied with Internet pornography. Sue Cebulko M. A. will carry out this work under the supervision of R. Dennis Shelby, Ph. D and conducted under the auspices of the Institute of Clinical Social Work, 180 N. Michigan Ave., Suite 1605, Chicago, Il60601, (312)726-8480.

### PURPOSE

The purpose of this study is to research the experiences of women whose husbands are preoccupied with Internet pornography. The results of this work will be used to further the understanding of how the husband's use of Internet pornography affects women and how women manage and cope as a result. The results are for use by other clinicians in the treatment of women in therapy.

### PROCEDURES USED IN THE STUDY

The time involved in the participation will be approximately three hours. This will involve completing a short demographic questionnaire, completing a 35-question survey that examines attitudes toward religious beliefs, happiness, marriage, and pornography and participating in a semi-structured, face-to-face or phone-to-phone interview. Each participant will be invited to review the draft of the results to check for accuracy.

## BENEFITS

There are several benefits associated with participation in this study. Some participants have never discussed their husband's preoccupation with the Internet with any other person. These women may discover that it is a relief to talk to someone and understand that there are other women who face a similar issue in the marriage. There may be some women who have discussed this issue with others. These women can still benefit from talking to a researcher who has some knowledge about the issues involved in Cybersex.

In addition, by participating in this study, the women may begin to look at the issues of Cybersex and begin to understand how it is affecting them and their families. The opening up of the topic may lead some of these women to begin conversations with their husbands concerning the preoccupation. This conversation is potentially beneficial to both husband and wife as it allows what was previously secretive and shameful, to be revealed and more honest communication between the couple could commence.

## COSTS

The costs involved for this will be only for time involved. There are no other monetary costs to the participant.

## POSSIBLE SIDE EFFECTS / RISKS

In addition to the three-hour inconvenience involved, there may be negative emotional responses that arise as a result of the examination of this issue. Perhaps you may not have shared your concerns or problems with anyone up to this point. By participating in the interview, it is possible that we could tap into other concerns or problems with which you were previously unaware.

I intend to make this interview as comfortable as possible by checking with you frequently to find if you are willing to continue.

If you encounter any negative emotional responses during or after the interview, I will be available for up to three debriefing sessions. If you need further therapy at this point, I will refer you to Catholic Social Services in your area or therapists on staff in your parish. I can also find appropriate therapists for you in your particular geographic area.

## Privacy / Confidentiality

I will protect your confidentiality throughout this process. The data will be used only for my research. I will keep your audiotapes, transcriptions, and notes separate from other data and in a locked file. Dennis Shelby Ph.D., the supervising chair, and myself will be the only people to have access to your confidential data. I will keep the audiotapes, transcriptions and notes for three years following the completion of this research. At that time I will shred all notes and destroy the audiotapes.

## Participant Assurances

By signing this consent form, I agree to take part in this study. I have not given up any of my rights or released this institution from responsibility for carelessness.

I may cancel my consent and refuse to continue in this study at any time without penalty or loss of benefits. My relationship with the staff of the ICSW will not be affected in any way, now or in the future, if I refuse to take part, or if I begin this study and then withdraw.

If I have any question about the research methods, I can contact Sue Cebulko M.A. at 317-580-4003 (day) or 317-843-2141 (evening) or R. Dennis Shelby at 312-943-2155 x8 (day) or 219-929-4314 (evening). If I have any questions about my rights as a research subject, I may call Daniel Rosenfeld, M.A., Chair of Institutional Review Board, ICSW, 180 N. Michigan Ave., Suite 1605, Chicago IL 60601, (312) 726-8480.

## SIGNATURES

I have read this consent form and I agree to take part in this study as it is explained in this consent form.

_____          _____

Signature of Participant                                    Date

I certify that I have explained the research to _____
and believe that she understands and that she has agreed to participate freely. I agree to answer any additional questions when they arise during the research or afterward.

_____          _____

Signature of Researcher                                    Date

# APPENDIX C

## DEMOGRAPHIC QUESTIONNAIRE

Please answer the following questions:
1. What is your age? _____
2. How long have you been married? _____
3. How long have you been a part of your denomination (identify which denomination)? _____
4. Please indicate your current household income.
   Rather not say
   Under $40,000
   $50,000–$65,000
   $66,000–$80,000
   $81,000–$90,999
   $91,000–$100,000
   $101,000–$120,000
   $121,000–$140,000
   $141,000–$150,000
   $151,000–$175,000
   Over $175,000
5. Please indicate the highest level of education completed.
   Grammar School
   High School
   Vocation Technical School (2 yrs)
   Some College
   Bachelor's Degree (4 yrs)
   Master's Degree (M.S. or M.A.)
   Doctoral Degree (Ph.D.)
   Professional Degree (M.D., J.D., etc.)
   Other
6. Number of children _____

7. Ages and gender of children

   M/F _____

   M/F _____

   M/F _____

   M/F _____

   M/F _____

8. What is your primary occupation?

   _____

9. Do you own a personal computer?

   Yes / No _____

10. How comfortable are you navigating the Internet?

    Extremely _____

    Very _____

    A little _____

    Not at all _____

11. Have you ever used birth control?

12. Has your husband ever used birth control?

# APPENDIX D

## GENERAL SOCIAL SURVEY RESULTS

Participant Code

Survey Questions: (Adapted from the General Social Survey, Queens College, 1972)

The first section of this survey addresses religious attitudes.

1. Would you call yourself a strong Christian (Muslim, Jew, etc.) or not a very strong Christian, Muslim, Jew?

|  |  | Results |
|---|---|---|
| Strong | 1 | **5** |
| Not very strong | 2 | **3** |
| Somewhat strong | 3 | **6** |
| Don't' know | 8 | **1** |

2. In what religion were you raised?

|  |  | Results |
|---|---|---|
| Protestant | 1 | **5** |
| Catholic | 2 | **8** |
| Jewish | 3 | **0** |
| None | 4 | **1** |
| Other | 5 | **1** |
| (Specify denomination) | | |

3. How often do you attend religious services?

|  |  | Results |
|---|---|---|
| Never | 0 | **1** |
| Less than once a year | 1 | **0** |
| About once or twice a year | 2 | **0** |
| Several times a year | 3 | **0** |
| About once a month | 4 | **0** |
| 2–3 times a month | 5 | **1** |

| | | |
|---|---|---|
| Nearly every week | 6 | **2** |
| Every week | 7 | **2** |
| Several times a week | 8 | **0** |
| No answer | | **9** |

4. Do you believe there is a life after death?

| | | **Results** |
|---|---|---|
| Yes | 1 | **7** |
| No | 2 | **1** |
| Undecided | 8 | **6** |
| No answer | | **1** |

5. There are many different ways of picturing God. I'd like to know the kinds of images you are most likely to associate with God. On a scale of 1–7 where would you place your image of God between the contrasting images?

A. Mother _____ **6. 0** Father

| 1 | 2 | 3 | 4 | 5 | 6 | 7 |
|---|---|---|---|---|---|---|

B. Master **2.7**_____ Spouse

| 1 | 2 | 3 | 4 | 5 | 6 | 7 |
|---|---|---|---|---|---|---|

C. Judge _____**3.8**_____ Lover

| 1 | 2 | 3 | 4 | 5 | 6 | 7 |
|---|---|---|---|---|---|---|

D. Friend _____**5.1**_____ King

| 1 | 2 | 3 | 4 | 5 | 6 | 7 |
|---|---|---|---|---|---|---|

6. People have different images of the world and human nature. I'd like to know the kinds of images you have. On a scale of 1–7, where would you place your image of the world and human nature between the contrasting images?

A. The world is basically filled with evil and sin     There is much goodness in the world which hints at God's goodness

_____**5.5**_____

| 1 | 2 | 3 | 4 | 5 | 6 | 7 |
|---|---|---|---|---|---|---|

B. Human nature is          Human nature is fundamentally
   basically good           perverse and corrupt

_____**3.6**_____

| 1 | 2 | 3 | 4 | 5 | 6 | 7 |

7. How often do you pray?

|  |  | **Results** |
|---|---|---|
| Several times a day | 1 | **4** |
| Once a day | 2 | **5** |
| Several times a week | 3 | **5** |
| Once a week | 4 | **0** |
| Less than once a week | 5 | **0** |
| No answer |  | **1** |

8. When it comes to your religious identity, would you say you are a traditional moderate, or liberal Christian, Muslim, Jew or do none of these describe you?

|  |  | **Results** |
|---|---|---|
| Traditional | 1 | **2** |
| Moderate | 2 | **5** |
| Liberal | 3 | **2** |
| None | 4 | **0** |
| Other (Specify) | 6 | **6** |

9. In the past month, about how many hours have you spent doing religious activities in your home (such as time spent praying, meditating, reading religious books, listening to religious broadcasts, etc.)?
   **8.1 hrs. (Range 0–30 hrs)**

10. In the past month, how many hours have you spent doing religious services activities outside your home (such as attending religious services, prayer groups Bible studies, church leadership meetings, etc.)?
    **12.5 hrs. (Range 0–60 hrs)**

11. People have many differing views about what makes a person a good Christian, Jew or Muslim. Please tell me how important is each of the following to you. Please indicate where you would place your feelings on a scale from 1 to 5.

| Very important | | Not important | | Don't know |
|---|---|---|---|---|
| 1 | 2 | 3 | 4 | 5 |

How important is it…

|  | | Rating |
|---|---|---|
| A. | To attend regularly religious services | **2.3** |
| B. | To believe in God without question or doubt | **2.3** |
| C. | To follow faithfully the teachings of their church | **3.3** |
| D. | To follow one's conscience even if it means going against what the churches or synagogues say and do | **2.4** |

12. How often have these problems caused doubts about your religious faith often, sometimes, or never.

 A. Evil in the world

| | | **Results** |
|---|---|---|
| Often | 1 | **2** |
| Sometimes | 2 | **6** |
| Never | 3 | **5** |
| Don't know | 8 | **2** |

 B. Personal suffering

| | | **Results** |
|---|---|---|
| Often | 1 | **2** |
| Sometimes | 2 | **9** |
| Never | 3 | **2** |
| Don't know | 8 | **2** |

 C. Did you receive any of your grade or high school education in Catholic or Christian parochial schools?

| | | **Results** |
|---|---|---|
| Yes | 1 | **7** |
| No | 2 | **8** |

 **If Yes:**

 A. How many years did you attend religious schools?
 **6.1 (Range from 1–12 Yrs)**

13. To what extent do you consider yourself a religious person? Are you?

|  |  | Results |
| --- | --- | --- |
| Very religious | 1 | **4** |
| Moderately religious | 2 | **9** |
| Slightly religious | 3 | **1** |
| Not religious at all | 4 | **1** |

14. Tell me whether you strongly agree, agree, disagree, or strongly disagree with the following statement:
    A. I believe in a God who watches over me.

|  |  | Results |
| --- | --- | --- |
| Strongly agree | 1 | **9** |
| Agree | 2 | **5** |
| Disagree | 3 | **0** |
| Strongly disagree | 4 | **1** |

15. Tell me whether the teachings of your Church are very important, important, not important or not very important in making decisions.

|  |  | Results |
| --- | --- | --- |
| Very important | 1 | **3** |
| Important | 2 | **8** |
| Not important | 3 | **2** |
| Not very important | 4 | **1** |
| No answer |  | **1** |

16. Tell me whether your personal judgment is very important, important, not important, or not very important in making decisions.

|  |  | Results |
| --- | --- | --- |
| Very important | 1 | **9** |
| Important | 2 | **5** |
| Not important | 3 | **1** |
| Not very important | 4 | **0** |

17.  Because of your religious or spiritual beliefs have you always, almost always, often, seldom, or never felt the following ways:

A.   I have forgiven myself for things I have done wrong.

|                          |   | **Results** |
|--------------------------|---|-------------|
| Almost or almost always  | 1 | **6** |
| Often                    | 2 | **6** |
| Seldom                   | 3 | **3** |
| Never                    | 4 | **0** |

B.   I have forgiven those who hurt me.

|                          |   | **Results** |
|--------------------------|---|-------------|
| Almost or almost always  | 1 | **9** |
| Often                    | 2 | **5** |
| Seldom                   | 3 | **1** |
| Never                    | 4 | **0** |

C.   I know that God forgives me.

|                          |   | **Results** |
|--------------------------|---|-------------|
| Almost or almost always  | 1 | **12** |
| Often                    | 2 | **2** |
| Seldom                   | 3 | **0** |
| Never                    | 4 | **0** |
| No answer                |   | **1** |

The following questions are about pornography—books, movies, magazines, and photographs that show or describe sex activities. (Extracted from the General Social Survey, (1972))

18.  Sexual materials provide information about sex.

|              |   | **Results** |
|--------------|---|-------------|
| Yes          | 1 | **8** |
| No           | 2 | **7** |
| Don't know   | 3 | **0** |

19.  Sexual materials lead to breakdown of morals.

|              |   | **Results** |
|--------------|---|-------------|
| Yes          | 1 | **14** |
| No           | 2 | **0** |
| Don't know   | 3 | **1** |

20. Sexual materials provide an outlet for bottled-up impulses.

|  |  | **Results** |
|---|---|---|
| Yes | 1 | **5** |
| No | 2 | **7** |
| Don't know | 3 | **2** |
| No answer |  | **1** |

21. Which of these statements comes closest to your feelings about pornography laws.
    1. There should be laws against the distribution of pornography no matter what age.
    2. There should be laws against the distribution of pornography to persons under 18.
    3. There should be no laws forbidding the distribution of pornography.

|  |  | **Results** |
|---|---|---|
| Illegal to all | 1 | **8** |
| Illegal to under 18 | 2 | **6** |
| Legal | 3 | **0** |
| Don't' know | 4 | **0** |
| No answer |  | **1** |

The following questions concern marriage and personal happiness.

22. How would you rate the importance of being married?

|  |  | **Results** |
|---|---|---|
| One of the most important | 1 | **4** |
| Very important | 2 | **6** |
| Somewhat important | 3 | **4** |
| Not too important | 4 | **1** |
| Not at all important | 5 | **0** |

Do you agree or disagree with the following statements?

23. Married people are generally happier than unmarried people.

|  |  | **Results** |
|---|---|---|
| Strongly agree | 1 | **0** |
| Agree | 2 | **5** |

| Neither agree nor disagree | 3 | 7 |
|---|---|---|
| Disagree | 4 | 2 |
| Strongly disagree | 5 | 1 |

24. Personal freedom is more important than the companionship of marriage.

| | | **Results** |
|---|---|---|
| Strongly agree | 1 | **0** |
| Agree | 2 | **3** |
| Neither agree nor disagree | 3 | **6** |
| Disagree | 4 | **4** |
| Strongly disagree | 5 | **2** |

25. The main advantage of marriage is that it gives financial security.

| | | **Results** |
|---|---|---|
| Strongly agree | 1 | **0** |
| Agree | 2 | **1** |
| Neither agree nor disagree | 3 | **6** |
| Disagree | 4 | **3** |
| Strongly disagree | 5 | **5** |

26. The main purpose of marriage these days is to have children.

| | | **Results** |
|---|---|---|
| Strongly agree | 1 | **1** |
| Agree | 2 | **1** |
| Neither agree nor disagree | 3 | **2** |
| Disagree | 4 | **6** |
| Strongly disagree | 5 | **4** |
| No answer | | **1** |

27. It is better to have a bad marriage than no marriage at all.

| | | **Results** |
|---|---|---|
| Strongly agree | 1 | **0** |
| Agree | 2 | **0** |
| Neither agree nor disagree | 3 | **0** |
| Disagree | 4 | **7** |
| Strongly disagree | 5 | **8** |

28. Divorce is acceptable.

|                            |   | **Results** |
|----------------------------|---|-------------|
| Strongly agree             | 1 | **2**       |
| Agree                      | 2 | **7**       |
| Neither agree nor disagree | 3 | **2**       |
| Disagree                   | 4 | **4**       |
| Strongly disagree          | 5 | **0**       |

29. Couple's don't take marriage seriously enough when divorce is easily available.

|                            |   | **Results** |
|----------------------------|---|-------------|
| Strongly agree             | 1 | **9**       |
| Agree                      | 2 | **3**       |
| Neither agree nor disagree | 3 | **3**       |
| Disagree                   | 4 | **0**       |
| Strongly disagree          | 5 | **0**       |

30. Taken all together, how happy would you say that you are today?

|              |   | **Results** |
|--------------|---|-------------|
| Very happy   | 1 | **2**       |
| Pretty happy | 2 | **10**      |
| Not too happy| 3 | **3**       |

31. Taking things all together, how happy are you in your marriage?

|              |   | **Results** |
|--------------|---|-------------|
| Very happy   | 1 | **3**       |
| Pretty happy | 2 | **5**       |
| Not too happy| 3 | **5**       |
| No answer    |   | **2**       |

The following questions are amended from Zillman and Bryant (1988).

32. How satisfied are you with your spouse's physical appearance?

|                |   | **Results** |
|----------------|---|-------------|
| Very satisfied | 1 | **3**       |
| Satisfied      | 2 | **10**      |

| Unsatisfied      | 3 | **1** |
| Very unsatisfied | 4 | **0** |
| No answer        |   | **1** |

33. How satisfied are you with your spouse's affectionate behavior towards you?

|                  |   | **Results** |
| Very satisfied   | 1 | **1** |
| Satisfied        | 2 | **4** |
| Unsatisfied      | 3 | **6** |
| Very unsatisfied | 4 | **3** |
| No answer        |   | **1** |

34. How satisfied are you with your spouse's sexual behavior?

|                  |   | **Results** |
| Very satisfied   | 1 | **1** |
| Satisfied        | 2 | **3** |
| Unsatisfied      | 3 | **6** |
| Very unsatisfied | 4 | **4** |
| No answer        |   | **1** |

35. How satisfied are you with your spouse's desire to explore novel sexual practices with you?

|                  |   | **Results** |
| Very satisfied   | 1 | **0** |
| Satisfied        | 2 | **3** |
| Unsatisfied      | 3 | **8** |
| Very unsatisfied | 4 | **3** |
| No answer        |   | **1** |

# REFERENCES

Akhtar, S. (1999). *Inner torment: Living between conflict and fragmentation.* Northvale, N. J: Jason Aronson Inc.

———. (2003). *New clinical realms: Pushing the envelope of theory and technique.* Northvale, N. J: Jason Aronson. Inc.

Akhtar, S., & Kramer, S. (Eds.). (1996). *Intimacy and infidelity: Separation individuation perspectives.* Northvale, N. J: Jason Aronson Inc.

Alperin, R. (2000). Barriers to intimacy: An object relations perspective. *Psychoanalytic Psychology, 18*(1), 137–155.

Amati Mehler, J., & Argentieri, S. (1989). Hope and hopelessness: A technical problem. *International Journal of Psycho-analysis, 70,* 293–303.

Anderson, K. (1997). *The pornography plague.* Retrieved Jan. 21, 2005, from http: www.leaderu.com/orgs/probe/docs/pornplag.html

Armstrong-Perlman, E. (1994). *The allure of the bad object.* In J. S. Grotstein, & D. B. Rinsley (Eds.). *Fairbairn and the origins of object relations* (pp. 222–232), New York: Guilford Press.

Baird, R. J. (2005) Clergy and cybersex: A motivational study. *Dissertation abstracts international: Section B: The sciences and engineering, 65 (12-B),* 6639. Retrieved July 20, 2006 from PsychINFO database.

Benjamin, J. (1986). The alienation of desire: Women's masochism and ideal Love. In C. Zanardi (Ed.), *Essential papers on the psychology of women* (pp. 455–479). New York: New York University Press.

———. (1988). *The bonds of love.* New York: Pantheon Books.

———. (1990). Recognition and destruction: An outline of intersubjectivity. In L. Aron, & S. Mitchell (Eds.), *Relational psychoanalysis: The emergence of a tradition* (pp. 181–210). New Jersey: The Analytic Press.

———. (1995). *Like subjects, love objects: Essays on recognition and sexual difference.* New Haven, CT: Yale University Press.

Bird, M. (2006). Sexual addiction and marriage and family therapy: Facilitating individual and relationship healing through couple therapy. *Journal of Marital and Family Therapy, 32*(2), 297–311.

Blair, C. (1998). Netsex: Empowerment through discourse. In B. Ebo (Ed.), *Cyberghetto or cybertopia?: Race, class, and gender on the Internet* (pp. 203–217). Westport, CT: Praeger.

Carnes, P., Delmonico, D., Griffin, E., & Moriarity, R. (2001). In *The shadows of the net: Breaking free of compulsive online sexual behavior.* Center City, MN: Hazelden Education and Publishing.

Casement, P. (1991). Learning from the Patient. New York: Guilford Press.

*Catechism of the Catholic Church.* (1994). New York: Doubleday.

Chasseguet-Smirgel, J. (1988). Feminine guilt and the Oedipus complex. In C. Zanardi (Ed.), *Essential papers on the psychology of women* (pp. 88–131). New York: New York University Press.

Chodorow, N. (1978). *The reproduction of mothering: Psychoanalysis and the sociology of gender.* Berkeley, CA: University of California Press.

———. (1980). Gender, relation, and difference in psychoanalytic perspective. In C. Zanardi (Ed.), *Essential papers on the psychology of women* (pp. 420–436). New York: New York University Press.

———. (1989). *Feminism & psychoanalytic theory.* New Haven, CT: Yale University Press.

Civin, M. A. (2000). *Male, female, email: The struggle for relatedness in a paranoid society.* New York: Other Press.

Cooper, A. (Ed.). (2002). *Sex and the Internet: A guidebook for clinicians.* New York: Brunner-Routledge.

Dines, G., Jensen, R., & Russo, A. (1998). *Pornography: The production and consumption of inequality.* New York: Routledge.

Dworkin, A. (1989). *Pornography: Men possessing women.* New York: E. F. Dutton.

Ethics in information processing. Retrieved November 25, 2006, from Encyclopedia of Business and Finance Web Site: <http://business.enotes.com/business-finance-encyclopedia/ethics-information-processing> html

Fairbairn, W. R. D. (1949). Steps in the development of an object-relations theory of the personality. *Psychoanalytic Studies of the Personality* (pp. 152–161). New York: Routledge & Kegan.

———. (1943). The repression and the return of bad objects (with special reference to the 'war neuroses'). In psychoanalytic Studies of the Personality (pp. 59–81). New York: Routledge & Kegan.

———. (1963). An object relations theory of the personality. In D. Scharff (Ed.), *From instinct to self: Selected papers of W. R. D. Fairbairn.* Northvale (pp. 55–56), NJ: Jason Aronson.

Frank, A. (1996). Intimacy and Individuation. In Akhtar, S. & Kramer, S. (Eds.). Intimacy and Infidelity: Separation-Individuation Perspectives (pp. 73–89). Northvale NJ: Jason Aronson.

Freud, S. (1933). Femininity. In J. Strachey (Ed. and Trans.) *New introductory lectures on psycho-analysis and other works* (pp.112–135). London: Hogarth Press and the Institute of Psycho-analysis. Vol. XXII.

————. (1905). Three essays on the theory of sexuality. In J. Strachey (Ed. and Trans.). *New introductory lectures on psycho-analysis and other works.* London: Hogarth Press and the Institute of Psycho-analysis. Vol. XXII.

Gilligan, C. (1982). In a Different Voice. Cambridge, MA: Harvard University Press.

————. (1986). Remapping the moral domain: New images of the self in relationship. In C. Zanardi (Ed.), *Essential papers on the psychology of women* (pp. 480–496). New York: New York University Press.

Goldberg, A. (1995). Sexualization and desexualization. *The problem of perversion* (pp. 29–45). New Haven, CT: Yale University Press.

————. (1999). *Being of two minds: The vertical split in psychoanalysis and psychotherapy.* Hillsdale, NJ: The Analytic Press.

Greenberg, J., & Mitchell, S. (1983). Object Relations in Psychoanalytic Theory. Cambridge, MA: Harvard University Press.

Griffiths, M. (2000). Excessive Internet use: Implications for sexual behavior. *Cyberpsychology & behavior, 3*(4), 537–552.

Grotstein, J. D., & Rinsley, B. R. (Ed.). (1994). *Fairbairn and the origins of object relations.* London: Free Association Books, Ltd.

Hoggs, C. (1990). What is pornography? In *Pornography and the Internet in The United States.* Retrieved Nov. 10, 2003, from the University of British Columbia, School of Archival and Information Studies, http:///www.slais.ubc.ca/courses/libr500/fall1999/www_presentations/c_hog/Define html

Jochen, P., & Valkenburg, P. M. (2006). Adolescents' exposure to sexually explicit material on the Internet. *Communication Research, 32*(2), 178–204.

John Paul II. (1979). On Catechesis in our time (Catechesi Tradendae). CD-ROM. Boston: St. Paul Media. 2000.

Kendrick, W. (1996). *The secret museum: Pornography in modern culture,* Berkeley, CA: University of California Press.

Kernberg, O. (1974). Barriers to falling and remaining in love. In Object Relations Theory and Clinical Psychoanalysis. pp. 215–239. New York: Jason Aronson Inc.

Kernberg, O. (1975). *The syndrome. Borderline conditions and pathological narcissism.* Northvale, NJ: Jason Aronson.

————. (1995). *Love relations: Normality and pathology.* New Haven, CT: Yale University Press.

Khan, R. M. (1979). Alienation in Perversions. New York: International Universities Press Inc.

Kibby, M., & Costello, B. (2001). Between the image and the act: Interactive sex entertainment on the Internet. *Sexualities, 4*(3), 353–369.

Klein, M. (1937). Love, Guilt, and Reparation. In Love, Guilt and Reparation: and other works 1921–1945. London: Vintage.

————. (1946). *Envy, gratitude, and other works: 1946–1963: The writings of Melanie Klein.* Boston: Free Press.

————. (1975). The Oedipus complex in the light of early anxieties. In C. Zanardi (Ed.), *Essential papers on the psychology of women* (pp. 65–87). New York: New York University Press.

Kramer, S. (1996). The Development of Intimacy. In S. Akhtar & S. Kramer (Eds.). Intimacy and Infidelity: Separation-Individuation Perspectives. pp. 3–18. Northvale, NJ: Jason Aronson Inc.

Lederer, L. (Ed.). (1980). *Take back the night: Women on pornography.* New York: William Morrow & Co.

Lincoln, Blanche (D-AR). (2005). Retrieved July 20, 2006, from http://lincoln. senate.gov/press_show.cfm?id=241537.

Lincoln, Y., & Guba, F. (1985). *Naturalistic inquiry.* Newbury Park, CA: Sage Publications Inc.

Lorde, A. (1980). Take back the night. In L. Lederer (Ed.), *Take back the night.* New York, William Morrow & Co.

Matheu, M., & Sobotnik, M. (2001). *Infidelity on the Internet: Virtual relationships and real betrayal.* Napierville, IL: Sourcebooks Trade.

MacKinnon, K. (1987). *Feminism unmodified: Discourse on life and law.* Cambridge, MA: Harvard University Press.

McKenna, K., & Bargh, J. (2000). Plan 9 from cyberspace: The implications of the Internet for personality and social psychology. *Personality and Social Psychology Review, 4*(1), 57–75.

Menaker, E. (1953). Masochism—A defense reaction of the ego. In C. Zanardi (Ed.), *Essential papers on the psychology of women* (pp. 221–233). New York: New York University Press.

Meyers, S. (1996). Sexuality and sexualization. In S. Akhtar, & S. Kramer (Eds.), *Intimacy and infidelity: Separation-individuation perspectives.* Northvale, NJ: Jason Aronson Inc.

*Microsoft Encarta Encyclopedia.* 1997. CD-ROM. Seattle: Microsoft Corporation.

Miller, J. B. (1984). *Toward a new psychology of women.* Boston: Beacon Press.

Miriam-Webster Online Dictionary. Retrieved Nov. 25, 2006. Web site: http://www.m-w.com/dictionary/pornography

Mitchell, S. (2003). *Can love last?: The fate of romance over time.* New York W.W. Norton and Co.

Pontifical Council for the Family. *Truth and meaning of human sexuality,* 1995. CD-ROM. Boston: St. Paul Media. 2000.

Perkins, B. (1997). *When good men are tempted.* Grand Rapids, MI: Zondervan.

Paul VI. *On christian marriage* (Casti Connubii), 1930. CD-ROM. Boston: St. Paul Media. 2000.

Philaretou, A. G., Mahfouz, A. Y., & Allen, K. (2005), Use of Internet pornography and men's well being. *International Journal of Men's Health, 4*(2), 149–169.

Pontifical Council for Social Communications. Pornography and Violence in the communications media: A pastoral response. (1989). CD-ROM. Boston: St. Paul Media. 2000.

Queen's College. (1972). General Social Survey.

Reik, T. (1941). Masochism in Modern Man. New York: Farrar, Straus & Giroux.

Rossetti, S. *Cybersex & the priesthood,* 2002. CD-ROM. Boston: St. Paul Media.

Rossney, R. (1995). Time's story on cyberporn of questionable validity, San Francisco Chronicle, p. C3. Retrieved November 11, 2003 from www.SFGate.com

Sacred Congregation for the Doctrine of Faith. *Declaration on certain questions concerning sexual ethics (Persona Humana),* 1975. CD-ROM. Boston: St. Paul Media. 2000.

Schnarch, D. (1997). Sex, intimacy, and the Internet. *Journal of Sex Education and Therapy, 22*(1), 15–20.

Schneider, J. P. (2000). A qualitative study of cybersex participants: Gender differences, recovery issues, and implications for therapists. *Sexual Addiction & Compulsivity, 7,* 249–278.

————. (2000). *Effects of cybersex addiction on the family: Results of a survey.* Retrieved November 11, 2003, from http://www.jenniferschneider.com.html

Schneider, J. P. (2002). The new elephant in the living room. In A. Cooper (Ed.), *Sex and the Internet*. New York: Brunner-Routledge.

Schneider, J. P., & Weiss, R. (2001). *Cybersex exposed: From fantasy to obsession*. Center City, MN: Hazelden Education and Publishing.

Searles, H., (1979). *Countertransference and related subjects: Selected papers*. New York: International Universities Press, Inc.

Smalley, G. (1996). *For better or for best*. Grand Rapids, MI: Zondervan.

Stern, D. (1985). *The interpersonal world of the infant: A view from psychoanalysis and developmental psychology*. New York: Basic Books.

Stoller, R. (1991). Eros and polis: What is this thing called love? *Journal of The American Psychoanalytic Association, 39*, 1065–1102.

Strauss, A., & Corbin, J. (1998). *Basics of qualitative research: Techniques and procedures for developing grounded theory*. Thousand Oaks, CA: Sage Publications.

Strean, H. (1976). The extramarital affair. *The Psychoanalytic Review, 63*(1), 101–113.

Summers, F. (1994). *Object relations theories and psychopathology*. Hillsdale, NJ: The Analytic Press.

Surrey, J. (1991). The self-in-relation: A theory of women's development. In J. Jordan (Ed.) *Women's growth in connection: Writings from the stone center* (pp. 51–66). New York: Guildford Press.

United States Senate Committee on the Judiciary (2005). *Why the government should care about pornography*. Retrieved July 20, 2006, from http://judiciary. senate.gov/hearing.cfm?id=1674

Weber-Young, J. (2001). *Exploratory study of intimate relationships on and translated through the Internet*. Unpublished doctoral dissertation, Institute for Clinical Social Work, Chicago.

Wood, H. (2006). Compulsive use of internet pornography. In J. Hiller (Ed.) Sex, Mind, and Emotion: Innovation in Psychological Theory and Practice. New York: Karnac.

Ybarra, M., & Mitchell, K. (2005). Exposure to Internet pornography among children and adolescents: A national survey. *Cyberpsychology & Behavior, 8*(5), 473–486.

Yoder, V. C., Virden, T. B., & Kiran, (2005). Internet Pornography and Loneliness: An Association. Sexual Addiction & Compulsivity, (12), 19–44.

Young, K. (1998). Caught in the Net. New York: John Wiley and Sons.

———. (2000). *Tangled in the Web: Understanding cybersex from fantasy to addiction.* New York: John Wiley and Sons.

Zillmann, D., & Bryant, J. (1988). Pornography's impact on sexual satisfaction. *Journal of Applied Social Psychology, 18*(5), 438–453.

# NAME INDEX

# SUBJECT INDEX

Printed in the United States
85696LV00002B/58/A